EZEKIEL

Published by
The Bible Reading Fellowship
First Floor, Elsfield Hall
15–17 Elsfield Way, Oxford OX2 8FG
ISBN 1 84101 040 5

First published 2002
10 9 8 7 6 5 4 3 2 1 0

Acknowledgments
Unless otherwise stated, scripture quotations are taken from
The New Revised Standard Version of the Bible, Anglicized Edition,
copyright © 1989, 1995 by the Division of Christian Education of the
National Council of the Churches of Christ in the United States of
America, and are used by permission. All rights reserved.

Scripture quotations taken from The Revised Standard Version of the
Bible, copyright © 1946, 1952, 1971 by the Division of Christian
Education of the National Council of the Churches of Christ in the
United States of America, are used by permission. All rights reserved.

The New Testament in Modern English, Revised Edition, translated by
J.B. Phillips. Published by HarperCollins Publishers Ltd.

A catalogue record for this book is
available from the British Library

Printed and bound in Great Britain
by Bookmarque, Croydon

EZEKIEL

THE PEOPLE'S
BIBLE COMMENTARY

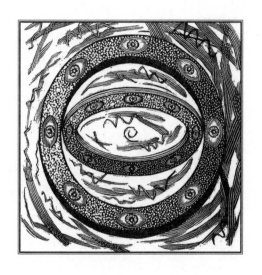

ERNEST
LUCAS

A BIBLE COMMENTARY FOR EVERY DAY

Introducing the
People's Bible Commentary
Series

Congratulations! You are embarking on a voyage of discovery—or rediscovery. You may feel you know the Bible very well; you may never have turned its pages before. You may be looking for a fresh way of approaching daily Bible study; you may be searching for useful insights to share in a study group or from a pulpit.

The People's Bible Commentary (PBC) series is designed for all those who want to study the scriptures in a way that will warm the heart as well as instructing the mind. To help you, the series distils the best of scholarly insights into the straightforward language and devotional emphasis of Bible reading notes. Explanation of background material, and discussion of the original Greek and Hebrew, will always aim to be brief.

- If you have never really studied the Bible before, the series offers a serious yet accessible way in.

- If you help to lead a church study group, or are otherwise involved in regular preaching and teaching, you can find invaluable 'snapshots' of a Bible passage through the PBC approach.

- If you are a church worker or minister, burned out on the Bible, this series could help you recover the wonder of scripture.

Using a People's Bible Commentary

The series is designed for use alongside any version of the Bible. You may have your own favourite translation, but you might like to consider trying a different one in order to gain fresh perspectives on familiar passages.

Many Bible translations come in a range of editions, including study and reference editions that have concordances, various kinds of special index, maps and marginal notes. These can all prove helpful in studying the relevant passage. The Notes section at the back of each PBC volume provides space for you to write personal reflections, points to follow up, questions and comments.

Each People's Bible Commentary can be used on a daily basis, instead of Bible reading notes. Alternatively, it can be read straight through, or used as a resource book for insight into particular verses of the biblical book.

If you have enjoyed using this commentary and would like to progress further in Bible study, you will find details of other volumes in the series listed at the back, together with information about a special offer from BRF.

While it is important to deepen understanding of a given passage, this series always aims to engage both heart and mind in the study of the Bible. The scriptures point to our Lord himself and our task is to use them to build our relationship with him. When we read, let us do so prayerfully, slowly, reverently, expecting him to speak to our hearts.

CONTENTS

PBC EZEKIEL: INTRODUCTION

Historical background

The Bible is a book that came into being over a period of time as people experienced God in a variety of ways, times and places. As the writer of the letter to the Hebrews put it, 'Long ago God spoke to our ancestors in many and various ways by the prophets' (Hebrews 1:1). The result is that the message of the Bible is often related to a particular historical setting, and this affects how it is expressed. This is clearly the case with the book of Ezekiel. Indeed, unlike some books within the Bible whose historical setting is hard to date with certainty, Ezekiel gives precise dates, and sometimes places, for some of his oracles. This enables us to determine the book's historical context and so helps us to understand its message. The opening verses tell us that Ezekiel was by the river Chebar in Babylonia in the fifth year of the exile of King Jehoiachin when he experienced the vision that marked the beginning of his ministry as a prophet (1:2–3). The latest date given to any of his oracles is the 27th year of the exile (29:17), so he was active for at least 22 years. The opening of the book raises the question of why Ezekiel and a group of his countrymen, including the king of Judah, were exiles in Babylonia. In order to understand that, we need to know something of the history of the ancient Near East.

Israel and Judah

Israel was a united kingdom for less than a century under David and Solomon. After Solomon's death in about 930BC the kingdom fell apart (1 Kings 12), with Israel (sometimes called Ephraim) becoming an independent kingdom in the north, its capital eventually settling at Samaria. The kingdom of Judah in the south kept Jerusalem as its capital and the descendants of David as its kings. These two kingdoms were at the south-western end of what is called 'the fertile crescent'. This is the relatively fertile area of land that curves around the north end of the Arabian desert. It is fertile along the Mediterranean coast because at certain seasons westerly winds bring in rain from the sea. The north-eastern part of the crescent is Mesopotamia, the fertile valleys of the Tigris and Euphrates rivers, which rise in the mountains of Turkey. To the south of the fertile crescent is another fertile river valley, that of the Nile. The great river valleys, with their constant supply of water, became the centres of major civilizations and the homes of great empires. The smaller states that lay in between them were sometimes caught like nuts in a nutcracker as these empires struggled with one another for supremacy. As a result, the history of Israel and Judah was affected by the regional superpowers to their north (Assyria and Babylon) and south (Egypt). In 722/1BC the Assyrians captured Samaria after a three-year siege. This brought the kingdom of Israel to an end. It was incorporated in the Assyrian empire and a considerable part of its population was deported to the upper Euphrates and Media.

Judah and the superpowers

About this time, Judah became a vassal kingdom, subject to Assyria. This involved paying annual tribute to Assyria and also the intro-duction of Assyrian forms of worship into the temple in Jerusalem (2 Kings 16:10–18). When the Assyrian King Ashurbanipal died in about 627BC, Assyrian power went into decline as his sons fought over the succession to the throne. At the same time, the power of the Babylonians and the Medes was growing. King Josiah had come to the throne of Judah in 640/39BC as an eight-year-old child. He brought about a major religious reform in Judah. Active steps in this direction seem to have begun at about the time of Ashurbanipal's death (2 Chronicles 34:3). Maybe Josiah was taking advantage of the weakening of Assyrian power, because the reform involved removing the apparatus of Assyrian worship from the temple (2 Kings 23:12) and so could be seen as rebellion against Assyrian rule. Indeed, revival of the worship of the God of Israel, and that God alone, could itself be seen as a reassertion of Judah's independence. The fact that Josiah extended his reforms to parts of the former kingdom of Israel (2 Kings 23:15–20) may indicate that he had hopes of reviving the united kingdom.

Nineveh, the capital of Assyria, fell to a combined assault by the Medes and Babylonians in 612BC. The Egyptians decided to come to the aid of the Assyrians, and in 609BC Pharaoh Neco marched north to help them. Josiah tried to stop him. Perhaps he was trying to assert Judah's independence. The result set off a tragic train of events. Josiah was killed in battle at Megiddo (2 Kings 23:29), and his son Jehoahaz succeeded him. When he failed in his attempt to bolster Assyrian power, Pharaoh Neco decided to establish his control over Judah. He deposed Jehoahaz, put his brother Eliakim on the throne, changing his name to Jehoiakim, and exacted tribute from Judah (2 Kings 23:31–35). In 605BC the Babylonians defeated the Egyptians at the battle of Carchemish on the Euphrates. Jehoiakim now became a vassal of the Babylonians. From then on, there seems to have been a struggle within the leadership in Judah between pro-Egyptian and pro-Babylonian factions. The pro-Egyptian faction seems to have hoped to re-establish Judah's independence by rebelling against Babylon with Egypt's help. The pro-Babylonian faction saw this as a recipe for disaster. Following Josiah's death, his religious reform crumbled.

Disaster came fairly soon. After a failed Babylonian attempt to invade Egypt in 601/600BC, Jehoiakim withheld tribute from the Babylonians. This was a declaration of independence. Nebuchadnezzar, the Babylonian king, was slow to react because of problems elsewhere in his empire. By the time his army reached Judah in 597BC Jehoiakim had died and been replaced by his son Jehoiachin. After a short siege of Jerusalem, Jehoiachin surrendered to Nebuchadnezzar. The king, queen mother, some high officials and leading citizens (including Ezekiel) and considerable booty were all taken to Babylon (2 Kings 24:10–16). The king's uncle, Mattaniah, was put on the throne, with his name changed to Zedekiah.

The picture we get of Zedekiah in the book of Jeremiah, who was active as a prophet during the turbulent last decades of Judah, is of someone who was well-intentioned but lacked the strength of character to control the factions among the Judean leaders. For reasons that are not clear, Judah rebelled against Babylon in 589BC. This time Nebuchadnezzar reacted swiftly. Jerusalem was soon besieged and the Babylonians began to reduce the other fortresses in Judah. An Egyptian army that tried to come to Judah's aid was driven off. In 587/6BC the city wall was breached and the Babylonians entered the city. Zedekiah and some of his soldiers escaped by night and fled towards the Jordan, but they were overtaken and captured near Jericho. When Zedekiah was brought before Nebuchadnezzar he was forced to witness the execution of his sons before he was blinded and taken in chains to Babylon, where he died (2 Kings 25:1–7). Some of the civil, military and religious leaders were executed and a further group of the population were deported. The city walls were broken down and the city and temple sacked and burned.

Judah ceased to exist as a state. It became a province of the Babylonian empire, with a governor. Initially the Babylonians appointed a prominent Judean, Gedaliah. He followed a conciliatory policy, but the die-hard nationalists, with the backing of the king of Ammon, hatched a plot and murdered him. This led Gedaliah's supporters to flee to Egypt, taking Jeremiah with them (Jeremiah 40—41). After this, Judah was probably absorbed into the Babylonian province of Samaria.

Ezekiel received his call to be a prophet in 593BC. Much of his book relates to the years leading up to and immediately following the cataclysmic disaster of the destruction of Judah, Jerusalem and the temple. The fall of Jerusalem is the central event in the book. The message of the book cannot be understood unless it is read against the background of that event, and what led up to it and its consequences for the Judeans.

Significant dates

Here, for quick reference, is a list of some key dates (all BC) with regard to the historical setting of Ezekiel's ministry. Scholars differ, usually only by a year of so, with regard to some of these dates.

640   Josiah becomes king of Judah
627   Death of the Assyrian king Ashurbanipal
         Josiah begins his religious reforms
         Call of Jeremiah (Jeremiah 1:2)
623   Birth of Ezekiel (?)
612   Fall of Nineveh—end of Assyrian Empire
609   Death of Josiah in battle at Megiddo
         Jehoahaz becomes king of Judah but is deposed by the Egyptians
         Jehoiakim is made king by the Egyptians
605   Battle of Carchemish. Judah becomes a Babylonian vassal
601   Jehoiakim rebels against Nebuchadnezzar
597   Jehoiakim dies and is succeeded by Jehoiachin, who is exiled to Babylon
         Ezekiel is among the exiles taken to Babylon
         Zedekiah is made king by Nebuchadnezzar
593   Ezekiel's call to be a prophet (Ezekiel 1:2)
589   Zedekiah rebels against Nebuchadnezzar

586　　The fall of Jerusalem and end of the kingdom of Judah
584(?)　Assassination of Gedaliah
571　　Ezekiel's last dated prophecy (Ezekiel 29:17)

Dates of Ezekiel's oracles

Here is a list of the dates given for Ezekiel's oracles, expressed in our modern calendar (again, all the dates are BC). Calculating these dates involves making some assumptions. Not all scholars would agree about them, so they should be taken as a general guide only, as far as day and month are concerned.

1:2	Ezekiel's call	31 July 593
8:1	Vision of idolatry in Jerusalem	17 September 592
20:1	Deputation of elders	9 August 591
24:1	Siege of Jerusalem begins	15 January 588
26:1	Oracle against Tyre	? ? 586
29:1	Oracle against Egypt	7 January 587
29:17	Oracle about Nebuchadnezzar	26 April 571
30:20	Pharaoh's broken arm	29 April 587
31:1	Oracle against Pharaoh	21 June 587
32:1	Lament over Pharaoh	3 March 585
32:17	Pharaoh in Sheol	17 March (?) 585
33:21	News of Jerusalem's fall	19 January 586
40:1	Vision of the future	28 April 573

See the relevant section of the commentary for more details about these dates and their significance. If the collection of oracles against the nations is removed (chs. 25—32) the other dates are all in chronological order.

Ezekiel: the man

All that we know of Ezekiel is what we can deduce from his book. He was the son of Buzi and a priest (1:3). Most scholars take the reference to 'the thirtieth year' in the opening verse of the book to refer to his age. If this is the case he would have been born a few years after Josiah's reform got under way and would have grown up with it. He would have been in his mid-teens when Josiah died. If he lived in Jerusalem he would have known of the preaching of Jeremiah, who was also from a priestly family (Jeremiah 1:1). This would have included his famous 'temple sermon' (Jeremiah 7:1–15) attacking a false reliance on the presence of the temple in Jerusalem as a kind of 'talisman' that would protect the city from capture and destruction. There are a number of similarities and parallels between the themes and images used by these two prophets. The fact that Ezekiel was taken into exile in 597BC shows that he belonged to a prominent family. He gained some standing in the community of exiles, since the elders came to consult him (8:1; 20:1). He was married, and his wife died at the time of the fall of Jerusalem (24:18). The community of which he was part lived at a place called Tel Abib near the river Chebar. This river is usually identified with an irrigation canal called the Kabari in Babylonian texts. It brought water from the Euphrates south-eastwards from Babylon to Nippur and then looped back to the main river near Uruk. Nothing is known of the geographical location of Tel Abib.

Ezekiel is one of the most visual of the major Hebrew prophets in the presentation of his message. A considerable proportion of it is presented as the description of visionary experiences: his call experience (chs. 1—3), a vision of the corrupt practices in the Jerusalem temple (chs. 8—11), and a vision of the restored land (chs. 40—48). Some of the other prophets occasionally perform symbolic actions, but Ezekiel performs what amounts to 'street theatre', for example when he acts out the siege of Jerusalem (chs. 4—5). Even in his 'straightforward' preaching he paints pictures with words as he makes use of allegories and poems, such as the allegory of the eagles (17:1–10) and the poem in which Tyre is depicted as a ship (ch. 27). His priestly background comes out in the language and imagery he uses: for example, the terms 'blood', 'clean/unclean', 'holy/profane' and 'glory' all reflect priestly concepts.

Some scholars have seen Ezekiel's concentration on the fate of Jerusalem and his reported visit there in a visionary experience as evidence that he in fact spent part of his ministry in Judah. Perhaps after being deported he was able to return to Jerusalem for a while, only to be deported again. This line of argument is not very convincing. As we shall see in the commentary, there was good reason why Ezekiel and the exiles with him should be seriously concerned about the fate of Jerusalem. Psalm 137 gives evidence of how deeply the exiles felt about the city. Also, the book of Jeremiah, particularly his letter to the exiles (Jeremiah 29), gives evidence that considerable communication was possible between the exiles and those in Jerusalem. What

Jeremiah was saying was being reported in Babylon, and the words of prophets speaking in exile were being conveyed back to Jerusalem.

Other scholars have seen in Ezekiel's visionary experiences and sometimes rather bizarre behaviour evidence of particular physical or psychosomatic disorders such as epilepsy or schizophrenia. However, the evidence we have from his book is too limited for any of these 'diagnoses' to be anything but speculative. What can be said is that Ezekiel felt deeply about the fate of his nation and was passionately involved in his message, and this had a physical effect on him. Although when proclaiming judgment because of the sinfulness of the people he can sound harsh, his sensitivity as a person is evidenced by the brief description of his feelings for his wife (24:15–18) and his pleas for God to spare his people (9:8; 11:13).

Ezekiel: the book

Authorship and date

In one sense it is difficult to talk about the 'authorship' of the prophetic books of the Old Testament. The Hebrew prophets were primarily preachers. Their oracles were proclaimed verbally, probably memorized by them and some of their hearers. One reason why much of the prophetic material is in poetic form in the original Hebrew is because poetry is easier to memorize than is prose. However, at some point this material was written down and put into book (strictly speaking, scroll) form. Who did this in the case of Ezekiel, and when?

The book of Ezekiel has a structural unity, a chronological flow, a degree of uniformity of style and language, and a coherence of message that have led many scholars to assume its essential unity as the direct product of the prophet Ezekiel. However, for a period in the mid-20th century this view was challenged. Some scholars argued that the poetic and visionary material in the book came from Ezekiel but that the considerable amount of prose was the result of later additions to the prophet's own material. After a period of popularity, this view has waned. This is partly because of the disagreements over identifying Ezekiel's own words, which call the criteria used into question. Also, there has been a fresh recognition of the unity that exists in the book at various levels from phraseology to its overall structure. There is now a general agreement that most of the book comes from Ezekiel himself, with some later expansions and additions that may have come from the prophet when the material was put into book form. Alternatively, they could be from 'disciples' of his, who may have been the ones who preserved the material before it was put together in one book. It may be that sections of the book, such as the oracles against the nations (chs. 25—32) and the great vision of the renewed land at the end of the book (chs. 40—48) once circulated as separate scrolls before the book took the form we know. In fact, the book is such a well-structured and unified composition that it can be readily studied as a coherent work in its present form, which is what we shall do in this commentary.

It needs to be said that to describe some material in the book as 'later expansion and additions' is in no way to downgrade its value or importance. There are many different ways in which God's message came to people in biblical times, and came to be incorporated in scripture. There is no reason why these later expansions and additions should not have inspired by the same Spirit who inspired the prophet Ezekiel.

Structure

The book has a clear outline structure:

- Chapters 1—3: The prophet's vision of the glory of God and his commissioning

- Chapters 4—24: Oracles of doom about Jerusalem

- Chapters 25—32: Oracles against the nations

- Chapters 33—48: Oracles of restoration and transformation

Within these large sections there are smaller sections of structure, which will be pointed out in the commentary.

This overall structure indicates the essence of Ezekiel's message. The turning point is the fall of Jerusalem or, more strictly, the arrival of the news of its fall in Babylon. Before that, the prophet is warning the people of the seriousness of their sins, which will lead to this catastrophe, and calling on them to change their ways. He also exposes their false grounds of hope that somehow God will avert the disaster because Jerusalem is the home of the temple, his Holy Place. Once the city has fallen, Ezekiel is recommissioned to bring the people words of hope. He assures them that God will act to restore them to their land, and will transform them and the land so that he can once again dwell in their midst and bless them. The 'Oracles against the Nations' section acts as a dramatic interlude, building up tension as the reader, like Ezekiel and the exiles, waits to see whether the prophet's oracle of doom will be fulfilled. They also prepare the way for the oracles of hope since they underscore the point that Jerusalem's destruction is not due to the inability of the God of Israel to defend the city, but is an act of judgment upon it in which God uses the other nations as his agents.

Text and translation

The Hebrew text of Ezekiel has suffered more than that of most books of the Old Testament in the process of transmission. The footnotes that are to be found in many modern translations bear witness to the many occasions when the translators had difficulty with the text. This is partly because Ezekiel used a number of rare words, especially technical ones, which later copyists could not be expected to know. There is a concentration of these in the vision in chapters 40—48. One source to which translators often turn for help is the early Greek translation of the Old Testament, called the Septuagint. It is often referred to in footnotes in abbreviated form as 'Gk' or 'LXX' (the Roman numerals for seventy, referring to an old tradition that seventy men translated it from Hebrew into Greek). Since the Septuagint is itself a translation, it has to be used with care as evidence of the Hebrew text, with due consideration given to the translation's own characteristics.

This commentary is based on the New Revised Standard Version English text, and all quotations are taken from this translation unless it is stated otherwise.

Ezekiel: some theological themes

The vision described in Ezekiel 1—3 stresses above all else the awesomeness of God and God's separateness from human beings, whose creaturely frailty is emphasized by the way the prophet is addressed as 'O mortal'. This awesomeness and separateness of God is just what the word 'holy' means in its most general sense in the Old Testament. The vision also presents the God of Israel as the creator and sovereign Lord of history, sitting on the throne of the universe. What Ezekiel actually sees is not God but 'the appearance of the likeness of the glory of the Lord'. The 'glory' of God is God's nature as it is revealed to humans and as comprehended by them. In Ezekiel the glory of

God is the mode of God's presence on earth. Much of Ezekiel's preaching can be directly related to these three aspects of God's nature—holiness, glory and sovereignty.

The holiness of God and the people's sinfulness

Ezekiel's grasp of the holiness of God as his awesome separateness ('otherness' is a term often used of this) strongly colours his attack on the sinfulness of Israel. His major concern is with religious sins, not social sins. Time and again he attacks the idolatry and apostasy of God's people. In the vision of chapters 8—11 it is the worship of other gods that is the centre of the prophet's concern. Such worship is an attack on the holiness of the God of Israel, his unique 'otherness' as the only true God. The God of Israel cannot tolerate being put on a par with other gods, and therefore withdraws his presence, his glory, from the temple and city.

Ezekiel is not blind to moral and social evil, but he sees these evils as the products of the nation's apostasy. Because they have gone after other gods they have rejected the covenant Law (20:16). Ezekiel uses priestly terminology to describe the result of the people's sin. They have defiled both themselves (20:30–31) and the land (36:17). There is a constant stress on the shedding of innocent blood in the land (11:5–7; 36:18). Jerusalem is called 'the bloody city' (22:2; 24:6). The word 'blood' here probably stands for all forms of social violence but is also used because of its sacrificial connotations. The people are shedding the 'blood' of social injustice instead of genuine sacrifices that atone for sin. The sacrifices they do offer are of no effect because of their idolatry.

It may have been Ezekiel's priestly upbringing that gave him such a sense of the seriousness of sin. He sees it as more than mere isolated acts of disobedience to God. Rather, it is a deep-seated resistance to God, an inability to obey God which is endemic to human nature. This is brought out in a rather horrifying way in three recitals of Israel's history (chs. 16; 20; 23). Because of their repeated sinfulness and refusal to repent, the nation must now bear God's judgment (23:28–35). This judgment is nothing other than the consequence of breaking the Sinai covenant (5:6–12). This is shown by the fact that to a large extent the detailed punishments that the prophet mentions echo the covenant curses listed in Leviticus 26.

These themes in Ezekiel have clear application today. They challenge us to consider our contemporary forms of worship. How far do those forms reflect a sense of the holiness of God? They also challenge us to consider the way we live. As the apostle Paul reminds us (Romans 12:1), worship is about how we live our life, not just what we do in church. How well do our lives reflect the holiness of the God to whom we claim to be committed? Ezekiel's sense of human sinfulness calls for realism about this when framing social policy, rather than the 'optimistic humanism' that sometimes prevails.

The glory of God and the people's hope

The sinfulness of the nation is so endemic that ultimately the prophet places no hope for the future on any genuine repentance on their part. His hope for the future rests on the very nature of God, especially God's concern for his glory, his 'reputation' among humans. It is self-evident to Ezekiel that since there is only one true God, all humans should come to recognize that god as God. For Ezekiel, God's glory is closely linked with God's 'name', because the 'name' is related to God's nature and how it is comprehended by humans.

In the recital of Israel's history in chapter 20 Ezekiel declares that in the past God has withheld judgment to prevent his name being profaned among the nations (20:9, 14, 22). The defeat of Israel and Judah by nations worshipping other gods would raise the question of whether the God of Israel really was the true God. The extent of Judah's sinfulness is seen in the fact that God must now invoke the covenant curses and risk the profaning of his name.

The prophet is convinced that hope for the future rests in God's concern for his glory. God will not let his name be profaned for ever, but will act to vindicate it by showing that he is not a weak and powerless God. Therefore the prophet proclaims that God will restore the nation to its own land, not because they deserve it, but for the sake of his name (36:22–23, 32). This restoration will be a miracle of divine grace and power, as is made clear by the vision of the valley of dry bones (37:1–14) and the promise of a new 'heart' (or, more correctly translated into our idiom, 'mind') (36:26–28). The contents of this promise make it nothing less than a promise of a new covenant, as can be seen when they are compared with Jeremiah's promise of a new covenant (Jeremiah 31:31–34).

The apostle Paul saw the fulfilment of the promises of both Ezekiel and Jeremiah in the work of Christ and the gift of the Holy Spirit

(2 Corinthians 3:6). Like Ezekiel, he realized that salvation is a miracle of divine power and grace, and not something that we can ever deserve: 'For by grace you have been saved through faith, and this is not your own doing; it is the gift of God—not the result of works, so that no one may boast' (Ephesians 2:8–9). The resurrection of Jesus, which for Paul is a crucial element in the Christian message (1 Corinthians 15:14), gives a new dimension to the understanding of the vision of the valley of dry bones, adding a firmer basis for hope for the future.

God's sovereignty and the nations

The universal sovereignty of God over history is evident in the oracles against the nations (chs. 25—32). Some scholars argue that the repeated refrain that God wants the nations to know that he is the Lord is merely a rhetorical device and that there is no real concern for the conversion of the nations. However, the condemnation of Israel for failing to witness to the holiness of God belies this. In 5:5–6 it is implied that Israel was to be a witness to God among the nations, and she is condemned partly because she has failed in this task (5:7–8). Ezekiel cannot have forgotten that God's purpose in calling Abraham (Genesis 12:3) and then in choosing Israel as a 'priestly nation' (Exodus 19:5–6) was so that his blessing might be made available to all nations. Jesus restated this purpose when he gave his Great Commission to his disciples (Matthew 28:18–20).

Conclusion

These themes do not exhaust Ezekiel's theology. However, as we study his book in some detail we shall find them woven into it like the themes of a theological symphony. They provide the general framework within which we should understand the specific pronouncements of his oracles.

Further reading

J. Blenkinsopp, *Ezekiel*, John Knox Press, 1990: A Bible commentary for teachers and preachers.

H. McKeating, *Ezekiel*, JSOT Press, 1993: A concise guide to scholarly study of the book.

C.J.H. Wright, *Ezekiel*, IVP, 2001: An exposition of Ezekiel with application for today.

SETTING *the* SCENE

The book of Ezekiel begins with two dates, both setting the scene for what follows. The easier date to understand is 'the fifth year of the exile of King Jehoiachin' (v. 2). In our dating system, that means 593BC. We are told about this king and his exile in 2 Kings 24:10–17. Judah had got caught up in the turbulent power politics of the Near East. Unwise actions by her leaders led to an invasion by King Nebuchadnezzar. Jerusalem and its temple were looted, and the king 'and the elite of the land' (2 Kings 24:15) were taken into captivity in Babylon. A puppet-king was put on the throne.

Exiles and aliens

It is not hard to imagine how those exiles would have felt. They had suffered the bitter experiences of the siege and capture of Jerusalem, perhaps losing loved ones in the fighting. They would probably have lost their material possessions. Then they were arrested and marched into captivity in Babylonia, a journey that took Ezra four months on horseback (Ezra 7:9). Now they were struggling to re-establish their life in an alien land on the banks of a large irrigation canal near the ancient city of Nippur, in what is now the plains of southern Iraq. This was a very different environment from the hill country of Judea. They would have experienced shock, grief, home-sickness, anger, despair and other similar emotions. To make matters worse for a people for whom religion was an integral part of their life, they were cut off from the temple in Jerusalem. This was the symbol of the presence of their God with them as a people, and the place where they experienced meeting God in a special way at the great pilgrim festivals. They must have felt cut off from God, not just by the physical distance but by the disaster that had struck the city and its temple. Did it mean that God had deserted them, or even that he was not powerful enough to protect them against the gods of their captors? They were soon to learn, through Ezekiel, that their God was the only God, and that the gods of Babylon were useless idols, mere human creations. Moreover, God was to assure them that he was in control of their destiny, a truth that was both unsettling and comforting.

Ezekiel the priest

While verse 2 puts the events of the book into the context of world history, and the history of one particular community—the kingdom of Judah—verse 1 puts those events into the context of the life of one person, Ezekiel, son of Buzi, a priest from Judah. The date 'the thirtieth year' is puzzling. The most likely explanation is that it refers to Ezekiel's age. Thirty was the age at which priests entered fully into the service of the sanctuary (Numbers 4:3, 30). Had events taken their normal course, Ezekiel could have expected a bright future. The Babylonians counted him among the 'elite' of his nation. These were the people whom they considered to have leadership potential and so, from their point of view, were potential troublemakers. As a priest, Ezekiel would have had the privilege of ministering in the temple, at the heart of his country's life. His book indicates that he was himself a deeply spiritual person, who would have greatly valued the spiritual privilege of serving as a priest. However, under the Mosaic Law, he could fulfil his priestly calling only in the temple in Jerusalem. That calling centred on performing the offering of sacrifices and the liturgical worship associated with them. The Israelites were not allowed to offer their sacrifices anywhere other than the Jerusalem temple (Deuteronomy 12). Now, in his thirtieth year, when he might have expected to begin to enter into everything for which he had been prepared and trained, Ezekiel finds himself a prisoner of war in an alien land, working as a labourer for a foreign power.

However, when all seemed lost, 'the heavens were opened' and Ezekiel 'saw visions of God' (v. 1). That very fact, quite apart from the substance of the visions, brought tremendous hope. The God of Israel could be met by the banks of the Chebar canal, not just in the Jerusalem temple. God had not forgotten his exiled people, nor this priest who longed to serve him. Fulfilment of his priestly calling might not be possible, but he could fulfil the calling of another kind of intermediary between God and people, that of a prophet.

MEDITATION

'May the God of hope fill you with all joy and peace in believing, so that you may abound in hope by the power of the Holy Spirit' (Romans 15:13). The background to that prayer is Paul's conviction that nothing 'in all creation will be able to separate us from the love of God in Christ Jesus our Lord' (Romans 8:39).

The VISION *of* GOD'S THRONE

Ezekiel's account of what he saw when 'the heavens were opened' is a complex and confusing description of a visionary experience of God's presence. Attempts to paint a coherent picture based on it have proved futile, and attempts to find some kind of meaning or significance in each detail of the vision have become exercises in reading things into it instead. Both approaches are misguided because they ignore the fact that Ezekiel is trying to describe the indescribable— God. This is especially apparent in the allusive language used in verse 28. Ezekiel can speak only of seeing 'the appearance of the likeness of the glory of the Lord'. Moreover, he is describing a vision that overwhelmed him. It is not surprising that his description of it is incoherent and hard to follow!

Imagery of God's presence

Although the vision is complex, it is possible to see within it a coming together of different strands of imagery that are used to speak of the presence of God in the Hebrew Bible. There is the imagery of the storm clouds, with thunder and lightning (v. 4; Exodus 19:16–20; Psalm 18:9–15). In Habakkuk 3 God is depicted as coming in awesome splendour in a great war chariot. Then there is the depiction of God as a sovereign seated on a throne (v. 26; Isaiah 6; Psalm 99). Cherubim are mentioned in both Psalm 18 and Psalm 99. In the ancient Near East, cherubim were not the rosy-cheeked, plump children with wings that appear in Renaissance paintings. They were hybrid creatures with wings, such as Ezekiel describes. In Psalm 18:10–11 the flying cherubim seem to be identified with the storm clouds. In Psalm 99:1 God is said to be 'enthroned' upon them. The background here is the use of the images of such creatures to act as 'throne guardians' symbolizing divine protection of the throne (1 Kings 10:18–20). In the Jerusalem temple there were images of two large cherubim overshadowing the ark of the covenant, the symbol of God's presence (1 Kings 8:16–28). This reflects an earlier tradition linking the ark with the cherubim-protected throne of God (2 Samuel 6:2).

God is with us!

With this background we can begin to appreciate the significance of Ezekiel's vision, even though we cannot understand all the detail. The appearance of the cherubim chariot-throne was an assurance that the exiles were not cut off from the God of Israel. He was not confined to the temple in Jerusalem. He could also be with them in Babylonia. Indeed the imagery of the vision depicts him as the Lord of creation, who can be present throughout the world he has created. The faces of the cherubim represent major groups of living creatures (v. 10, humans, wild animals, domestic animals, birds). Above them is the 'firmament' (v. 22, the same word as in Genesis 1:7, RSV), which is the 'roof' over the earth. Above this, God sits on the throne. The imagery not only assures the exiles that God is with them because he is, in fact, everywhere in his creation. It also assures them that God knows their plight because he sees everything. That is the probable significance of the eyes in the rims of the wheels of the chariot-throne (v. 18). Of course, as the one who sits on the throne, God is the all-powerful one, and so is in control of the destiny of his people.

In one sense, this was a reassuring vision. The all-knowing, all-powerful, ever-present Creator God is with his people in exile just as he was in the temple. However, when God comes to his people, that coming is not always welcome. He may come to deliver and bless, or he may come to execute judgment. But even if the coming does mean judgment, there is a ray of hope. In the vision this is seen in the rainbow (v. 28), a reminder of God's promise after the great flood that judgment would be tempered with mercy (Genesis 9:8–17). The exiles were already experiencing God's judgment on his disobedient people, and there was more to come. However, the rainbow in the storm clouds was an assurance that there was a future for them beyond the judgment.

MEDITATION

Ezekiel is the most visual of the prophets. He uses mental pictures and dramatic actions to convey his message. The truth has to be 'seen' in order to be understood and accepted. Meditate for a while on this awesome vision, praying that you might 'see' in it some truth about God that will encourage you in your situation.

EZEKIEL'S VOCATION

As Ezekiel lay prostrate on the ground, overwhelmed by the vision, he heard a command to stand up. It was not something he could do in his own strength. He was able to obey only because the Spirit empowered him to do so (v. 2). The voice addressed him as 'son of man' (translated as 'mortal' in the NRSV). This is a Hebrew way of saying 'human being'. It is the usual way in which Ezekiel is addressed by God, and seems intended to stress his weakness and frailty as a creature over against the power of the Creator God.

A daunting task

Ezekiel is commissioned to go as a prophet to his fellow Israelites. At this point he is not told the content of his message, only its character. He is to proclaim the word of the Lord God (v. 4), to be God's spokesman. The task is a daunting one. The people to whom he is to speak are described as impudent, stubborn and rebellious—hardly a very promising congregation—and their rebelliousness is not a mere passing phase. In verse 3 these people are called, in Hebrew, 'the sons of Israel' and it is then said that their fathers transgressed against God. Their rebelliousness has the character of an ingrained, inherited trait. The prophet's task is therefore a difficult one, described as being like wading through briers and thorns and sitting on scorpions (v. 6). But he is to go on declaring God's word to the people. Why should he persist in this fruitless ministry? It is so that 'they shall know that there has been a prophet among them' (v. 5). This knowledge will come only in retrospect, when Ezekiel's warnings about the consequences of their stubborn rebelliousness have come true. With that knowledge will come the realization that they cannot blame God for what has occurred. His spokesman gave them due warning and the chance to change their ways, but they failed to heed his words.

Career or calling?

Some Old Testament prophetic books contain an account of the prophet's call by God (for example, Isaiah 6 and Jeremiah 1). Prophecy in Israel was not a career but a calling, a vocation. This passage highlights some of the differences between a career and a vocation.

- A career is something that people simply choose for themselves, for whatever reason. A vocation rests on the sense that God has chosen you to do the job (v. 3). The issue is not what is done, but why it is done. One person may be a shop assistant or teacher or computer programmer because that is their choice of career, while another person can do the same job with the sense that it is their God-given vocation.

- A career is self-centred, concerned with 'personal advancement' in order to get as near the top of the 'ladder' as possible, with mate-rial gains, personal status and power as rewards. A vocation is centred on obeying God and making God known by the way the job is done—words of testimony spoken when appropriate and, most fundamentally, the quality of the life lived. The aim is that people might know that God's spokesperson is among them (v. 5).

- In a career, people depend on their own strengths—gifts, energy, personality, and so on. In a vocation, people use these same things in dependence on the power of God's Spirit (vv. 1–2).

- A person's career is judged by their measure of 'success' as defined by society. A person's vocation is judged by their faithfulness to God.

Few people in ancient Israel were called to be prophets, but all were called to be obedient to God in some way. The charge against the Israelites to whom Ezekiel spoke was that they refused to hear what God said to them, and so failed to obey him. Few Christians today are called to be prominent spokespeople for God—well-known evange-lists, preachers, musicians, or leaders of other kinds. However, every Christian, not just such notable people, has a vocation from God. There is some way in which we are all called to serve God obediently and so be God's spokesperson by the way we work, speak and live.

MEDITATION

Do you know what your vocation is? If so, how faithful are you in living it out? If not, pray that God will give you a clear sense of what it is. It could be the job you are doing now, but done with a different motivation.

EATING *the* SCROLL

In contrast to those to whom he is to prophesy, Ezekiel provides a model of submission and obedience to God. When he came face-to-face with the vision of God's glory, he fell down in humble submission (1:28). When God spoke to him, he listened, and obeyed the command to stand up (2:1–2). Now he obeys a command to open his mouth and to eat what he is given.

A double-edged message

As Ezekiel looked, he saw a hand appear, carrying a scroll, the ancient counterpart to the modern book. Scrolls were usually made of papyrus or parchment. Words would be written on one side of the scroll, and the scroll would then be rolled up with the writing on the inside. Unusually, the scroll Ezekiel saw had writing on both sides. This suggests a very full and complete message. We are told that it was one of 'lamentation and mourning' (2:10). This probably does not mean that the words themselves were mournful laments, but that their effect on those who read or heard them would be to cause lamentation and mourning. A message of liberation and hope to an oppressed people will be one of punishment and woe to their oppressors. In the same way, the word of God, which can bring joy to the godly, will make the ungodly mournful. When Ezekiel ate the scroll it was 'sweet as honey' to him (3:3). Jeremiah had spoken of God's words in a similar way. He found them to be 'a joy and the delight of my heart' (Jeremiah 15:16).

An unwelcome message

The eating of the scroll was a symbolic act of 'internalizing' the word of God, so that it became part of Ezekiel's very being, and thus it set the seal on his vocation to be a prophet. As Ezekiel pondered over this visionary experience, he may have remembered an event concerning a prophet and a scroll which had taken place ten years earlier in Jerusalem, and which he may even have witnessed. Jeremiah had instructed his scribe Baruch to write down his prophecies of warning and judgment on a scroll, and to read it out in the temple. At that time Jeremiah himself was banned from the temple. When Baruch read the scroll in public, it caused consternation, and the scroll was taken to be read to King Jehoiakim. He treated the message with contempt, burning the scroll piece by piece as it was read. Jeremiah and Baruch had to go into hiding to avoid arrest (Jeremiah 36). Ezekiel would have realized that the contents of the scroll that he had to proclaim would get no better reception than had the contents of Jeremiah's scroll. His ministry was not going to be an easy one.

The imagery of eating the scroll carries with it the idea of food and sustenance. What food is to the body—the source of its strength to carry out its daily tasks—God's word was to be to Ezekiel's ministry. As these words became part of him they would give him the strength to carry out his vocation of being a prophet to a stubborn and rebellious people.

Living out the message

Whatever our vocation may be, if we are to carry it out faithfully, as Ezekiel did his prophetic ministry, we need to learn from his example. Like him, we must be humble and submissive before God. This is not easy. At one point (2:2) it was the Spirit who gave Ezekiel the power to obey God's command. In the Old Testament the Spirit of the Lord comes and goes in mysterious ways. Since Pentecost the Holy Spirit comes to indwell Christians and be a permanent source of strength. Christians also have the privilege of God's word being available all the time in the Bible. This word can be 'eaten' by being read, studied, memorized and meditated upon so that it becomes part of us. In this way it will nourish us spiritually and give us the strength we need to carry out our vocation faithfully.

MEDITATION

'O taste and see that the Lord is good,' says the psalmist
(Psalm 34:8). Having 'tasted', we need to go further.
'You have been born anew, not of perishable but of imperishable
seed, through the living and enduring word of God…
Like newborn infants, long for the pure, spiritual milk,
so that by it you may grow into salvation—if indeed you have
tasted that the Lord is good' (1 Peter 1:23; 2:2–3).

EZEKIEL'S TASK

As Ezekiel's visionary experience draws to a close, God addresses him
again as 'son of man', reminding him of his frailty and mortality (v. 4,
'mortal' in NRSV). This seems an unpromising prelude to a description of the difficulty of his task. It would have been difficult enough
if he had been sent to a foreign nation. The communication problem
would then have been linguistic. But that could have been overcome
by effort on the prophet's part. He could have learnt the foreigners'
language. In all likelihood they would then have been willing to listen
to what he had to say to them. However, the problem with his compatriots was not that they could not understand what he said. It was
that they would not want to listen: they would refuse to hear what
God was saying to them through the prophet.

Closed minds

The Israelites are described as having 'a hard forehead and a stubborn
heart' (v. 7). This is another way of expressing what has been said
before, that they are 'impudent and stubborn' (2:4). The 'hard forehead' means an attitude of defiance, even belligerence. In Hebrew,
the heart is not the centre of the emotions, but of thinking, deciding
and willing. To have a 'stubborn heart' is to have a closed mind and
a set attitude that you are unwilling to change. This was the communication blockage that faced Ezekiel. How was he to respond? God
says that he is to 'face them out' (v. 8). This is not something he can
do just because of the strength of his own personality. God has 'hardened' Ezekiel's face and forehead, so that his determination to speak,
and go on declaring God's word, will be stronger than Israel's refusal
to listen.

Toughened prophets

In verse 8 there is a play on Ezekiel's name. His name is made up of
two parts. The ending, 'el', is a Hebrew word for 'god'. The first part
comes from the verb used in verse 8 to mean 'to harden'. So, the
name 'Ezekiel', which is usually taken to mean 'God will strengthen',
is here given the more specific meaning 'God will harden'. There is
an important implication here. Reading the book of Ezekiel, one

might conclude that the prophet was a rather tough, unfeeling person. However, verses 8–9 suggest the opposite. He was a sensitive person who needed to be toughened for his task. In general, the Hebrew prophets who declared God's judgment (excepting Jonah) seem not to have enjoyed their task. They were not vindictive people. Amos was appalled at the idea of God's judgment falling on Israel, and protested against it (Amos 7:1–6). Hosea expressed God's anguish at having to punish his people (Hosea 11:8). Jeremiah is renowned as 'the weeping prophet' because of the tears he shed over Judah. The toughness of these prophets was not the result of vindictiveness. It was the toughness of love which knew that, for their own good, the people had to be faced with the seriousness of their situation. Such is the love of God.

Tough love

We see this tough love in Jesus. He had some hard things to say to the religious leaders of his day (Matthew 23:1–36), yet he wept because of the disaster that awaited them (Matthew 23:37–39). He did not let a would-be disciple get away with a half-hearted commitment, despite his love for the man (Mark 10:17–22). When he sent his disciples out on a preaching tour he told them that they were not just to preach a comforting message of 'peace'. If the people in a town would not listen to the gospel, the disciples were to wipe its dust off their feet publicly as they left, as a warning to them of impending judgment (Matthew 10:13–15).

None of us likes offending people or being unpopular. As a result we are always tempted to 'soften' the hard bits of the message. That is why God calls on Ezekiel to go on listening to his word and taking it to heart (v. 10). Eating the scroll was not a once-for-all act. It symbolized what was to go on throughout his ministry.

His commissioning complete, Ezekiel returned to the people among whom he was to be a prophet. He seems to have experienced the kind of reaction that quite often follows a deep spiritual experience, and took time to come to terms with it before he spoke (v. 15).

PRAYER

Pray for Christians who are ministering in situations where they need the same kind of toughness that Ezekiel needed.

The WATCHMAN

The image of the prophet as a watchman was not new to Ezekiel. A century and a half earlier, Hosea had used it: 'The prophet is a sentinel (watchman) for my God over Ephraim' (Hosea 9:8). Ezekiel's contemporary, Jeremiah, used it, condemning Judah for being like people who do not heed the warning trumpet of the watchman (Jeremiah 6:17). It is a powerful image. The watchman has a key role, whether as the lookout on a ship, the sentry guarding the army encampment or the watchman on the city walls. In Ezekiel's day, without radar, sonar or other electronic listening devices, the watchman's warning was crucial in giving people time to prepare for, or avoid, impending danger. The reason prophets were compared to watchmen in ancient Israel is expressed in two ways in the Old Testament. First, one of the terms used of a prophet is 'seer' (Amos 7:12), that is, one who sees things that other people do not or cannot see. The prophets had a spiritual sensitivity that enabled them to discern things that others missed. The second reason is also expressed in Amos: 'Surely the Lord God does nothing without revealing his secret to his servants the prophets' (Amos 3:7). Perhaps God looks for those who have developed some spiritual discernment to be the recipients of such revelation.

The prophet's responsibility

The importance of the watchman image for Ezekiel is indicated by its repetition in chapter 33. It acts as both the introduction and conclusion to Ezekiel's prophecies of judgment, indicating their significance. By this image God brings home to the prophet that the privilege of his visionary experience of God's presence brings with it responsibility. The prophet differs from the mystic or the guru (and there is a place for both of these in any religious community). The mystic is concerned with deepening his or her own knowledge of God and relationship with God. For some, this then overflows into action in daily life, but that is not the mystic's primary concern. The guru gives teaching to those who deliberately come to learn, so showing their willingness to receive it. The prophet's primary concern is other people, and the target audience is everyone, whether or not they are willing to listen. By using the watchman image, God brings home to Ezekiel the awesomeness of his responsibility as a prophet. He is responsible to God for the spiritual life or death of those to whom God has sent him. It is common in Hebrew speech to indicate a totality by referring to its two extremes, and so the inclusion of 'the wicked' and 'the righteous' is a way of saying that Ezekiel has to speak to everyone without discrimination, warning them of God's impending judgment.

God's mercy

This awesome responsibility is to be seen as an expression of God's love and mercy. In terms of strict justice, God had no need to send his people yet another prophetic watchman. They had his covenant Law, so they knew what was right and wrong, and had failed to live by it. Numerous prophets had come to call them back to the covenant, and had been ignored or rejected. If summary judgment came, the people could hardly plead innocence or ignorance. Yet God wanted to give them one more chance to repent. This was Ezekiel's mission.

The hearer's responsibility

It is important to take in the fact that the prophet's responsibility is limited, however. It is limited by the responsibility of the hearers. He is responsible for the faithful proclamation of the warning (v. 18). They are responsible for whether or not they heed it (v. 19). There is an important lesson here that relates to all Christian vocations. As we have seen already, we are called to be faithful to God, not to be 'successful' by human criteria. Christians who think that they have ultimate responsibility for the spiritual well-being of their family, friends, work colleagues, church members, or anyone else, are in danger of burn-out and breakdown. If you are fulfilling your vocation faithfully, then the responsibility for the outcome rests between the other person and God. You have discharged your responsibility.

MEDITATION

Being a lookout requires constant vigilance. In spiritual terms this means a patient, receptive waiting upon God, as expressed by Habakkuk: 'I will stand at my watchpost, and station myself on the rampart; I will keep watch to see what he will say to me'
(Habakkuk 2:1).

7

EZEKIEL 3:22–27

EZEKIEL'S DUMBNESS

Ezekiel's call experience reaches its climax with a second vision of
God's glory. In this second experience he is told that he is going to be
housebound and dumb for most of the time. This is totally contrary
to what one might expect of a prophet who is God's spokesman.
Though we are not told it here, these restrictions are to last until he
receives news of the final destruction of Jerusalem (Ezekiel 33:21–22).

The nature of Ezekiel's dumbness

This passage has been the centre of much debate. It has been understood in several different ways, including the following alternatives.

- The language is metaphorical, but represents the fact that the
  leaders of Ezekiel's community put him under house arrest and
  prevented him from prophesying freely in public. There are a few
  references in the book to people coming to his house to consult
  him (14:1; 33:31), but it is far from clear that he was prevented
  from prophesying in public before the fall of Jerusalem.

- The actions of staying indoors, being bound with cords and not
  speaking unless uttering a prophecy are symbolic acts. They are
  intended to symbolize the state of the exiles—in bondage—and to
  add weight to the prophecies: the prophet only speaks (at least in
  public) when he has a message from God to proclaim. Symbolic
  acts were certainly part of the repertoire of the Hebrew prophets
  from an early period (1 Kings 11:29–33). They were the ancient
  equivalent of modern audio-visual aids. Jeremiah, Ezekiel's contemporary, made use of them (Jeremiah 19:10–13), and Ezekiel
  himself acts out some of his messages, as we shall see.

- The language is metaphorical and refers to the fact that Ezekiel was
  afflicted with some psychosomatic condition, no doubt of a spiritual origin, with the result that he was paralysed and dumb except
  when he had a word from God to proclaim, either verbally or by
  acting it out.

Given the brevity and ambiguity of this passage, it is not easy to
choose between these different interpretations, especially the last

36

two. What is clear is that Ezekiel's vocation to be a prophet was something that affected his whole being and way of life. The restrictions highlight the fact that he was first and foremost God's spokesman and a watchman for Israel. That life-shaping element should be true of every Christian's vocation, though it will rarely take such a dramatic form as it did in the case of Ezekiel.

True communication

God's closing words to Ezekiel, 'Let those who will hear, hear; and let those who refuse to hear, refuse' (v. 27) have the ring of both a promise and a threat. Jesus used similar words (Mark 4:9, 23), and a Christian prophet echoes them (Revelation 2:7). They are a reminder that it takes two to communicate. A message can be proclaimed, but there is no communication unless there is hearing, understanding and acceptance of the message. The messenger can only go so far, by expressing the message in as clear and compelling a way as possible. The rest is up to the hearers. They have the privilege of hearing God's word, but then have the responsibility for how they receive it. In the case of Ezekiel's audience, as we have seen, the problem was not with their ability to hear the sound of what he said. It was in their readiness to hear with understanding and then to act on that understanding.

Our responsibility

The account of Ezekiel's call carries a message not only for those who are proclaimers of God's word, in whatever way, by speech or action. There is also a message for all those who are confronted with God's word in any form. It comes to us and requires a reaction, for which we are responsible. God's word is powerful, but God respects us as people and we have a measure of freedom in our response to his word. We can listen or refuse to do so. Having listened, we can ignore the message or seek to understand it. Having understood, we can obey or disobey. Our spiritual well-being depends on the response.

MEDITATION

The parable of the sower, or of the four soils (Mark 4:1–20), is about the responsibility of hearing God's word. Meditate on it prayerfully as a way of assessing your preparedness to receive God's word so that it will bear fruit in your life.

JERUSALEM BESIEGED

The account of Ezekiel's public ministry begins with the description of three symbolic acts. The account of each act begins with the words, 'And you (O mortal), take…' (4:1, 9; 5:1). In the first of these acts (vv. 1–3), Ezekiel is told to take a brick and inscribe on it a sketch-map of Jerusalem. Babylonian houses were made of mud bricks. Presumably Ezekiel made his sketch-map on a brick while it was still soft, before it was dried. (Archaeologists have found Babylonian bricks with sketch-maps or architectural drawings on them.) It may be that the siege equipment was also depicted on the brick. Alternatively Ezekiel may have made models of siegeworks, camps, battering rams and so on, to place around the brick. When all this was set up, the prophet was to take a large iron plate and fix it up between himself and the model of the besieged city. He was then to gaze towards the city from behind the plate. Presumably, all this was done outside his house in Tel Abib so that people could see it.

Symbolic actions

What was the point of all this? Most obviously it was an acted-out prophecy that Jerusalem would once again be besieged, as she had been in 596BC before the city was taken by the Babylonians, and Ezekiel and others were taken into captivity. If this was not bad news enough, the prophet behind the plate represented God, who was fully aware of the plight of the city but, because of the people's sinfulness, represented by the iron plate, was leaving the city to its fate. The message being driven home was that the people should not put any false hopes in the deliverance of Jerusalem. It is clear from the book of Jeremiah (see, for example, Jeremiah 7) that in the last decades before the destruction of the temple, there were those in Judah who believed that because the temple was in Jerusalem, God would never let the city be destroyed. Somehow he would act miraculously to deliver it, as he had in the time of Hezekiah (2 Kings 19:35–37). By his dramatic action Ezekiel sought to destroy such false hopes.

Symbolic numbers

The precise details of the other part of Ezekiel's actions (vv. 4–9) are not clear, nor is the significance of the numbers. There is space here to offer only one interpretation. First, the action of lying on his side facing the model with an arm bared (v. 7) as a sign of threatening action was probably something he did for a part of each day. Verse 8 indicates that Ezekiel felt a sense of divine compulsion about this 'acted prophecy', just as prophets did about their spoken prophecies (for example, Jeremiah 20:9). The actions described in the following two sections (4:9–17 and 5:1–4) were probably carried out during this period. The cooking, eating and drinking, at least, would need to be done daily. We are told that lying on his side facing the model represented periods of punishment enacted by God against his people (v. 4). The numbers are probably round numbers symbolizing particular significant periods, rather than exact figures. The 390 years corresponds roughly to the time from the building of the temple to its eventual destruction by the Babylonians. The forty years is a new period 'in the wilderness', namely the Babylonian exile.

On the one hand, the message of this aspect of Ezekiel's actions is just as depressing as the actions described in verses 1–3. The sinfulness of the people is seen as something that has characterized their whole history as a nation. Throughout they have provoked God's displeasure by their sinfulness. Now they will lose the promised land and find themselves in the wilderness once again. However, there is also a message of hope implicit in the numbers. God did look after his disobedient people in the wilderness and eventually brought them into the promised land. So perhaps the exile would end and there would be a return to Jerusalem. Also, the two figures, 390 and 40, add up to 430. That is no accident. It was the number of years the Hebrews spent in slavery in Egypt (Exodus 12:40). That period ended in the mighty deliverance of the exodus. Here is a hint that a new exodus may lie ahead.

MEDITATION

When we are caught up in a seemingly hopeless situation, it is not easy to keep hope alive or to see possible glimmers of hope. Do you know someone in such a situation whom you could support by prayer and in other ways? Alternatively, pray for some of the 'hopeless' situations that are in the news headlines at present.

SIEGE RATIONS

Ezekiel's second form of silent drama was to make bread out of a mixture of cereals, baked over a fire of dung. He was to eat a small loaf (v. 10, about 225 grammes or 8 ounces) and drink a small amount of water (v. 11, about three-quarters of a litre or one and one-third pints) daily. This action carried a twofold message. On the one hand, it depicted the sparse rations that would be eaten in Jerusalem as a city under siege. The staple foods would eventually be in short supply, and so whatever odds and ends of cereals were available would have to be used to make bread. The supply of both bread and water would be limited (vv. 16–17). On the other hand, it also symbolized the outcome of the siege—exile in foreign lands where observance of the laws of ritual purity would be difficult, if not impossible.

Identification with his hearers

It is a matter of debate whether or not the daily ration of food and water described here was all that Ezekiel consumed during the time he was acting out the siege of Jerusalem. It is possible that this is all that he ate in public, but that he also ate and drank in private at home. Even if he did supplement this ration, the demands of acting out the siege of Jerusalem by lying on his side and eating and drinking restricted rations for a good part of each day made it a far from comfortable way of proclaiming his message. The prophet did not simply stand apart from those to whom he had been sent with a message. He did not gloat over their misfortunes, well-deserved though they were. In some measure at least, he identified with them in their sufferings. This suffering identification with a sinful people in order to bring their plight home to them is a pale foreshadowing of God's ultimate means of communicating with a sinful world—the word becoming flesh in Jesus of Nazareth.

God's kindness

The prophet's plea that he be spared from having to use human excrement as the fuel for his fire to bake the bread, and God's response (vv. 12–15), provide some glimmers of hope. Ezekiel's reaction to the original command arose from more than just the natural human repugnance at the idea of cooking food over human dung. It was rooted in his upbringing as a priest. This had given him a profound awareness of the importance of ritual purity if one was to preserve a relationship with God. The purpose of the purity laws under the Sinai covenant was to give the people a sense of the holiness and awesomeness of God, who was therefore not to be approached lightly. At the same time the laws made clear his grace in making it possible for them, despite their sinfulness, to approach him at all. Ezekiel reacts with horror to the command to defile himself by eating food that was ritually unclean because of the way it was cooked, as this would put a barrier between him and God. The response he gets shows that God is not unfeeling—far from it. In an act of kindness and respect towards his faithful messenger, God changes his original command. It seems legitimate to see here the hint of the possibility of a faithful 'remnant' coming through the disaster of judgment and providing the basis for a new beginning for God's people.

God's provision

We have seen that Ezekiel's symbolic action of lying on his side for forty days implies that the time in exile in Babylon is a new 'wilderness experience'. Concern about food had featured in the original wilderness experience. When the people complained about the lack of food and water, or the monotony of their diet, God provided manna, quails and water. At the end of that wilderness time, Moses declared that the purpose of the experience of having to depend on God for their food was to teach them that 'one does not live by bread alone, but by every word that comes from the mouth of the Lord' (Deuteronomy 8:3). Jesus reaffirmed the importance of these words (Matthew 4:1–4). The prophet's message shows the reverse side of this truth. Those who continually reject the spiritual bread of God's word may eventually be reduced to emergency rations for the body as they experience his judgment.

PRAYER

Sadly, wars are frequent items in our news. Pray for those who are suffering because of current wars. Pray for the relief agencies that are trying to meet their needs, including the Christian ones which are also working to provide the spiritual nourishment that people need to help them cope in such situations.

The FATE of the BESIEGED

Ezekiel's three symbolic acts roughly follow the sequence of events that the inhabitants of Jerusalem did experience. First came the mounting of the siege. Then followed increasing hardship as the siege cut off supplies and they had to be rationed. Finally, the walls were breached, the city was put to the sword and torch and the survivors were rounded up for punishment and exile (2 Kings 25:1–12).

The fate of the city's inhabitants at the hands of the Babylonians is graphically portrayed by the prophet's actions. Shaving the head and beard could be a sign of mourning (Leviticus 21:1–5). However, it could also be done to someone as an act of humiliation (2 Samuel 10:4). The prophet's action of shaving his head and beard with a specially sharpened sword carries something of both meanings. The Judeans would be thrown into deep mourning by the destruction of Jerusalem. At the same time, the destruction of the city in a military disaster would be a great humiliation for them.

The prophet's treatment of the hair spoke of the different fates of its citizens (v. 2). Some would perish in the destruction of the city. Some would die fighting to defend it or as they tried to flee from it. The rest would be scattered in exile.

Glimmers of hope

The starkness of this tragedy and the awfulness of the judgment behind it must not be played down. However, as in Ezekiel's other prophecies of judgment, there are signs of hope. To begin with, the prophecy makes clear that what will happen to Jerusalem is a deliberate act of the God of Israel. It is not a result of his weakness and inability to defend his people and city. In fact, the prophet's actions are probably an allusion to an earlier prophecy given by Isaiah (Isaiah 7:20) concerning God's use of the Assyrians to punish Israel for her sins. The deliberateness of Ezekiel's actions, especially the careful weighing of the hair into three piles (v. 1), speaks of a considered and measured act of judgment by God. This is no indiscriminate over-reaction. Then there is the prophet's action of collecting up some of the scattered hairs and binding them in the folds of his robe (v. 3). Here there is a promise that some of the survivors who go into exile will be kept safe—although even they will not have an easy time. There will be casualties even among them, as symbolized by the burning of some of the hairs that were hidden in the robe (v. 4).

God's judgment

While this symbolic action makes clear the nature and extent of God's judgment, we have to wait for the prophetic oracle that follows to get the explanation for the judgment. It is enough at this point to recognize the reality and awfulness of God's judgment on sin and evil. In case we are tempted to dismiss this as something that belongs only to the old covenant, we need to heed the words of the New Testament that it is still true that 'our God is a consuming fire' and that 'it is a fearful thing to fall into the hands of the living God' (Hebrews 12:29; 10:31). In 1 Peter the writer speaks of our being born anew into God's family through what Jesus has done for us. But he then warns us not to forget that the one whom we now know as our heavenly Father is still the holy God and that this has implications for how we should live. 'As he who called you is holy, be holy yourselves in all your conduct,' he says, and goes on, 'If you invoke as Father the one who judges all people impartially according to their deeds, live in reverent fear during the time of your exile' (1 Peter 1:15, 17). The 'fear' spoken of here is not abject terror of a despot, but reverent respect for God which will lead us to seek to please and honour our heavenly Father in the way we live as God's obedient children.

PRAYER

Heavenly Father, thank you for adopting me as one of your
children because of the work of your Son Jesus Christ.
Forgive me for the times I have been a disobedient child.
Please enable me to understand what it means to live a life
that reflects your holiness, and grant me the power of your
Holy Spirit to live it out day by day.

JERUSALEM *the* REBEL

During the 'street theatre' of his symbolic actions, Ezekiel remained dumb. His strange antics probably drew an audience of onlookers who wondered what he was up to and what it all meant. His behaviour would have become a topic of conversation, with different people offering various understandings of what it meant. In this way his actions prepared the ground for the spoken oracle when it came. People's interest had been aroused and their minds engaged.

False hopes ended

Although it is obvious to us that the city at the heart of Ezekiel's actions was Jerusalem, it may not have been so obvious to some of his audience. Maybe, moved by wishful thinking, some even thought that it was Babylon. The book of Jeremiah tells us that both in Jerusalem (Jeremiah 28) and among those exiled in 596BC with Ezekiel (Jeremiah 29), there were prophets who declared that Jerusalem would be safe and that the exiles would return soon because God was about to punish Babylon. As soon as Ezekiel begins to speak, however, he dispels such hopes. 'This is Jerusalem,' he says (v. 5), referring to the plan of the city on the brick that has been the centrepiece of his street theatre. The symbolic actions have portrayed graphically what is going to happen to Jerusalem. Through the prophet, God now explains the reason for his judgment. To understand fully, it is important to recognize that the background to what is said is the covenant relationship between God and Israel.

God's purpose for Israel

When God called Abraham and Sarah, his declared purpose was that through them all the nations of the earth should be blessed (Genesis 12:1–3). Later this was linked with the responsibility of Abraham and his descendants to 'keep the way of the Lord by doing righteousness and justice' (Genesis 18:19). When God made a covenant with Israel at Sinai he declared that they were to be 'a priestly kingdom and a holy nation' (Exodus 19:6). As priests they were to stand between God and the other nations, so making God's blessing available to the nations. This could be so only if they remained a holy nation. What this meant was made clear by the covenant laws, which laid down a pattern of holy living. Eventually God made a covenant with King David (2 Samuel 7), establishing the importance of Jerusalem and its temple as the place where God was to be encountered in a special way. In a sense, his presence on earth was 'focused' here. So, the prophets Isaiah (Isaiah 2:1–4) and Micah (Micah 4:1–3) had visions of the nations flocking into Jerusalem to meet God there and to be taught his ways.

Privilege and responsibility

This vision of Israel attracting other nations to God by their holy way of life and so mediating God's blessings to the nations has now been shattered, declares Ezekiel. It has been shattered because of Israel's rebellion against the covenant laws and statutes. Far from living by them and setting a good example to other nations, the people have rejected them. When God says that Israel has been 'more turbulent than the nations that are all around you' (v. 7), what may be in mind is the kind of thing that Amos said. He declared that Israel's privileged position made her even more culpable than other nations because she ought to have known better how to behave rightly (Amos 3:2).

The principle that privilege brings with it responsibility was one that Jesus taught to his disciples: 'From everyone to whom much has been given, much will be required' (Luke 12:48). In the New Testament both the Church (1 Corinthians 3:16: the 'you' is plural) and the individual believer (1 Corinthians 6:19–20) are spoken of as God's temple. God is present on earth in a special way through the gift of the Holy Spirit in both the fellowship of the Church and the life of the individual Christian. The quality of the life of Christians, both individually and corporately, is intended to have the same effect as the quality of life of Israel. It should attract people to God and so bring them the blessings that flow from knowing God for themselves.

MEDITATION

'You are a chosen race, a royal priesthood, a holy nation, God's own people, in order that you may proclaim the mighty acts of him who called you out of darkness into his marvellous light' (1 Peter 2:9). These words echo Exodus 19:6, but describe the Church. What a responsibility they imply!

JERUSALEM *the* MOCKED

The language of these verses is horrifying, as are the judgments that are threatened. However, this is not the outburst of a God who has lost control of his temper and is simply lashing out at his people in anger. We have already stressed the covenant background to this oracle. When the Israelites accepted the covenant, they accepted both its blessings and its curses, as set out in Leviticus 26 and Deuteronomy 28. The judgments threatened in Ezekiel are not arbitrary or unfair; they are fulfilments of the covenant curses, and so no more or less than the people might expect. God's face will be set against them (5:8; Leviticus 26:17). As a result they will suffer plagues of wild animals (v. 17; Leviticus 26:22), the sword and pestilence (v. 17; Leviticus 26:25), famine (v. 16; Leviticus 26:26), even to the extent of cannibalism (5:10; Leviticus 26:29). They will be scattered among the nations, while being pursued by the sword (5:12; Leviticus 26:33).

A fearful lesson

Israel had failed to be the beacon to the nations that she should have been. As a result she faced judgments that would make her an object of taunting and mockery because of her desolate state. The irony of the situation would be that whereas she was meant to demonstrate God's righteousness and justice to the nations by the way she lived out the laws she had been given, she would now display those qualities through the judgments that would fall upon her. By becoming an object of horror she would be a warning to others of what happens when God's laws are flouted (v. 15). We have here an example of how the message of God will get out somehow, even if the messenger fails to deliver it in the way originally intended. This is a lesson that we need to take to heart.

Love and wrath

This passage brings to a climax the message of judgment that was portrayed by Ezekiel's symbolic actions. It is a hard and unpalatable message. Some people get very upset at talk of God's anger or fury. They feel it to be at odds with the New Testament message of God's love. However, it is not. Surely someone who sees a child being abused and does not react with anger and outrage is lacking in compassion and love for the child. Similarly, parents who see the child they love destroying itself by getting deeper and deeper into some form of evil cannot just sit back and let it happen without expressing anger and taking what steps they can to halt the slide into evil. Those steps might be painful. They might involve harsh words and strong, hurtful actions. But they will be taken in love, and will be evidence of love. To do nothing and say nothing would be a betrayal of love, and a betrayal of goodness and morality.

Hope

The people who argue that because there is so much evil and suffering in the world, they cannot believe in God, are sometimes also the people who reject the idea of a God who can be wrathful. Yet it is in the idea of God's wrath against evil that there is hope for the final triumph of goodness in the world. A God who is incapable of wrath against evil is a God who is indifferent to morality and therefore to injustice and the suffering it brings.

So, the harsh words and awful judgments of Ezekiel 5:5–17 are not evidence of an uncaring, vengeful God. The reverse is the case. Only a God who cared deeply for his people, and for what is good for them, could speak and act like this. Here, then, is another ray of hope. Maybe God's love for his people will ensure that judgment is not the last word. Perhaps the outcome will be the eventual restoration of a chastened child to its loving parent. How God's love and justice can be reconciled is not something that Ezekiel or any of the Hebrew prophets could fathom. The ultimate answer is found in the death of Jesus on the cross and his resurrection.

MEDITATION

'On the mount of crucifixion fountains opened deep and wide;
through the floodgates of God's mercy flowed a vast and gracious tide.
Grace and love, like mighty rivers, poured incessant from above;
and heaven's peace and perfect justice kissed a guilty world in love.'

William Rees and William Edwards (19th century)

A MESSAGE *to the* MOUNTAINS

The whole of Ezekiel 6 is addressed to 'the mountains of Israel', but this message has three parts. The first seven verses constitute the first part of the message. The phrase 'the mountains of Israel' (vv. 2–3) has a double significance. It can mean the whole of the land of Israel as, for example, in Isaiah 14:25 and 65:9. Although the territory that was under the control of the kingdoms of Israel and Judah fluctuated, the constant heartland was the mountainous area that forms the western ramparts of the Jordan valley from Lake Galilee to the Dead Sea.

Canaanite worship

However, in this passage the main emphasis is on the land's being desecrated by the worship of false gods (vv. 4–6). When the Israelites settled in the promised land, they found there 'high places' where the Canaanites worshipped their gods, especially Baal and Asherah. These worship centres were called 'high places' because, as archaeological excavations have shown, their major feature was a large raised stone platform, which provided the stage for various ritual acts. On it were altars for offering animal sacrifices and burning incense. The male gods, such as Baal, were represented by stone pillars and the females, such as Asherah, by a wooden pole or a tree. Central to Canaanite worship was the search for the fertility—of crops, animals and women—on which prosperity depends for an agricultural people. The activity at the 'high places' included ritual prostitution. This mimicked, and so was thought to encourage, the fertilization of the earth by the rain sent by the storm-god Baal. The 'high places' could be situated anywhere, including towns (2 Kings 17:9; 23:5) or valleys (Jeremiah 7:31; 32:35), but most were situated on elevated sites such as hill-tops.

Israel's idolatry

The Israelites were supposed to have nothing to do with this Canaanite religion. However, when they settled in the land, they took over some of the 'high places' for the worship of their own God. Even after the temple had been built in Jerusalem, worship continued at these local shrines. This sometimes resulted in syncretism, the mixing of the worship of the God of Israel with that of other supposed 'gods' such as Baal and Asherah. At certain times and places there was outright apostasy, a turning away from the God of Israel to the worship of Baal. From Elijah onwards, various Hebrew prophets fought against this apostasy. Two kings of Judah, Hezekiah and Josiah, attempted to destroy the 'high places' and centralize worship in Jerusalem. In each case their success was short-lived.

In verses 3–6, Ezekiel is saying that the 'high places' will now be destroyed, and the offering of worship at them ended. Israel's idolatry will at last be brought to an end. However, this will not be as a result of the reforming zeal of prophets and kings, since the people have not responded to this. Instead it will be the result of military disaster ('a sword', v. 3) sent by Israel's God. Again, this is a fulfilment of the covenant curses (verses 3–5 echo Leviticus 26:30).

Some modern idols

Idolatry can take many forms, but its essence remains the same. At the heart of it is the human desire for security and well-being, which are often seen as tied up with power, prosperity and pleasure. The Canaanites believed that these qualities were to be obtained by the worship of gods who were personifications of the powers of nature. In following them the Israelites forsook the worship of the Creator, the Lord of nature, for the worship of the forces of nature. Modern people do the same kind of thing when they believe that they can find security and the meaning of life by gaining a position of power, amassing material possessions, pursuing pleasure, or anything else other than worshipping their Creator.

As Christians we may avoid such blatant idolatry, yet fall into the trap of syncretism by transposing some of our society's values into religious forms. For example, the search for 'spiritual power' can replace the search for the kingdom of God and his righteousness. Belonging to a 'successful' church can become more important than serving God in the world, and a sense of security in the fellowship of the church can replace finding true security in fellowship with God.

PRAYER

Lord God, help me to see any idols that I am harbouring,
and give me the strength to remove them and instead let you
be supreme in those parts of my life.

'THEY SHALL KNOW
that I AM *the* LORD'

The phrase 'and you/they shall know that I am the Lord' is a refrain in this chapter (vv. 7, 10, 13, 14), and variants of it occur elsewhere in the book of Ezekiel. Here it summarizes the purpose of God's judgment. It is a reminder that the harsh judgments pronounced by Ezekiel reflect the opposite of God's desire and intention for his people. The essence of the covenant relationship is expressed in Exodus 6:7: 'I will take you as my people, and I will be your God. You shall know that I am the Lord your God.' As long as Israel 'knew' her God, she would enjoy the blessings he longed to give her. Moses warned the people of the danger of taking these blessings for granted and forgetting God: 'Take care that you do not forget the Lord your God, by failing to keep his commandments, his ordinances and his statutes, which I am commanding you today' (Deuteronomy 8:11). That 'forgetting' is exactly what happened. As a result, instead of experiencing the blessings of the covenant, Israel would experience the curses. In the second and third sections of Ezekiel 6 the prophet holds out to his hearers two different ways of coming to 'know' God again.

The way of hope

The first is described in verses 8–10. It centres on 'remembering'. God promises that some of those who survive the coming events will look back on what has happened and begin to perceive the causes of the disaster. They will realize that it is not just the result of the accidents of history, or the weakness of their God compared with the gods of Babylon. With horror they will come to see and accept that their own evil deeds and idolatry have brought it about. Only then will they be in a condition to be able to return to the Lord their God and once again 'know' him. In the Old Testament the true knowledge of God means recognizing him for who he is and being committed to him. This will necessarily result in living by his 'commandments, ordinances and statutes'. Coming to know God by this process of 'remembering' will be painful, but it is greatly to be preferred to the alternative way spoken of by Ezekiel. It brings with it hope for the future.

The way of despair

In verses 11–14 there is something of a repetition of what has been said in chapter 5. Words alone cannot express the prophet's horror at what is about to befall Israel, and his words are prefaced by a kind of 'dance of death' in which he expresses his agitation. He cannot be dispassionate about his message. After repeating the essence of the oracle in 5:5–17 the prophet homes in on the major topic of chapter 6, the idolatry at the 'high places'. These places will be desecrated by having slain worshippers strewn around them (v. 13). Dead bodies were ritually defiling, and the burning of corpses or bones on an altar was a common way of desecrating it (1 Kings 13:2; 2 Kings 23:16). Here in Ezekiel, though, there seems also to be an allusion to Leviticus 26:30 in which the lifeless bodies of the corpses seem to be represented as fitting 'worshippers' for lifeless idols: 'I will destroy your high places and cut down your incense altars; I will heap your carcasses on the carcasses of your idols.' The idols are shown to be powerless to protect their worshippers from the judgment of the Lord God of Israel. As a result of this calamity the people will come to 'know' that the God of Israel is 'the Lord' in the same kind of way that the Egyptians came to know it through the experience of the plagues and the disaster at the Reed Sea. It is the knowledge of despair, not hope.

Parental discipline

Hebrews 12:5–11 reminds us that, like a good and loving parent, God chastises us when we go astray. When this happens, two outcomes are possible. The pain can move us to remember God's grace and to be disgusted at our sin and repent of it, or we can be unmoved, even perhaps hardened in our disobedience. The responsibility for the outcome lies with us, as it did with those who heard Ezekiel's message.

MEDITATION

'My child, do not despise the Lord's discipline or be weary
of his reproof, for the Lord reproves the one he loves,
as a father the son in whom he delights.'

Proverbs 3:11–12

The END HAS COME

This lengthy, melancholy oracle concludes the warnings of judgment
that began in chapter 4. It repeats much of what has been said before,
but expands on it. First, it expands the geographical extent of the
judgment. Chapters 4—5 concentrated on Jerusalem; chapter 6
spoke to 'the mountains of Israel', the heart of the promised land.
This could imply the whole land, and if there was any doubt about
that, chapter 7 dispels it. Judgment is to fall on 'the four corners of
the land' (v. 2), the land in its entirety. No part will escape.

The Day of the Lord

A second, even more horrifying expansion is the repeated assertion
that doom is not just around the corner, it has arrived! The prophet
refers to this judgment in two ways. It is 'the end' (vv. 3, 6), and it is
'the day' (vv. 7, 10, 12). Behind this language and indeed the whole
oracle is the concept of 'the Day of the Lord'. The origin of this
concept is unclear, but it probably arose out of the experience of 'holy
war' in the early days of Israel's settlement in Canaan. There were
occasions when the Israelites won some amazing victories against the
odds, and believed that this was because 'the Lord of hosts' fought for
them against their (and his) enemies. Sometimes the Israelites hardly
had to fight at all as some unusual happening threw their enemies into
a panic (see, for example, 1 Samuel 7:5–11). So, the hope grew of a
great and final battle when all God's enemies would be routed and
Israel would reign supreme. The first explicit reference to this concept
is by the prophet Amos. He turns the hope on its head, declaring that
the Day of the Lord will not mean deliverance for Israel, but destruction, because her sinfulness has put her among God's enemies (Amos
5:18–20). Therefore the Day of the Lord will be 'the end' for Israel
(Amos 8:1–3). Amos announced the end of the kingdom of Israel.
Ezekiel announces the end of the kingdom of Judah.

Utter disaster

The third area of expansion is in the description of the thorough-
ness of the judgment. It is 'Disaster after disaster!' (vv. 5, 26). All
the common grounds of human confidence and security will be

removed—the pomp and show that are the trappings of power (v. 11), military might (v. 14), wealth (v. 19), even the temple, which had become the symbol of their false religiosity (vv. 20–22). Once again the point is made that this is no arbitrary, unfair punishment. God is dealing with them 'according to their ways' (vv. 3, 8, 9). As in chapter 6, God's declared aim in bringing about this disaster is that the people will 'know that I am the Lord' (vv. 4, 9, 27).

A day of reckoning

The very immediacy and completeness of the judgment described by Ezekiel might seem to make his message irrelevant to us. However, it does have relevance to us, rooted in the reality of God's judgment as an expression of both his love and his total rejection of evil. He will not let evil disfigure his creation and bring suffering to his creatures for ever. There must be a day of reckoning for evil and for evildoers. This conviction has always been part of Christian belief, stemming from Jesus' own teaching. In both parable (for example, Matthew 13:24–30, 36–43) and apocalyptic language (for example, Matthew 25:31–46), he spoke of ultimate judgment. The New Testament writers continue this teaching. Paul says, 'For all of us must appear before the judgment seat of Christ, so that each may receive good or evil according to what they have done in the body' (2 Corinthians 5:10). Hebrews puts it simply and clearly: 'It is appointed for mortals to die once, and after that the judgment' (Hebrews 9:27). This passage goes on to sum up the good news of the Christian message: 'Christ, having been offered once to bear the sins of many, will appear a second time, not to deal with sin, but to save those who are eagerly waiting for him' (Hebrews 9:28). Yet even those who are saved from eternal judgment for their sins will have to give account to God for how they lived their lives. The apostle Paul speaks of this using the imagery of a refining fire, and says that if any one's work is burned up they will suffer loss, though they themselves will be saved, but only as through fire (1 Corinthians 3:15).

PRAYER

*'Search me, O God, and know my heart; test me
and know my thoughts. See if there is any wicked way in me,
and lead me in the way everlasting.'*

Psalm 139:23–24

The VISION *of* JERUSALEM

Ezekiel 8—11 forms a distinct section in the book. The elders of the Jewish exiles came to Ezekiel, presumably seeking an oracle about the fate of Judah and Jerusalem. In their presence Ezekiel had a visionary experience, and afterwards he described it to them (11:24–25). However, this is not an isolated section. It fills out what has been said briefly in the previous chapter about the idolatry of the Judeans (7:20).

A visionary journey

The date of the vision (v. 1) puts it fourteen months after Ezekiel's vision at the river Chebar (1:1–2). It therefore took place during the time he was acting out the siege of Jerusalem, assuming that the periods of 390 days and 40 days (4:5–6) followed each other. As the prophet and the elders waited for a word from the Lord, Ezekiel saw a human form like the one he had seen in his first vision. He had a sense of being plucked away from his house and transported to Jerusalem, where he found himself in the temple compound, inside the north gate. This gate had a double significance. Since the palace was north of the temple, this was the gate through which the king and his entourage would normally enter the temple. Perhaps more significantly for this vision, the north was the direction from which invaders often came to Judah. Ezekiel's contemporary, Jeremiah, warned the Judeans of judgment coming through an invasion from the north (Jeremiah 1:13–16).

An image of jealousy

The first thing that Ezekiel saw in the temple was 'the glory of the God of Israel' as he had seen it in Babylon (vv. 2, 4). One would expect the presence of the glory of God in the temple. After all, the temple was where God's presence was 'focused' on earth, and the glory was a symbol of that presence. It had appeared when Solomon dedicated the temple (1 Kings 8:11). The shocking thing is what Ezekiel saw next, when his gaze was directed to the north. In the entrance of the temple he saw an 'image of jealousy' (v. 3). Any image used for idol-worship would provoke the God of Israel to jealousy.

That is why the Ten Commandments begin with commands about not worshipping any other god or making any images (Exodus 20:3–5). However, the phrase here can mean an 'image of lust'. If that is the meaning, it would refer to an image of Asherah, the Canaanite goddess of love and fertility. Her image was placed in the temple by the apostate king of Judah, Manasseh (2 Kings 21:7). It had been destroyed during Josiah's reform (2 Kings 23:6), but may have been replaced when the reform lapsed after his death.

God's jealousy

This vision is the first of four in this chapter in which Ezekiel is shown the kinds of 'abominations' that are going on in the very sanctuary dedicated to the 'jealous' God of Israel. It is these, the divine voice tells the prophet, that are driving God out of his temple.

Jealousy is something that we tend to think of as a vice. This is because in humans it readily becomes selfishly possessive, and therefore destructive. However, even in our experience we recognize that it can have a legitimate place and a positive role. There is a right sense in which a married couple should be jealous of their relationship and protect it from intrusions that would weaken it. We can be rightly jealous of the good reputation of a group or organization to which we belong, and so seek to uphold it by our behaviour. In the Old Testament, God's jealousy of his relationship with Israel is not selfish. It is centred on what is good for Israel and, through them, for the nations to whom they are meant to mediate God's blessing. There was no way that God was going to share the temple with other gods, false gods. Either they had to be removed or the true God would withdraw his presence. That withdrawal would be the ultimate act of judgment on Israel.

God will not accept a divided loyalty. As Jesus put it, 'No one can serve two masters; for a slave will either hate the one and love the other, or be devoted to the one and despise the other. You cannot serve God and wealth' (Matthew 6:24).

PRAYER

'The dearest idol I have known, whate'er that idol be,
help me to tear it from Thy throne, and worship only Thee.'

William Cowper (1731–1800)

IDOLATRY *in the* TEMPLE

Ezekiel's vision continues with three scenes of idolatrous worship, each bringing him closer to the inner sanctum of the temple proper. He has been standing in the outer courtyard, looking out to the gate that led into it. Now he is brought to the northern gatehouse of the inner court. Here he sees a hole in the wall and is told to dig into the wall or, possibly, to examine it closely (v. 8). In either case, the point is that he finds a concealed door and is told to enter it. The secret room he enters is lined with pictures or carvings of all kinds of creatures (v. 10). This is reminiscent of an Egyptian burial chamber, the walls of which would be covered with brightly painted images of deities in animal forms. Seventy elders are burning incense before these images (v. 11). If this was the worship of Egyptian gods, one reason for secrecy would be fear of the Babylonians, who were in control of Judah at this time. Worship of Egyptian gods would probably be linked with a nationalistic desire to rebel against Babylon, with Egyptian support.

In the entrance of the north gate itself, the prophet sees a group of women 'weeping for Tammuz' (v. 14). Tammuz was an ancient Mesopotamian fertility god, whose worship was linked to the cycle of the seasons. In the hot, dry summer season he was thought to have descended to the underworld. The rites of mourning for his death were intended to ensure his rebirth in the spring, and with it the return of fertility.

Finally, when Ezekiel enters the inner court, he sees 25 men with their backs to the temple. They are facing east and worshipping the sun (v. 16). Throughout the ancient Near East there were forms of sun-worship because the sun was regarded as one of the most powerful gods. It was another form of worship that Josiah had tried to eradicate (2 Kings 23:11–12). We are not told who the men are, but to be where they are in the inner court, they must be priests.

The extent of idolatry

These four tableaux showed the nature and extent of idolatry in Judah. It encompassed all sections of society—civil leaders, priests, ordinary men and women. It was a 'pick and mix' kind of pluralism, drawing on the religions of Canaan, Egypt and Mesopotamia.

There was a tragic irony in this idolatry. Time and again in the past, prophets had made clear to Israel and Judah that drought, crop failure, infertility of cattle and so on were not due to the inability of the God of Israel to give fertility. Rather, they were forms of his chastisement, meant to remind them of the covenant curses (Leviticus 26:14–20; Deuteronomy 28:15–24) and to bring them back to him. When the people returned to God, he would bless them with fertility (see, for example, Hosea 2). Faced with his chastisement, neither Asherah nor Tammuz would be of any help to them. In worshipping the gods of Egypt they were worshipping the gods of the nation that once enslaved them and whose powerlessness had been demonstrated at the time of the exodus. If they wanted deliverance from Babylon, the answer was to return to the God of the exodus. In worshipping the sun they were worshipping a derivative source of life in place of the true giver of life. In worshipping a dead god, Tammuz, they were forsaking the living God.

The outcome of idolatry

How had the Judeans got into this state? They had ignored what was at the heart of Josiah's reform and the preaching of Jeremiah following Josiah's death—the call to recognize that they had forsaken the covenant, broken its laws, and so forsaken the covenant God. Because they refused to acknowledge this, they thought that God had forsaken them (v. 12) for no good reason, and so were looking to other gods for help. The tragedy was that they were therefore forcing God to forsake the temple. Jeremiah provides a powerful commentary on this: 'Has a nation changed its gods, even though they are no gods? But my people have changed their glory for something that does not profit. Be appalled, O heavens, at this, be shocked, be utterly desolate, says the Lord' (Jeremiah 2:11–12).

MEDITATION

'My people have committed two evils: they have forsaken me, the fountain of living water, and dug out cisterns for themselves, cracked cisterns that can hold no water' (Jeremiah 2:13). Are there any ways in which this could be said of you?

The SEVEN EXECUTIONERS

The prophet's four visions end with the statement that God will no longer listen to his people even if 'they cry in my hearing with a loud voice' (8:18). This is immediately followed by the prophet reporting that God 'cried in my hearing with a loud voice' (v. 1). It was an awful cry because it summoned an execution squad, consisting of six men with weapons and one with a writing-case.

A nightmare

Ezekiel's vision now turns into a nightmare. Up to this point the movement in the vision has been inwards, towards the temple. This is now reversed as the glory of God leaves its place in the 'holy of holies' in the temple, where the ark of the covenant stood guarded by cherubim, and comes to the threshold of the temple (v. 3). This is the first stage in God leaving his sanctuary and city. Disaster is going to happen, not because God cannot defend his city but because he is removing his protection and calling down judgment on its sins. What follows is indeed terrible, but it is not indiscriminate slaughter. It is justly administered judgment on evil. Therefore, the first act is the marking of those who grieve over the evil that is going on in Jerusalem (v. 4). These people are to be spared. The slaughter then begins with the elders who have turned their backs on the temple to worship the sun (v. 6). Their blood defiles further the sanctuary that their idolatry has already desecrated.

Ezekiel intercedes

The prophet is horrified by the slaughter and begins to intercede with God for the people (v. 8). This is as much part of the prophetic office as is the proclamation of judgment. Once again we see that the prophet does not gloat over the fulfilment of the judgment he has prophesied. The prophet is an intermediary, speaking to people on God's behalf, but also speaking to God on their behalf. He is one of the people and feels for them.

The reply from God seems devoid of any comfort for his anguish. The people are far gone in sin and are only getting what justice demands (vv. 9–10). Yet there is a ray of hope. The scribe returns, saying that he has done his work (v. 11). We are not told how many people have been marked and spared, but the very fact that the scribe was part of the execution squad implies that he had a job to do and that there were some faithful people whose lives would be spared.

God's wrath and mercy

We have noted earlier in this commentary that the idea of God's wrath and judgment is not a popular one today. Yet it is clearly part of the biblical portrayal of God. Moreover, as we have already commented, without it we would have no assurance that God is good and that good will ultimately triumph over evil. But there is a tension between God's wrath and God's mercy. At the heart of it is the sacrificial love of the cross. The marking of the faithful to save them from slaughter in Ezekiel's vision is reminiscent of the Passover in Egypt that preceded the exodus. There, the sacrificial giving of an animal life brought deliverance. For Christians this foreshadows a greater deliverance: 'Our paschal [passover] lamb, Christ, has been sacrificed,' said the apostle Paul (1 Corinthians 5:7). His death dealt with our sin so that we can be spared judgment and experience the forgiveness of God.

In Ezekiel's vision, the word for the 'mark' that the scribe is told to put on people's foreheads is actually the Hebrew letter *tav*. In Ezekiel's day this had the shape of our letter X. In the book of Revelation John sees a vision of those who have refused the mark of the beast and who have been redeemed. On their foreheads they have the name of the Lamb. This would no doubt be 'Christ', which in Greek begins with the letter *chi*, which has the shape X. There is a continuity in God's saving activity down through history, and it finds its ultimate expression in the cross of Jesus Christ.

MEDITATION

'In Christ God was reconciling the world to himself, not counting their trespasses against them… For our sake he [God] made him [Christ] to be sin who knew no sin, so that in him we might become the righteousness of God' (2 Corinthians 5:19, 21). Meditate on the mystery and wonder of these verses.

The BURNING COALS

Having completed his first commission, the man dressed in linen is given another. Up to this point in the vision it has not been clear from where God has been speaking. The opening verse of chapter 10 implies that this command comes from the divine throne. The man is told to take burning coals from beneath the throne and between the cherubim and to scatter them over the city of Jerusalem like incendiary bombs (v. 2). This is clearly intended to symbolize the judgment of God on the city.

Devastating destruction

When Jerusalem was captured by the Babylonians for the first time in 598BC, there was considerable loss of life, pillaging and devastation. However, the basic structure of the city was left intact. This may have helped to encourage the idea that God would not let utter disaster befall Jerusalem and the temple. Jeremiah had to do battle with this kind of attitude (Jeremiah 7:1–4). What Ezekiel sees in this vision implies the impending destruction of the city as well as the slaughter of its inhabitants which has been depicted in the previous chapter, and this is what happened when the Babylonians took the city for the second time in 587BC.

The details of verses 3–5 are not clear, perhaps not surprisingly in an account of a visionary experience. What is clear is that this act of judgment is related to the beginning of the movement of the chariot-throne and the glory of the Lord away from the sanctuary. God's abandonment of the sanctuary is in itself an even more devastating judgment than the destruction of the city.

The glory of the Lord

The fact that the burning coals of fire come from the chariot-throne, and are indeed handed to the man by one of the cherubim (v. 7), makes a close link between the judgment and the glory of the Lord. In the Old Testament the glory of the Lord is often depicted in terms of bright light and fire. It is something that is both beautiful and dangerous. As Isaiah found in his great vision (Isaiah 6), to be brought into the presence of God is to be made aware of God's moral purity and of human sinfulness. Faced with these realities, Isaiah cried out, 'Woe is me! I am lost, for I am a man of unclean lips' (Isaiah 6:5). In his case a heavenly being, a seraph, took a burning coal from an altar and touched his mouth with it, so purifying him and taking away his sin and guilt.

Burning purity

A theme running throughout scripture is that God's burning purity can be either a threat or a promise. For those who recognize their moral state and throw themselves on God's mercy, wanting to live in his ways, the burning coals of God can purify and restore. However, those who refuse to recognize their impurity and live with a false self-confidence find that those same burning coals produce a conflagration that consumes and destroys them. The destruction of Sodom and Gomorrah and the other cities of the Dead Sea region by fire from heaven is held out as an example of the awfulness of God's judgment, more than once in the Bible. Earlier prophets had warned the rulers of Judah that they were in danger of such judgment (Isaiah 1:9–10). Ezekiel sees this as about to happen. The glory of the Lord will not share the temple with the worship of other gods, the idols of other nations. The holy God will not condone the impurity of his people and his city. The message of this vision is that things have gone so far that the only outcome is for the burning coals of God's judgment to consume all the impurity and so destroy it.

In the New Testament the mode of God's presence with people is through the Holy Spirit. It is not surprising, therefore, to find the imagery of fire associated with the Holy Spirit, symbolizing both purifying judgment (Matthew 3:11–12) and blessing (Acts 2:1–4).

PRAYER

*'Come down, O love divine, seek thou this soul of mine
and visit it with Thine own ardour glowing;
O Comforter, draw near, within my heart appear,
and kindle it, Thy holy flame bestowing.
O let it freely burn, till earthly passions turn
to dust and ashes, in its heat consuming;
and let Thy glorious light shine ever on my sight,
and clothe me round, the while my path illuming.'*

R.F. Littledale (1833–90), after Bianco de Siena (d. 1434)

The GLORY LEAVES *the* TEMPLE

The action of Ezekiel's vision halts for a while as the prophet gives a lengthy, but not easily understood, description of the divine chariot-throne. Much of it repeats what has been said in chapter 1, and this has led some scholars to regard the description here as an editorial addition to the original account of the vision. Whether or not that is so, the presence of the description here does make theological sense.

A mobile God

In comparison with the description in chapter 1, there is more attention given here to the wheels of the chariot (vv. 9–13). This is probably to stress the mobility of God. He is not confined to his sanctuary. He can roam the world. In chapter 1 this is a comforting truth, assuring the Judean exiles that, although they are cut off from the temple and the worship there, God is with them. Here it is a threatening truth, as the Lord prepares to leave the temple in Jerusalem. Of course, the imagery of the chariot and its mobility is just one way of visualizing the truth of the omnipresence of God. He is everywhere at all times. This makes all the more terrible the message that God is withdrawing his presence from Jerusalem. Paradoxically the omnipresent God can withdraw his presence and become absent, leaving a void of God-forsakenness.

An abandoned city

In the ancient Near East it was a widely held belief that a city could not be captured unless its gods were either defeated or had abandoned it. The so-called 'Cyrus Cylinder' inscription (now in the British Museum) records the victory of the Persians over Babylon in 539BC. It ascribes the defeat of Babylon to the anger of its god, Marduk, over the religious and social sins of the Babylonian king, which led Marduk to leave the city and hand it over to Cyrus the Persian. Similarly, the prelude to the impending destruction of Jerusalem is the departure of the Lord, caused by his wrath at the sins of the people. It is destroyed, but not because he is too weak to defend it. Here is at least a glimmer of hope for the future.

Ezekiel twice emphasizes that the cherubim he describes here are the same as the living creatures he saw in the vision by the River Chebar in Babylonia, which he did not name there as cherubim (vv. 15, 20, 22). Why is this important? In the ancient Near East in general, cherubim were the guardians of the throne of the high god and divine messengers. In monotheistic Hebrew religion, they were angelic beings guarding the throne of God. In the temple, golden cherubim stood over the ark of the covenant, the symbol of the presence of God in the Holy of Holies. So Ezekiel is making the point that the cherubim who take the enthroned glory of the Lord from the temple in Jerusalem are the same creatures that bring it to the exiles in Babylon. This anticipates what is to be said in the next chapter. Although the Lord is leaving the temple, he may then come to, and work through, his people in exile. So there is more than a glimmer of hope for the future of God's people Israel.

God's presence

The essence of Hebrew religion was the enjoyment of God's presence: '"Come," my heart says, "seek his face!" Your face, Lord, do I seek' (Psalm 27:8). Time and again the psalmists plead with God, 'Do not hide your face from me' (Psalm 27:9). The most awful loss they could imagine was the removal of God's presence. Ezekiel's vision makes clear that when this does happen, it is not done lightly or without very good cause. On the cross Jesus took on his lips a psalmist's expression of his sense of God's absence (Mark 15:34; Psalm 22:1) as he experienced the God-forsakenness of the sinful people for whom he gave his life as a ransom (Mark 10:45). As the apostle Paul puts it, he 'became a curse for us' (Galatians 3:13), for all who have broken and flouted God's law as did the Judeans of Ezekiel's day. As a result we can be reconciled with God and enjoy his presence for ever (Romans 5:10–11).

MEDITATION

In Psalm 139 the psalmist rejoices in the fact that God accepts him as he is and is always present with him. Make time to read and meditate on that psalm.

DEATH *at the* TEMPLE GATE

The overall meaning of this section is clear, but the details are not. The prophet is brought to the east gate of the temple, where he sees a meeting of what is no doubt the Royal Council. He recognizes two 'officials of the people', or royal officials (v. 1). They were probably people he knew before his deportation from Jerusalem. He is told that these people, who are meant to be giving the king and country good advice, are instead leading them astray because they 'devise iniquity' and give 'wicked counsel' (v. 2). The background is found in 2 Kings 24—25 and the book of Jeremiah. King Zedekiah was a rather weak person. His court was torn between a faction advocating continued submission to Babylon and a militant faction advocating rebellion, relying on support from Egypt. Jeremiah pleaded with the king not to listen to the militants, warning that rebellion would lead to utter disaster. Despite his own misgivings, Zedekiah eventually gave in to the militants, and the disaster prophesied by Jeremiah came about.

A difficult saying

The exact meaning of what the counsellors are reported to say in verse 3 is unclear. Scholars differ over whether the first part of the quotation is a question ('Is not the time at hand to build houses?') or a statement ('The time is not at hand to build houses'). The significance of the following metaphor of the cauldron and the meat is also a matter of debate. Perhaps the key to understanding the first part is Jeremiah's 'letter to the exiles' (Jeremiah 29) in which he encourages them to build houses and settle down in Babylonia because they are going to be there for 70 years (that is, 'a lifetime'). The counsellors may be rejecting this as defeatist talk and urging action to break free from Babylonian domination. Some see the reference to the cauldron and the meat as a statement of confidence—a belief that they will be secure within Jerusalem if they are besieged again by the Babylonians. However, this seems unlikely. Meat is put in a cauldron to be cooked, not preserved. They are more likely to be saying that unless they take action they will be 'dead meat' for the Babylonians.

A word of judgment

God tells Ezekiel to give a prophecy of judgment. It refers to the loss of life that followed the first rebellion against Babylon (v. 6). The policy now being advocated will lead to fresh slaughter of the inhabitants of Jerusalem. The counsellors themselves will not simply die in the general slaughter. They will have to face individual punishment at the hands of the Babylonians. The prophecy that this will happen 'at the border of Israel', repeated in verses 10 and 11 for emphasis, has a twofold significance. These militants were nationalists, seeking to regain control of the lost territory of Israel and revive the importance of the nation. Far from achieving this, they were going to lose control of the land altogether. Secondly, the prophecy refers to what actually happened, as recounted in Jeremiah 39:4–7. The king and his entourage were captured trying to flee from Jerusalem when it fell. They were taken to Hamath, the traditional northern border of Israel (Joshua 13:5; 2 Kings 14:28), where Nebuchadnezzar executed 'all the nobles of Judah'.

As Ezekiel was prophesying, Pelatiah fell down dead (v. 13), prompting an anguished cry from the prophet. Perhaps he saw it as an indication of the imminence and severity of judgment, especially as Pelatiah's death seems a negation of the meaning of his name, 'the Lord delivers'. Ezekiel is afraid that its severity will mean the end of Israel altogether.

A challenge

The most challenging thing about this episode is the blindness of the Judean leaders. Their nationalist ideology has made them blind to God's purposes. In verse 12 there is an indication of how this had come about. They had stopped following God's ways and adopted those of the nations around them. If we are not careful, we can easily fall into the same kind of error, as we are bombarded day by day with the ideas and outlook of the non-Christian world around us. We can combat it, though, by reading and studying God's word to gain guidance.

MEDITATION

'Don't let the world around you squeeze you into its own mould, but let God remould your minds from within, so that you may prove in practice that the plan of God for you is good.'

Romans 12:2 (J.B. Phillips)

A WORD *of* HOPE

Since there is no indication that the vision of Ezekiel 8—11 was ever communicated to the people in Jerusalem, one might wonder what was the purpose of its horrifying message of judgment on Jerusalem. If the exiles in Babylon had hopes for the deliverance of Jerusalem and a subsequent return to the city, the vision would certainly have destroyed those hopes. It also deals with the question of whether the destruction of Jerusalem and the temple indicated the powerlessness of the God of Israel. However, the major purpose of the vision comes out in this closing section. Having had their false hope destroyed, the exiles are given a firm hope for the future. Whereas Ezekiel's cry of anguish in 9:8 did not receive a comforting response, his second cry is met with a ringing declaration that the future of Israel lies with the exiles.

The Judean perspective

It is ironic that while the exiles had been pinning their hopes on a possible turn of events in Jerusalem, the people left behind in Judah had written them off (v. 15). Behind their words was the self-righteous belief that those who had gone into exile must have been the ones deserving punishment. God had cast them off by casting them out of his land. Those remaining felt that the future of the land lay with them, and that the land was theirs. The way their words are phrased suggests that they set about occupying the land left vacant by those in exile. When the exiles heard of this, they must have felt betrayed and dispirited. Clearly their compatriots did not expect or want them to return.

God's plans

God's plans for the two groups of people were very different from what they supposed. He had not deserted the exiles. In fact, he was about to complete his departure from the temple and Jerusalem, leaving the people there to their fate at the hands of the Babylonians. But he was not deserting his people completely. He was leaving the profaned sanctuary in Judah and going to the exiles in Babylon to be a sanctuary for them (v. 16). Although they were cut off from the temple and its ritual, they were not cut off from their God and could continue to worship him even in exile. This was only going to be a temporary state of affairs, anyway, because God was eventually going to gather them together and bring them back to Judah again (v. 17). Since those who were now profaning the temple by their worship of idols were unwilling to recognize the error of their ways and return to worship the true God, they were going to face destruction. It would be the returned exiles who would do away with the idols and their trappings and re-establish pure worship in Jerusalem (v. 18).

God's initiative

Yet, how could this come about? Were the exiles any better than their compatriots in Judah? The real word of hope comes in verses 19–20. God promises that the exiles will be able to do things differently because they are going to be different. He is going to take the initiative to change them. He will give them an 'undivided heart' and 'a new spirit'. As mentioned previously, in Hebrew thought the heart is not the centre of the emotions, but of the thinking and willing processes. The promise being given is for a change of understanding and attitude—a single-minded commitment to God. This will replace their former stubborn attachment to doing things their way. Now they will become sensitive to God and his way. With this new attitude will go a new inner motivation to enable them to live up to, and live out, their commitment. This amounts to nothing less than a renewal of the covenant relationship: 'They shall be my people, and I shall be their God' (v. 20).

These words provide hope for God's people whenever they feel cast off, abandoned, worthless or helpless. Down through the history of his people, God has shown that he can renew them and radically transform situations. Jesus demonstrated this when he took the good news of the kingdom of God to the outcasts of his society—the lepers, tax collectors and prostitutes—and the apostle Paul spoke of God using what is foolish, weak, low and despised to achieve his purposes (1 Corinthians 1:27–29).

PRAYER

Maybe you need to appropriate this word of hope for yourself,
by asking God to renew you or transform some situation you are
facing. If not, think of someone else for whom you can
appropriate it in prayer.

EXILE ENACTED

It is not always easy to see why the material in the prophetic books is in the order in which it appears. However, in Ezekiel so far there is a recognizable general development of thought. In chapters 4—7 he warns of a new siege of Jerusalem. This is followed by a vision of the destruction of the city and its temple, with all the loss of life that this will bring. Now he declares that there will be a new exile, like the one he and his compatriots in Babylon have already experienced.

An acted parable

Once again the prophet acts out his message in a piece of street theatre. In daylight, so that everyone can see, he prepares 'an exile's baggage' (v. 3). Presumably this would have contained a few clothes, a little food and some cooking utensils, with other necessities of life, all wrapped in a cloak or blanket. He puts this where it can be seen and so will attract attention. After dark he digs through a wall, no doubt one made of mud-brick, and goes out through it, carrying his baggage (v. 7). This may have been the wall of Ezekiel's own house, or a wall surrounding the refugee settlement in which he lived. As he leaves, he covers his face, perhaps to symbolize grief at leaving or an attempt at concealment. His fellow exiles who are watching this mime are left wondering just what it means.

What Ezekiel performs is, in effect, an acted parable. It is an attempt to get a message through to those who 'have eyes to see but do not see, who have ears to hear but do not hear; for they are a rebellious house' (vv. 2–3). Such people will simply reject an 'up-front' proclamation. So the prophet uses a method of communication that might get through their defences by catching their interest, making them intrigued by what they see, and leaving them to think about it. This was Jesus' reason for telling parables (Mark 4:10–12). We need to consider how we can do the same kind of thing in our generation. However, success in communication is not guaranteed, as Jesus' parable of the four soils makes clear (Mark 4:1–20). At least Ezekiel's actions aroused interest and gave him the opportunity of a hearing for his message when, in the morning, people asked him what it was all about.

The parable explained

The meaning may seem obvious to us, knowing what did happen to Jerusalem and its inhabitants. Nevertheless, the more optimistic among Ezekiel's fellow exiles might have interpreted his actions as meaning that their exile was about to end and that they would be able to start the trek back home. If there were such hopes, the prophet shattered them, explaining that his actions depicted the fate of the 'prince in Jerusalem and all the house of Israel in it' (v. 10). In 2 Kings 25:4–7 we read of what happened to Zedekiah. When the Babylonians breached the wall of the city, he fled by night but was captured and taken to face Nebuchadnezzar's wrath. His sons were killed before his eyes. He was then blinded and taken as a prisoner to Babylon.

Once again the prophet portrays a dark picture of judgment. Yet there are a couple of glimmers of hope. God commands him to act out his parable with the words, 'Perhaps they will understand…' (v. 3). God does not want his people to face judgment because of their rebelliousness. He longs for them to understand and repent. When judgment looms, grace is not far away. This is made clearer at the end of the oracle: a few will escape (v. 16).

The use of the word 'prince' (vv. 10, 12) may reflect the legal status of Zedekiah, as regent for his nephew Jehoiachin who was in exile in Babylon (2 Kings 24:17); or a theological point may be intended. God is the true king of Israel. Certainly the purpose of the judgment is that the people should return to the recognition that God is 'the Lord' (v. 16). Failure to recognize this is what brought about the judgment in the first place.

PRAYER AND MEDITATION

Pray that God will help you, and the church to which you belong, to be imaginative in the ways in which you communicate the Christian message. Remember also that the very way we live is an 'acted parable' whereby the people around can see Christ portrayed in us, as individuals and as a community. How good is the representation they see?

TERROR ENACTED

In another acted parable, Ezekiel is to portray the shock and terror
that will overtake the inhabitants of Judah as their lands and cities are
ravaged by the invading army. Unlike the previous parable, there is a
command telling Ezekiel how to act, but no account of his carrying
out the actions. This adds some support to the suggestion of some
scholars that in this case Ezekiel was not just 'play-acting'. Rather, he
identified so completely with the plight of those of whom, and to
whom, he was prophesying that he was himself overcome with terror
as he contemplated the awfulness of the judgment that was to befall
his people. As a result, he found himself trembling so violently that
when he tried to drink he spilt the water from the cup as he lifted it
to his lips, and he had difficulty putting his food into his mouth. If
this is the case, he might have preferred to hide his state from others,
but instead, by eating and drinking in public, he presented himself as
another parable to the people.

Violence

The main point of this short prophecy is not the fact that the people
of Judah will be overcome with terror, but the reason for the judgment that will provoke this terror. It will come about 'on account of
the violence of all those who live in [Judah]' (v. 19). Jesus said, 'All
who take the sword will perish by the sword' (Matthew 26:52). The
reality that violence does not solve problems, but in fact provokes
further violence, is one that humans have always found hard to
accept. Perhaps this is because violence seems to offer a quick way
to get what you want, or a short-term solution to an intractable
problem. The violence that had been done by the people of Judah is
not specified, but no doubt at the heart of it was the violation of
God's covenant laws. The laws had been given to ensure that everyone in the community was treated justly and given their due rights,
and when they were not kept, people inevitably suffered in various
ways. When the prophet Habakkuk was faced with a society in which
the law was not adhered to, he summed up the consequences in the
cry, 'Violence!' (Habakkuk 1:2–4).

Moral laws

Part of the message of the prophets is that we live in a world where there are consequences to our actions. There are moral laws at work. Hosea expressed this graphically: 'For they sow the wind, and they shall reap the whirlwind' (Hosea 8:7). Moral laws do not operate in the obvious and inexorable way that physical laws do. If you jump off a high cliff, you will suffer serious physical damage within seconds. The consequences, for good as well as ill, of our moral actions can take a long time to appear. Some of the most difficult problems in the world today are the result of injustices done long ago that have festered for decades, or even centuries, and then broken out in open violence. Wrongs we personally have done in the past may come back to haunt us, or kindnesses done may bring us future blessing. This is a reminder to us of the justice of God, and may be a ground for hope that one day evil will finally be overcome.

Breaking the chain

In the physical world, we can use the effect of one law to overcome another. The laws of aerodynamics can be used to ensure that the lift generated by an aircraft wing overcomes the effects of the law of gravity. Something similar is true in the moral realm. A chain of wrong actions and their consequences can be broken by acts of repentance and restitution or forgiveness and reconciliation. That is why both repentance and forgiveness have a high priority as Christian virtues in the New Testament.

Of course, the definitive 'chain-breaking' act was Jesus' death on the cross. Here he took on himself the consequences of our wrong-doing and experienced God-forsakenness for us. As a result, God holds out to us forgiveness instead of judgment.

PRAYER

Think of someone you know, or someone mentioned in the news media recently, who has reason to be afraid today. Pray both about the cause of this fear and that they will have the strength to overcome their fear.

TWO PROVERBS REVERSED

This section gives us some insight into how the prophet's hearers responded to his preaching. The fact that they responded with proverbial sayings is an indication of widespread attitudes that had grown up towards prophets and prophecy. The two proverbs express two different attitudes.

Scepticism

The first is outright scepticism. Some people were saying, 'Time goes by and nothing happens!' (v. 22). They were doubting the truth of the prophet's words. They had heard this kind of prophecy of doom before, and it had not come true. They had some reason to say such things: there had been false prophets, and of course their prophecies had not come about. There had also been prophecies by people whom we, with hindsight, recognize as true prophets, which did not find fulfilment for a long time. In the latter half of the eighth century BC, Micah spoke of the destruction of Jerusalem and of the temple (Micah 3:12). Nearly 150 years later, both were still standing. How could anyone tell the difference between false prophecies and true ones that were merely delayed in their fulfilment? There is no simple answer, but perhaps, in the case of Micah, there was a pointer in the fact that some of his prophecies, such as the destruction of Samaria (Micah 1:6), had happened. Ezekiel's response to the sceptics is clear-cut: 'The time has come, it is all going to happen!' (v. 23). It is backed up by a twofold promise from God: he is going to put an end to false prophecy, and is going to bring about the fulfilment of the true prophecies very soon (vv. 24–25).

Complacency

The second attitude is one of complacency. The hearers played safe in as far as they did not question the veracity of the prophet's words. Instead they questioned the relevance of those words for their own day. The fulfilment would not come about in their generation (v. 27). Again, there were some grounds for this assumption, in view of unfulfilled prophecies such as the one already referred to in Micah. Yet it was a complacent attitude because a good many of the prophecies of earlier prophets, such as Amos, Hosea, Isaiah and Micah, had come about within a few years or decades of their utterance. Again, Ezekiel gives a clear-cut response. His prophecies would be fulfilled very soon (v. 28).

Faced with these attitudes of scepticism and complacency, and the fact that there was a measure of justification for each, it would not be surprising if Ezekiel suffered from some self-doubt. Yet he responds with clear-cut, defiant answers. How could he have been so sure that his prophecies were true? The answer has to lie in the strength of his relationship with God, which in turn was rooted in the vision of God that constituted his call to be a prophet.

Spiritual blindness

Why couldn't these sceptical and complacent people accept the truth of Ezekiel's warnings of judgment? To some extent, the answer lay in a wilful spiritual blindness. They saw only what they were disposed to see. Their view of earlier prophets and prophecies was a very partial one: they remembered only the unfulfilled and delayed prophecies. Perhaps more seriously, their understanding of God was deficient in that they failed to reckon with his grace. Some of Jeremiah's supporters recalled Micah's unfulfilled prophecy about the destruction of Jerusalem and the temple, but realized that its fulfilment had been postponed because God responded graciously to Hezekiah's repentance (Jeremiah 26:17–19). Prophecies are not magical words which, once spoken, have a power of their own to act automatically. They are the words of a personal God who is looking for a response from his hearers, to whom he wants to do good and not harm. The way in which his words are fulfilled depends on their response.

It is an act of grace, not evidence of God's failure to keep his word or inability to act, when judgment is delayed. 'The Lord is not slow about his promise, as some think of slowness, but is patient with you, not wanting any to perish, but all to come to repentance' (2 Peter 3:9).

PRAYER

Lord, forgive me for the times when I have heard you speak to me, but have then used excuses to avoid taking seriously what you have said. Thank you for graciously continuing to speak—through your word as I read it or hear it preached, through the advice of Christian friends, and in other ways. Please give me the discernment to recognize your voice and the determination to obey it.

FALSE PROPHETS

People get the prophets they deserve. Ezekiel's hearers refused to take his message seriously, and so made themselves prey to false prophets. Throughout the history of Israel false prophecy existed alongside the genuine article. Distinguishing between them was often not easy, but what Ezekiel says in his condemnation of false prophets provides some guidance for making the distinction. In his condemnation he uses some striking imagery.

Scavengers

In verses 1–7 he paints a picture of a ruined wall with two kinds of creature to be found among the ruins. There are jackals—scavengers, whose only concern is the picking they can get among the ruins. These are the false prophets, who make their living out of the people's misfortunes. They gain status and income by giving groundless comfort and building up false hope. The other creatures among the ruins are those people who are working to repair the breaches and so rebuild a solid protective wall. They put aside self-interest and work for the good of the community. That is what true prophets do. Their concern for the good of the people leads them to speak uncomfortable and unwelcome truths about things that need to be put right if the community is to be strong and stable.

Whitewash

Ezekiel follows this with a picture of a badly built wall, coated with whitewash to cover the defects (vv. 8–16). A severe storm washes away the whitewash, exposing the defects in the wall, and the wall itself collapses under the battering. The pronouncements of the false prophets are like the whitewash on the jerry-built wall. They prophesy '*shalom*'. This means more than is conveyed by the English word 'peace'. It means a state of harmony, well-being and blessing. However, this can come about only when people live in accordance with God's laws. The Judeans of Ezekiel's day were flouting the covenant and its laws, and it was the job of the true prophet to expose this, not to cover it up by proclaiming oracles of '*shalom*'.

True and false prophets

The prophets whom Ezekiel labels as 'false' may well have been sincere in what they proclaimed to be words from the Lord, but they were really prophesying out of their own imaginations. They were colluding with their hearers in saying what they both wanted to hear and believe. How did Ezekiel know that they were wrong? His closeness to God gave him a deeper spiritual insight. He could see that Judah was like a ruined wall that needed to be rebuilt properly and not just whitewashed. In the end, only the course of events would prove, to those who lacked this insight, who was the true prophet and who the false one.

False prophecy is a continuing danger in the Church. John urges his readers to 'test the spirits to see whether they are from God; for many false prophets have gone out into the world' (1 John 4:1). We must never accept what someone says simply because they claim that it is 'a word from the Lord'. This applies as much to interpretations of scripture as it does to words that are claimed as direct revelations from God. We need to follow the example of the Beroeans, who examined the Scriptures for themselves to test the truth of what Paul and Silas preached (Acts 17:11).

In ancient Israel, prophecy was a ministry open to both men and women: we can read of some prominent prophetesses, such as Miriam, Deborah and Huldah. In verses 17–23 Ezekiel turns his attention to a group of prophetesses whose activity he condemns. In fact, they are witches rather than prophets. They make use of certain magical practices, the details and meaning of which are obscure to us. There is always a temptation to try to control God by certain formulae and rituals instead of listening for God's word and obeying it. Christian prayer can sometimes descend to that level, when people rely on such things as the frequency or length of prayers, the form of prayer used or its fervency. All this treats prayer as a way of coercing God, instead of being a conversation with God in which we open ourselves up to him and seek to understand his will for us.

PRAYER

Lord, help me not to collude with false prophets by listening only to what I want to hear or believe. Give me the discernment I need to 'test the spirits' and recognize your authentic word. Then give me the courage both to obey it and proclaim it.

27 EZEKIEL 14:1-11

IDOLATROUS ELDERS

Here we get a glimpse of Ezekiel's life as a prophet. A group of people come to visit him because they are seeking guidance from God. In this case it is a group of elders—community leaders. We are not told the question they are asking. The substance of the issue is not important. What matters to God is the spiritual condition of the questioners.

Request refused

The answer comes in two parts. The first part is the retort that they do not deserve any answer because they are guilty of 'taking idols into their hearts', which have become a stumbling-block to them. The seriousness of this charge is shown by its threefold repetition in the passage (vv. 3, 4, 7). It is emphasized by the language of the charge, which echoes that of the laws in the Old Testament. It is as if God is laying the charge against them in a court of law. Exactly what form this idolatry took is not made clear. It is probable that, faced with their desperate situation, the elders were 'hedging their bets' and getting involved with the worship of Babylonian gods, while keeping a veneer of the orthodox worship of the God of Israel. However they were doing it, they were breaking the first of the Ten Commandments. God's response is that since they have done so, and turned away from him, they have no right to expect guidance from him.

A harsh reply

The second part of the response is even harsher. God says that he will answer them, but not through the prophet or in the way they desire. He will do it by direct action, through the disaster that will overtake them (v. 8). Then the error of their ways will be all too clear. Yet God's purpose in this is not simply to bring upon them well-deserved retribution. His ultimate purpose is to regain the commitment of Israel to himself (v. 4). So, to start with, he gives this warning and appeals for repentance, a turning away from the idols to himself (v. 6). If this does not happen, then the disaster has to come to shock the people into realizing the folly of idolatry and that the God of Israel is indeed 'the Lord', the only true God (v. 8).

Hedging bets

It is all too easy to fall into the same kind of error as these elders of Israel, by 'hedging our bets' in various ways instead of being fully committed to God. This is especially true when such commitment may seem risky. Maybe we know that we ought to make a stand on some moral principle in our place of work. However, we don't want to risk the loss of the goodwill of other workers, or jeopardize the chance of promotion. As a result we soft-pedal on the issue, or say nothing at all. Despite this, we still expect God to guide us and bless us in our work.

As well as having a warning for the elders, Ezekiel has a warning for his fellow prophets (vv. 9–11). If the elders did not like what Ezekiel had to say, they might go to other prophets seeking a 'second opinion', one more favourable to them. As in Ezekiel 13, prophets who simply tell people what they want to hear are warned that they will share the destruction to be meted out to the people whose disobedience they have encouraged.

We need to heed this warning when faced with the temptation to avoid confronting people with their sin and to speak words of assurance and comfort because we want to avoid unpleasantness, or out of a misplaced sense of compassion. Of course we have to be as careful and gentle as we can when seeking to get people to face up to the wrong they are doing, but ultimately, hiding the truth from them is not true compassion. It is like a doctor refusing to give a true diagnosis of a disease, so preventing the sufferer from seeking the cure and letting the disease gain a stronger hold.

PRAYER

Lord, show me if there are ways in which I am 'hedging my bets' rather than being fully committed to you. Give me the strength to turn away from these idols, which are displacing you, and turn wholeheartedly to you. Please also give me the strength to speak the truth, and the right words with which to speak it, so that I may help others to turn from idols to you.

NOAH, DANIEL & JOB

One of the functions of the prophet was intercessory prayer. On the one occasion when Abraham is described as a prophet, it is in the context of intercessory prayer (Genesis 20:7). However, such prayer has its limits. There are certain situations in which it is too late for anything but judgment. On two occasions Amos' intercession postpones God's judgment, but on a third occasion there is no room for intercession (Amos 7:1–9). Jeremiah is eventually forbidden to intercede for Judah (Jeremiah 14:11–12), and is told that not even the intercessions of such spiritual giants as Moses and Samuel would be of any avail (Jeremiah 15:1). What is said in Jeremiah 15:1 and here in Ezekiel suggests that in the last days of Judah there were some who were clinging on to the hope that the presence of a remnant of righteous people in Jerusalem would save it from catastrophe. That hope is destroyed by Ezekiel's oracle.

God's justice

In verses 12–20 the prophet again adopts a legal form of language to enunciate a general principle of God's justice. He speaks in general terms of 'a land' and gives four 'test cases' covering a range of forms of judgment. All this makes clear the universality of what is being said. This is how God treats all nations: Judah is not being treated unfairly. The three intercessors mentioned are all non-Israelites, in accordance with the universality of the principle being expressed. Noah is the biblical name for the hero of the flood, who was known by other names in the traditions of other ancient Near Eastern peoples. The Daniel mentioned is not the hero of the biblical book of Daniel but a wise and good Phoenician king, to whom Ezekiel refers again in a poem about the prince of the Phoenician city of Tyre (Ezekiel 28:3). Job, the righteous sufferer of the biblical book of Job, was probably an Edomite. All three were upright men of great integrity, but the sin of a land can become so great that their combined prayers would be of no avail. God can be pushed too far.

Covenant curses

The four judgments mentioned are all found in the covenant curses of Leviticus 26:22–26, and have already been mentioned in Ezekiel 5 as things that will befall the inhabitants of Jerusalem. It is therefore no surprise when, in verses 21–23, the principle enunciated in verses 12–20 is said to apply with particular aptness to Jerusalem. The flouting of the covenant has gone on for too long. Finally God must act, and nothing can now prevent well-deserved judgment from falling. The fact that all four forms of disaster will be combined indicates the seriousness of the situation. Amazingly, there will be survivors (v. 22), but this will not be because of their righteousness. Rather it will be so that when they join their compatriots in exile their impious behaviour will show Ezekiel's hearers that their judgment was well-deserved. In a sense this will be a 'consolation' to them, because it will underline what the prophet has been saying time and again, that the disaster that befalls Judah and Jerusalem is not evidence of the weakness of the God of Israel, or of his inability to protect his people. Rather, it is evidence of his justice and of his power, as he uses other nations as agents of his judgment.

No salvation by proxy

This passage warns that there is no salvation by proxy. One person cannot depend on the righteousness of another. This acts as a limit on, and is to some extent in tension with, the general acceptance in the Old Testament of corporate responsibility. The ultimate resolution of the tension is central to the Christian gospel. By his righteousness Jesus does save others. However, he did not simply intercede for us. He accepted the judgment due to us for himself. Moreover, he was not just another, albeit totally righteous, human being. He was God incarnate, upholding his own justice by accepting its demands. As a result, 'There is therefore now no condemnation for those who are in Christ Jesus' (Romans 8:1). For the apostle Paul the phrase 'in Christ' expresses the corporate solidarity that follows from faith in him as Saviour. That faith has to be exercised by individuals for themselves.

MEDITATION

*'And can it be that I should gain
an interest in the Saviour's blood?
Died he for me, who caused his pain?
For me who him to death pursued?
Amazing love! How can it be
that thou, my God, shouldst die for me!'*

Charles Wesley (1707–88)

The PARABLE *of the* VINE

We've commented already that it is often difficult to discern why material in the prophetic books occurs in the order that it does. The next long section in Ezekiel, chapters 15—23, seems to have been brought together because much of it consists of various forms of figurative language—parable, proverb and allegory. Some striking images are used—the vine, the dissolute woman, the eagle, the lioness and her cubs, the forest fire, the sword, the two sisters. This reminds us of the value of learning to communicate God's word in a variety of ways so as to be able to choose the one that will be most appropriate and effective for a particular message on a specific occasion. Ezekiel, like the other Hebrew prophets, was certainly adept at this.

The luxuriant vine

The fact that a single vine root can support many branches and produce an abundance of sweet-tasting grapes made the vine a symbol of fruitfulness in the ancient world. Moreover, the fact that grape juice can be made into wine also made it a symbol of luxury and happiness. So, when Amos speaks of the day of restoration and salvation that lies beyond judgment, he includes the promise, 'They shall plant vineyards and drink their wine' (Amos 9:14). Isaiah's vision of the new heaven and the new earth includes, 'They shall plant vineyards and eat their fruit' (Isaiah 65:21). The luxuriant vine became a symbol of Israel (Psalm 80:8–11; Isaiah 5:7; 27:2–6).

The useless vine

The power of a good parable lies in its meaning being at first concealed in a down-to-earth illustration that catches the hearers' interest and gains their consent. At that point the deeper, and sometimes uncomfortable, significance of the parable can be revealed so that it hits home with considerable force. This is how Ezekiel uses his parable of the vine. To start with, his audience must have been intrigued by the fact that he talked not about the luxuriance of the vine and its fruit, but about its wood (vv. 2–3). Vine wood lacks the firmness of straight-grained timber and so is useless for any kind of woodwork. All one can do with the cuttings from a vine, or with a dead plant, is to burn it. If, among the ashes of the fire, there are some half-burnt bits, with the ends burnt away and the middle charred, they are still of no use as anything other than fuel (vv. 4–5). The parable is expressed as a series of questions, so drawing the hearers in and getting their assent to what is said, while they must still be wondering what it is all about. Having grabbed their attention and engagement, the prophet reveals the point of the parable and drives it home. Instead of being the luxuriant and fruitful vine she should have been, Israel was like the wood of a dead vine or vine-prunings— fit only to be burnt by the fires of judgment (vv. 6–8). Once again the message is a bleak one. The vine that had been transplanted from Egypt (Psalm 80:8) has become useless dead wood, fuel for the fire. In the light of what has been said about the exiles in Ezekiel 11:16–20 there might be the hope of a new transplant from Babylon, but that is not hinted at here.

The true vine

Jesus takes up the imagery of the vine in John 15. He declares that he himself is the 'true' or 'genuine' vine. All that Israel should have been in terms of bearing spiritual fruit is fulfilled in him. He 'abides' in his Father's love (15:10) and so gives life and fruitfulness to all who 'abide' in him (15:5). There is some debate about what 'bearing fruit' means in John 15. If, as many commentators think, verses 9–17 expand on the statement about bearing much fruit in verse 8, then the essence of it is to do with becoming more and more Christ-like. In particular, this means growing in the kind of self-giving love that Jesus showed. This fruit of a Christ-like character will lead to fruit of another kind, the winning of others to be disciples of Christ through the selfless love that is shown to them.

PRAYER

Lord Jesus, help me to abide constantly in you so that your life and love may flow into me, like the sap of the vine into its branches, causing me to grow and develop into a disciple who truly reflects the character of the one I follow. May the quality of my life be such that it bears fruit by attracting others to be your disciples.

The BEGINNING *of* LOVE

The parable in the previous chapter made its point with some subtlety. The opposite is the case with the long, satirical extended metaphor contained in Ezekiel 16. It makes its point with a bluntness arising from its shocking imagery and coarse language. Ezekiel spares no blushes in trying to bring home to his audience that Jerusalem, far from being the 'golden girl' of their dreams, has behaved like a depraved prostitute. Some of the early rabbis argued against this passage being read in public, and the 19th-century Baptist preacher C.H. Spurgeon agreed with them. No doubt the original hearers would have found the story as shocking as we do. However, the reasons for shock may have been different, because of the differences between their culture and ours.

Jerusalem's origins

The story is a complex one, and in places Ezekiel's metaphor is stretched close to breaking point in order to accommodate aspects of the history of Jerusalem, or the kingdom of Judah which the city represents. Jerusalem is depicted as a women of mixed ethnic origin (v. 3). This reflects the fact that it had a long history as an important city before David captured it and made it the capital of Israel. The Amorites were one of the major ethnic groups in Canaan, and in Joshua 10:5 the king of Jerusalem is called an Amorite. In the Old Testament the term 'Hittite' is used in two senses. It can refer, as it no doubt does here, to an ethnic group indigenous to Canaan, or to the people who invaded the fertile crescent from Asia Minor and established kingdoms in Syria. So, the prophet begins by reminding his audience of Jerusalem's pagan origins.

God's grace

Modern readers are no doubt shocked by the depiction of Jerusalem as an abandoned baby (vv. 4–5), partly because of the graphic description but even more so by the very idea of leaving an unwanted baby to die in the open. However, the exposure of such children, often baby girls, was common practice in some ancient Near Eastern societies. Probably, what Ezekiel's hearers would have found most surprising, if not shocking, would have been the fact that a stranger noticed the child, rescued it and cared for it with good intentions in mind (v. 6). Occasionally a stranger might pick up an abandoned baby, but it would usually be with the aim of raising the child for the purposes of prostitution or slavery. So, what seems the most natural element of the story to us, someone taking pity on a abandoned baby girl, would seem the most unnatural to Ezekiel's contemporaries. As a result, the main point of this part of the story would hit them with greater force than it does us—the sheer grace and goodness of God towards Jerusalem. There was nothing about her that meant she deserved to become 'the city of God, the holy habitation of the Most High' (Psalm 46:4).

God's covenant

The sequence of events in verses 6–9 is rather strange. God finds the baby and rescues it, but it grows to maturity before he washes it and anoints it with oil. Here the metaphor is being stretched to reflect the history of the city. The prophet is saying that in its pre-Israelite days the city existed and prospered at the Lord's command. The spreading of the edge of the cloak over a girl (v. 8) was an act of a quasi-legal nature affirming the choice of a bride (as in the case of Ruth and Boaz; see Ruth 3:9). The historical reality behind this part of the prophecy is God's covenant with David and his descendants (2 Samuel 7). This involved not only God's election of David, but also of Zion, David's city, as the city of the great King (Psalm 48:2). Symbolically, that was when a clean break was made with the city's pagan past. The finery in which the young woman is dressed contains materials that are associated with the tabernacle (vv. 10, 13; cloth, fine linen, leather, gold and silver), a reminder of the city's religious status within Israel.

So the story begins by depicting the mystery of God's love and grace, which leads him to choose the unlovely one and to enable her to become lovely through his loving care and gifts.

MEDITATION

'My song is love unknown, my Saviour's love to me:
Love to the loveless shown, that they might lovely be.
O who am I, that for my sake
My Lord should take frail flesh, and die?'

Samuel Crossman (1624–83)

LOVE GOES ASTRAY

Beauty brings its own dangers. Down through history men's lust for beautiful women has caused conflict and devastation. Part of the tragedy of Jerusalem's story is that it is the woman's trust in her own beauty and the fame it has brought her that causes things to go so badly wrong. Yet that beauty is due largely to what her husband has done for her.

The awfulness of sin

Ezekiel's portrayal of the woman's descent into sexual depravity is graphic. Some English translations soften the shocking nature of the language. However, the language is not being used gratuitously. The prophet's sharing of something of God's hurt, pain and outrage may contribute to the violence of the language. He wants to bring home the true awfulness of sin. In particular, this sin has not been forced on Jerusalem, as when destitution drives a woman to sell herself as a prostitute. Here is someone who has had everything provided for her, when she had no reason to expect or deserve it. Yet with great ingratitude she abuses the love that has been shown her and prostitutes herself out of pure lust. The very gifts that her husband has given her she showers on those with whom she commits adultery.

The historical reality behind the story comes through quite clearly in this section. In verses 15–22 there is a reference to the way the Israelites, time and again, gave in to the temptation of idolatry, adopting the gods and ways of worship of the peoples around them. Many of these modes of worship were fertility cults that involved ritual prostitution. This is why the prophets, from Hosea onwards, used the language of adultery and prostitution to speak of Israel's unfaithfulness to her God. Some of the pagan cults even involved child sacrifice, and some of the kings of Judah practised this abomination (2 Kings 16:3; 21:6; Jeremiah 7:31). The picture in verses 23–34 reflects the fact that time and again Israel and Judah relied on political alliances, seeking security in the arms of a foreign power instead of relying on her covenant partner, the Lord. Since these alliances were sometimes sealed by political marriages, they could themselves lead to the promotion of idolatry—as in the cases of

Solomon's wives and Ahab's marriage to the Phoenician princess Jezebel.

The importance of remembering

This is more than just the tragic story of one nation that went astray. It illustrates a spiritual process that is of general significance. What led the lovely bride to become a lewd prostitute? The story depicts a four-stage process.

- The root of evil in the story is forgetfulness (v. 22). Human love for God springs from a response to his initiative of love towards us. The person who forgets love can no longer respond to it.
- Forgetfulness encourages pride. When we forget that we owe all that we have and are to God, we begin to believe that the success we have had is all our own doing. As a result we begin to rely on our own resources (v. 15).
- Related to forgetfulness and pride is ingratitude to God. Forgetting their source, we use his gifts for our own selfish ends (vv. 16–20).
- Finally, there is the descent into outright depravity.

The pivotal place of memory in this story illustrates its importance for healthy spiritual life, and why, for Israel, an act of remembrance, the Passover meal, had a central place in worship. Perhaps it is significant that, according to the Old Testament, for decades at a time Israel and Judah failed to keep the Passover (2 Kings 23:22; 2 Chronicles 30:5). When they forgot what God had done for them, Israel and Judah drifted into unfaithfulness.

Jesus knew that his disciples would face the same danger of forgetfulness, and so instituted a simple ceremony to be done 'in remembrance of me'. The Lord's Supper, Communion, Eucharist, or whatever name we might give it, is more than simply an act of remembrance, but it is at least that, and that aspect of it has great importance and value in itself, as this tragic history of Jerusalem shows us.

PRAYER

Read slowly through Paul's account of the institution of the Lord's Supper in 1 Corinthians 11:23–26. Meditate on what it is that we are remembering when we take part in it. Turn the remembrance into words of gratitude and love to God for what he has done for you.

ADULTERY PUNISHED

The phrase 'make known to Jerusalem her abominations' (16:2) has a quasi-judicial ring about it. Now, in these verses, it becomes clear that the recital in 16:3–34 has been in the nature of a speech by the council for the prosecution in a court of law. The judge now passes judgment.

The crimes committed

In verse 36 the reasons for the judgment are given, introduced by the word 'because'. There are three reasons—self-prostitution, idolatry and child sacrifice. The first refers to Judah's political alliances, the second to the adoption of pagan cults and the third probably includes both ritual child sacrifice and the loss of innocent lives in some of the disastrous wars that resulted from the political alliances.

The punishment declared

The judgment passed is introduced in verse 37 by the word 'therefore'. It relates the penalty directly to the crime. The guilty woman is paraded in public and all her former lovers are called to gather around her. Each may have thought that she had given herself to him alone. Now they can see that they have been played off against each other by this unfaithful wife. Although the description of the sentence that is to be carried out (vv. 39–41) is based on the exposure and stoning to death which was a common punishment for a proven adulteress in the ancient Near East, it goes beyond that. It clearly relates to the destruction of the city of Jerusalem in 586/7BC. The Babylonians broke down its walls and stripped it bare of anything valuable. It was burned with fire and many of the inhabitants put to the sword. Although the Babylonians were the prime agents of destruction, other of Judah's former 'lovers' took the opportunity to plunder the land, as Ezekiel 25 makes clear. At the end of it, Jerusalem will have returned to the state in which God originally found her—naked, bare and bloodied. Only then will God's wrath be finally turned aside (v. 42).

God's wrath

The kind of words said in verses 42–43a about God's jealousy and rage can be readily misunderstood by readers of the Old Testament if they forget that the language used is strongly anthropomorphic. All language about a personal God has to be so, but it needs to be understood in a way that removes from it the connotations that come from human sinfulness and puts it instead in the context of God's holiness. As we have seen in considering earlier passages in Ezekiel, anger can be a legitimate reaction in certain situations. There is such a thing as 'righteous anger' in the face of various forms of injustice and abuse. Where human anger goes wrong is that it so readily becomes infected with vindictiveness or malice. It also tends to get out of control. God's wrath is free of these human failings. There are also situations where jealousy has a rightful place. Marriage is meant to be an exclusive relationship in which each partner is committed wholeheartedly to the other alone. Each partner is right to be jealous of the integrity of that relationship, and to seek to protect it from being violated by others. Human jealousy goes wrong when it becomes motivated by selfishness rather than self-giving love for the other. God's jealousy for his people is always motivated by his love for them and his desire for their good.

The pronouncements of judgment that appear in many of the prophetic books, and that are especially strong in Ezekiel, can seem harsh and uncaring. However, to read them in this way is to fail to grasp that they are the expression of great grief, experienced by someone who has loved deeply and is rightly angry at how the beloved has behaved. That anger springs partly from revulsion at the evil that the beloved has done to others, and partly from seeing what that behaviour has done to the beloved, who has become depraved. Only an unjust and unloving person could ignore such behaviour.

PRAYER

Think of recent news items that have made you feel angry, and examine the reasons for your anger. How far was it righteous anger? Have there been things in the news about which you should have been angry, but instead have been indifferent? Turn your thoughts into prayers, confessing your wrong attitudes and praying for justice and love to prevail in the situations you have thought about. You can use the same approach to things that people have said or done recently that have angered you.

33   EZEKIEL 16:43b–52

LIKE MOTHER, LIKE DAUGHTER

The imagery now changes from that of husband and wife to that of a
mother and her daughters (v. 44). Some commentators see this as a
later expansion of the original extended metaphor. That may be so, but
the transition is a fairly natural one, and it builds on the statement at
the beginning of the metaphor about Jerusalem's origins. Jerusalem has
proved to be a chip off the old block. She is like her mother, the Hittite,
who was married to an Amorite, the people whose sins led to their
expulsion from the land of Canaan (Genesis 15:16). The implication is
that the same fate will befall the Judeans, whose capital is Jerusalem.

Sister Samaria

Not only is Jerusalem like her mother, she has a family resemblance to
her two sisters, Samaria and Sodom (v. 46). The description of Samaria
as her 'older/greater' sister must refer to the fact that Samaria was the
capital of the northern kingdom of Israel, which was larger than Judah.
Samaria itself was a new foundation by King Omri of Israel (1 Kings
16:24). Samaria's 'daughters' are the villages that surrounded it (this
was a common Semitic idiom for such villages). The sins of Samaria are
not elaborated upon in this section. They would have been well known
to Ezekiel's hearers. Jeroboam, the first king of the northern kingdom
after it split away from Solomon's son Rehoboam, founded national
shrines at Bethel and Dan. In them he put golden images of calves
and installed non-levitical priests. He also altered the religious calendar
(1 Kings 12:28–33). This does seem to have encouraged a greater
degree of open idolatry and adoption of pagan worship in Israel than
occurred in Judah (2 Kings 17:7–18).

Sister Sodom

Sodom is the 'younger/smaller' sister because it was probably a smaller
city, but what it lacked in size was made up for by its reputation. In the
Old Testament, Sodom is proverbial for its sinfulness, and its destruction
is one of the archetypal acts of judgment (Genesis 19:24–29; Isaiah
1:7–11). In Ezekiel, Sodom is not condemned explicitly for the sexual
sins with which its name became linked (although these may be included in the 'abominable things' of v. 50), but because its prosperity

induced a pride and callousness that led to the neglect of the poor and needy.

Shock therapy

According to Ezekiel, both of these outstanding examples of sinful cities, which had suffered complete and terrible destruction, had now been surpassed in sinfulness by Jerusalem (v. 51). The conclusion is inescapable: if God punished these cities severely for their sins, how could Jerusalem hope to escape his judgment (see 2 Kings 21:13)? But this is not the main point of the comparison. Its main purpose is to evoke a sense of shame on the part of the Judeans. Because of their adherence to the house of David and the cult of the temple in Jerusalem, the 'holy city', they looked down on the northern kingdom as semi-apostate. Sodom was to them the epitome of wickedness (16:56). Ezekiel's audience of Judeans would have been deeply shocked by the assertion that they were more corrupt than Sodom (v. 47) and more than twice as wicked as Samaria (v. 51). No doubt the prophet uses hyperbolic language to administer 'shock therapy' to his hearers. A sense of shame would at least be the starting point for a return to God (v. 52).

Jesus used a similar kind of shock tactic when faced with unrepentant stubbornness in his day (Matthew 11:20–24). What both Ezekiel and Jesus faced was a common human weakness. We are all much better at seeing the moral failings of others than at perceiving them in ourselves. Jesus summed this up memorably in his question, 'Why do you see the speck in your neighbour's eye, but do not notice the log in your own eye?' (Matthew 7:3) and went on to demand that we remove the log in our own eye before trying to remove the speck in our neighbour's. History teaches us the log-spotting is not easy and that those who have grounds for believing that they are among God's people often find it particularly difficult.

PRAYER

Use these words from the Psalms to ask God to show you any 'logs' you need to get rid of and to help you deal with them.

'Search me, O God, and know my heart; test me and know my thoughts. See if there is any wicked way in me, and lead me in the way everlasting.'

Psalm 139:23–24

The COVENANT RESTORED

The grim and shocking oracle ends with a surprising and amazing word of hope, a promise of restoration. The statement in verse 57 that Jerusalem is a 'mockery to… those all around who despise you' suggests that this section may well be a later addition to the oracle, added some time after the destruction of Jerusalem and the second deportation of Judeans to Babylon in 587/6BC.

Restoration

The word of hope begins with a promise of the restoration of Sodom and Samaria. In a sense this will further disgrace Jerusalem (v. 54), because the fact that her sins have surpassed theirs means that if she is to be restored, so should they, who have been less guilty than she became. Jerusalem too will be restored; indeed, she will be given responsibility for Sodom and Samaria (v. 61). But none of this will happen because Jerusalem deserves it. She has despised and broken the covenant, and so deserved nothing from God but punishment (v. 59). However, although she has forgotten the days of her youth (16:22), God has not. He will take the initiative to establish a new relationship with her. In doing so he will create in her the two things that have previously been lacking—memory and shame (vv. 61, 63).

Law and grace

In God's promise to Jerusalem we can see a classic theological tension, which can be expressed in a number of ways—judgment and mercy; justice and love; law and grace. On the one hand God declares, 'I will deal with you as you have done' (v. 59). On the other he says, 'I will remember my covenant with you in the days of your youth, and I will establish with you an everlasting covenant' (v. 60). As a matter of law and justice, the breaking of the covenant required that judgment be passed against Jerusalem. For God to do otherwise would have been to condone evil. It would also mean that he was not being true to the covenant. The covenant was a contractual relationship in which each partner took on certain obligations. The history of Israel that led up to the destruction of Jerusalem was one of repeated violation of the covenant. From the legal point of view, this could only end with the invocation of the covenant curses (Leviticus 26; Deuteronomy 28) and the final termination of the covenant.

As the first section of Ezekiel 16 expresses so poignantly, however, the covenant came into being only because of God's initiative of love. Whether one thinks in terms of the covenant with Abraham, or at Sinai, or with David, the human partner had never earned the right to be drawn into this special relationship with God. It had been a sheer act of unmerited love, of grace. Since that was the case, the returning of Jerusalem to her former state (v. 55) might indeed provide the opportunity for a new beginning. Once before when she was naked and bare, bloodied and unlovely, God had loved her by his own free choice. Might he not do so again? After her unfaithfulness this might well be too much to hope for, but it is just this that is promised. The first act of love produced loveliness of one kind in the beloved (16:13). This second act would produce loveliness of another kind— penitence and humility (v. 63).

A new commandment

There is an important insight here that Christians often fail to grasp. Keeping the covenant law was never the way by which Israel earned her relationship with God. The covenant existed only because that relationship was already established as a gift of God's love. The covenant law expressed how the relationship was to be lived out in practice. The same is true of the new covenant. It too is grounded in a gift of God's love—reconciliation with God through our Lord Jesus Christ. The new covenant has its own law, summed up in the 'new commandment' given by Jesus to his disciples that they should love one another as he had loved them (John 13:34–35). This is a radical expression of the heart of the law of the old covenant, the commandments to love God with our whole being and our neighbour as ourselves (Mark 12:29–31).

MEDITATION

'For the love of Christ urges us on, because we are convinced that one has died for all; therefore all have died. And he died for all, so that those who live might live no longer for themselves, but for him who died and was raised for them.'

2 Corinthians 5:14–15

An ALLEGORY of EAGLES

Ezekiel tells his fellow exiles another story. It is described as both a 'riddle' and an 'allegory'. The Hebrew word translated as 'riddle' (*chidah*) indicates a saying that hides the truth it imparts, while an 'allegory' (*mashal*) clarifies the truth that underlies it by putting it in a new light. In other words, the prophet's story serves both to conceal and reveal. It has a surface meaning that is fairly easy to understand, even if its message is unwelcome. However, for the discerning reader there is a deeper, underlying meaning.

Scene one

The allegory is rather like a modern political cartoon. Living creatures and plants are personified as symbols for nations or their rulers. This allegory has two 'scenes' and refers to the people and events that are recorded in 2 Kings 24—25. In the first scene (vv. 3–6), a great eagle, which is described as both powerful and beautiful, comes to Lebanon, breaks off the newest growth of a great cedar and takes it off to a 'land of trade' and 'city of merchants'. In the light of Ezekiel 16:29 it is clear that this is Babylon. In place of the cedar the eagle plants a vine, providing it with ideal conditions for growth, in which it begins to flourish. The eagle of this scene represents the imperial power of Babylon in general, and King Nebuchadnezzar in particular. The shoot of the cedar represents the most recent descendant of King David, in this case King Jehoiachin. He was taken into exile in Babylon in 597BC. The vine seed planted by the eagle represents his uncle, Zedekiah, whom Nebuchadnezzar set up as regent in Jehoiachin's place. To begin with, he ruled as an obedient vassal of the Babylonians.

Scene two

In the second scene (vv. 7–8), another great eagle appears, though it is not described in as glowing terms as the first. The vine turns its branches towards this eagle, hoping to receive better sustenance from it, and the second eagle transplants it in the hope that it will flourish and produce more fruit. The book of Jeremiah makes it clear that Zedekiah was caught between two groups of advisors. Some were pro-Babylonian, others pro-Egyptian. The pro-Egyptian party played the nationalist card, arguing that alliance with Egypt would bring hope of Judah regaining her independence. In the end they won the argument and Zedekiah rebelled against Nebuchadnezzar.

The allegory's message

On the political level, the message of the allegory is fairly clear, and the rhetorical questions in verses 9–10 drive it home. The eagles, the international superpowers, are not really interested in Judah's well-being, but in their own interests. Judah is a buffer state between them. To keep switching sides is not going to do her much good. It just makes her a pawn collaborating in their power play, and it will be her downfall, not her salvation. In this way the prophet is once again undermining the false hopes of those who may have been heartened by news of Zedekiah's adoption of a pro-Egyptian policy.

But there is a deeper meaning to the allegory, which is hinted at by some elements which do not quite fit the simple surface analysis. Why is the home of the cedar called 'Lebanon'? Is it just because Lebanon was the proverbial home of the best cedars? May it not be because it was also the name of one of Solomon's palaces (1 Kings 7:2)? The thoughtful reader is then prompted to consider who planted this cedar in the first place. Who established the Davidic dynasty in Jerusalem? Also, the phrase 'land of trade' (v. 4) is literally 'land of Canaan'. So, again the reader is reminded of Israel's initial settlement in Canaan. Who brought them there? Again, the eagle's provision for the vine echoes what is said in Psalm 80:8–11 about God's provision for the vine that he brought out of Egypt. Judah's political unfaithfulness is only a reflection of her spiritual state. Indeed it arises out of her lack of trust in God. The prophet's allegory draws the more thoughtful reader into an appreciation of the spiritual dimension of the events it describes, the dimension that we all too often fail to discern.

PRAYER

*Lord, it is so easy to live life on the pragmatic level,
seeking to understand and solve problems in purely practical terms.
Help me to give time to seeking your wisdom so that I gain
spiritual insight into what is happening and discover your way
of dealing with situations.*

The ALLEGORY EXPLAINED & EXTENDED

Although the meaning of the allegory was fairly clear as far as its reference to political events was concerned, Ezekiel did not want to leave his hearers in any doubt, so he explained it to them. Perhaps he suspected that the people could be deliberately obtuse when faced with unpalatable truths. In any case, in the course of the explanation he makes explicit the spiritual dimension that we have suggested is at least hinted at in the allegory itself. This is brought out in two places. Behind the questions in verse 15 lies the 'law of the king' in Deuteronomy 17:14-20, which prohibited any return to Egypt to acquire horses. Such action is seen as a lack of trust in the Lord God who had delivered the Hebrew slaves from Egypt. Whatever the political calculations involved in Zedekiah's policy of appealing to Egypt, it was doomed to failure. God's blessing could not be acquired by a policy that breached his covenant with Israel.

Zedekiah's sin

More surprising, perhaps, is verse 18 with its condemnation of Zedekiah for breaking his covenant with the king of Babylon. Why is God so concerned about a covenant with a pagan king, in which Zedekiah probably felt he had had little choice? Part of the answer may lie in the stress in the Old Testament on the importance of keeping one's word (for example, Psalm 15:4). To this can be added the fact that when Zedekiah swore his oath of loyalty to Babylon he would have done so in the name of his own God. That is why, in verse 19, God refers to it as 'my oath that he despised, and my covenant that he broke'. In breaking the oath, he was breaking the commandment not to take God's name in vain. However unwise Zedekiah's policy may have been politically, it was his disobedience towards God that really sealed his fate, says the prophet.

Hope for the future

The chapter ends with another allegory (vv. 22-24). As we shall see, Ezekiel's prophecies take on a very different character once Jerusalem has fallen and there is no more danger of false hopes for its deliverance, and no more opportunity to repent and avoid disaster. He then brings the people explicit words of hope, rather than just the hints of it. The final section of this chapter probably belongs to that period. It promises a new start that is the result of what God does, not anything that the Judeans do. God takes a new, tender shoot from the top of the cedar tree and plants it 'on a high and lofty mountain… the mountain height of Israel'. There is no doubt that this is a reference to Mount Zion, the site of Jerusalem (see Psalm 48:1). Here the shoot will grow into a great tree, providing abundant sustenance and shelter. As a result, the Lordship of Israel's God will be plain to all.

It is important to note that God does not promise to rescue the cedar shoot from Babylon, to restore Jehoiakim to the throne. Nor does he hold out any hope for the vine, Zedekiah. He will keep his promise to David (2 Samuel 7:16) by going back to the same cedar tree, but will take from it a new shoot. Here is one of the early expressions of the Jewish messianic hope—that God will intervene in history by sending a descendant of David who will truly establish God's kingdom.

Transformation

Christians see this promise fulfilled in Jesus (Luke 1:32–33). Ezekiel's allegory may have been in Jesus' mind when he told his parable comparing the kingdom of God to a mustard seed. He spoke of that seed growing until it becomes 'the greatest of all shrubs, and puts forth large branches, so that the birds of the air can make nests in its shade' (Mark 4:32). Both the allegory and the parable speak of a God who can transform seemingly unpromising situations. In doing so, he may start small, but a tender young shoot or a tiny mustard seed can grow into something great. What is more, the result is an expression of God's kingdom.

PRAYER

Think of a situation that seems unpromising at present.
Can you see in it some 'shoot' or 'mustard seed' that might be an
indication of hope? Whether or not this is the case, pray that God
will act to transform that situation, to make it in some way an
expression of his kingdom.

ACCEPTING RESPONSIBILITY

'It isn't fair!' is a common complaint. Sometimes we use it when seeking to avoid responsibility for something by blaming it on someone else or on impersonal 'fate'. Many of the Judeans of Ezekiel's generation sought to excuse themselves from responsibility for the disasters that befell them by blaming their parents. They kept repeating the proverb, 'The parents have eaten sour grapes, and the children's teeth are set on edge' (v. 2). It is not only Ezekiel who reports this. Jeremiah was faced with it too (Jeremiah 31:29), and a similar outlook is expressed in Lamentations 5:7: 'Our ancestors sinned; they are no more, and we bear their iniquities.'

The person who sins shall die

Behind the use of this proverb lies a combination of fatalistic despair ('It's not our fault and we can't do anything about it') and a questioning of God's justice ('Why should we have to suffer for what our parents did?'). The prophet's response is a categorical denial of the applicability of the proverb (v. 3). His argument falls into two parts. The first, in verses 4–20, is framed by the assertion, 'The person who sins shall die.' Here the argument is presented in the form used for priestly case law. The formula 'If a man...' followed by the judicial verdict is found, for example, in Leviticus 19:20–21. Ezekiel describes the behaviour of three generations, perhaps because this is normally the maximum number alive and active as morally responsible people at any one time. He asserts that if a man behaves righteously, he will live (vv. 5–9). If he has a son who behaves wickedly, the son will die. His father's righteousness will not save him (vv. 10–13). However, if this wicked man has a son who is righteous, that son will live because of his righteousness (vv. 14–18). The hypothetical objection that the prophet introduces in verse 19 enables him to point up the absurdity, in terms of morality and justice, of the outlook expressed in the 'sour grapes' proverb.

The 'checklist' of righteous behaviour (vv. 5–9) covers three basic areas—religious worship, sexual morality and social justice. The individual items in the list are clearly based on commandments found in the collections of the laws of the covenant in Exodus and Leviticus.

Thus Ezekiel is describing not some abstract pattern of right behaviour, but what it means to live in a right relationship to the God who is Israel's overlord under the covenant made at Sinai. In this context, what Ezekiel means by 'live' is 'to enjoy the fullness of relationship with God that flows from obedience'. To be cut off from God is to be 'dead', even though physically alive, because what is being referred to here is not merely physical existence. This is the sense in which the words are used in Deuteronomy 30:15 when, having laid out before the Israelites the demands of the covenant, with its blessings and curses, Moses says, 'See, I have set before you today life and prosperity, death and adversity.'

Accepting responsibility

Ezekiel was trying to bring his hearers to a more balanced view of things than the one they held. But his words were uncomfortable for them. They had found some comfort in the thought that their plight was not of their own making. Their conclusion that the wickedness of previous generations invited divine judgment was correct. However, the prophet asserts that divine judgment is not an uncontrollable juggernaut that crushes all in its path. It could be halted if people recognized and exercised their responsibility. It is true that the evil actions of one generation can have harmful consequences for the next. It is not true, however, that God holds people responsible for the actions of others. If people will recognize their responsibility, reject the evil ways of their predecessors, and admit their own faults, then there is hope for the future. God is ready to forgive people and set them free to enjoy the fullness of life that comes from having a right relationship with him.

MEDITATION

We sometimes like to believe that we are trapped in a situation through no fault of our own. This absolves us from trying to do anything about it. Ezekiel challenges us to accept that if we are to find freedom we must recognize our responsibility before God. That may mean admitting that we are at fault and taking appropriate action. This might seem too heavy a burden to assume, but for the knowledge that God is waiting to forgive and to restore.

RESPONSIBILITY & REPENTANCE

The second part of Ezekiel's argument (vv. 21–32) is marked by the call to 'turn' from sin (vv. 21, 32) and the repeated statement that God does not take pleasure in anyone's death (vv. 23, 32). The focus of what the prophet says changes from the relationship between one's situation and one's responsibility, to the relationship between responsibility and repentance.

Not trapped in the past

In 18:1–20, Ezekiel was speaking about the different generations, which meant treating an individual's life as if it were wholly good or bad. Now he deals with different phases in a single person's life (vv. 21–24). The reality is that a good person may 'go off the rails' at some point and subsequently live an evil life. Similarly, someone who has been living an evil life may see the error of their ways, turn over a new leaf, and live a good life from then on. How does God respond in these cases? The prophet's answer is that God recognizes these 'turnings' immediately. People are not trapped by their past, for good or ill. What matters is how they are living 'now'.

To some today this seems unjust, as it did to Ezekiel's audience. If a woman has lived a blameless life for more than sixty years, but then turns bad and lives a wicked life for a few years before she dies, surely those few years will be outweighed by the many years of good living? That's how many think it should be. And then there is a man who lives an evil life but, just before he dies, changes his ways and lives a life of great goodness. Is it fair that that should wipe out all the evil he has done? Surely not, many would think. Ezekiel disagrees with them, as does Jesus, to judge by his words to the thief on the cross, 'Truly I tell you, today you will be with me in Paradise' (Luke 23:43).

Turning to God

What is wrong with the popular view of justice in these cases? First of all, it treats God's justice as simply a matter of keeping a tally sheet, of weighing the quantity (and perhaps the quality) of good deeds against that of bad deeds. In the Bible, God's justice is not primarily about deeds, but about the relationship of a person to God. It asks the question, does that person stand in a right relationship to God? Is he or she 'turned' to God or away from God? The possibility of 'turning' is always there and each person is responsible for whether or not they are 'turned' to God. This means that fundamentally the issue is not one of deeds but of the direction and quality of a person's life. This is why Ezekiel uses the simple verb 'to turn' so often. Many English versions translate it as 'repent', but that tends to make us think of a psychological process. Ezekiel is talking about taking responsibility for the direction of your life. God takes no pleasure in anyone's death, and so is always ready to forgive the wicked person who 'turns' to him, forgetting their past. For God, to forgive is to forget. Since to enjoy life is to know God, those who turn away from him reject life and so will die. Their past righteousness will not save them.

Never too late

This is both a comforting and a disturbing teaching. It is comforting to those who are aware of their faults and failures. It assures them that they are never too bad, and it is never too late, to 'turn' to God and receive forgiveness and life. This is the message that Ezekiel emphasizes in his address to the Judean exiles. It might, however, seem a disturbing message to those who feel that they are living in a right relationship to God. How can they be sure that it will not all go wrong in the end, that they will not 'turn' away from God and be lost? Ezekiel gives a hint of an answer to that in verse 31. You cannot live in a right relationship to God without being transformed by it. That transformation, described here as getting a 'new heart and a new spirit', enables you to go on living 'turned' to God. This makes all the more glorious God's final invitation, 'Turn, then, and live' (v. 32).

MEDITATION

'Sin is not a cul-de-sac, nor is guilt a final trap.
Sin may be washed away by repentance and return,
and beyond guilt is the dawn of forgiveness.'

Abraham Herschel, *The Prophets* (Harper & Row, 1969, Vol. 1, p. 174)

A LAMENT *for* LION CUBS

In Old Testament times, lions were still to be found in Palestine, especially in the more fertile terrain of the Jordan valley. Sometimes villages might be terrorized by lions, and people dug pits to trap them. This is the background to Ezekiel's allegory. The 'king of beasts' was also a common symbol of royal power. It is used in that sense to describe Judah in the ancient Israelite poem known as 'Jacob's Blessing' (Genesis 49:8–12). So the story of two lions that threatened whole neighbourhoods and had to be hunted and trapped would have been readily understood by Ezekiel's hearers as an allegory about two Judean kings.

A Hebrew lament

Ezekiel's poem is not just an allegory. It is an allegory set in a particular form, that of the Hebrew lament, which was a distinctive form of song frequently sung at funerals. David's lament over Saul and Jonathan (2 Samuel 1:19–27) is a classic example, extolling their virtues and grieving over the tragic circumstances of their death. In Hebrew, the lament has a distinctive irregular 3+2 pattern of stress. Some prophets take up the lament form in their oracles as a striking way of communicating the certainty of the future tragedy of which they are speaking. In effect, they conduct a funeral service for a person who is still alive.

Who are the cubs?

It is not difficult to identify the first of the lion cubs in the allegory, since he is said to have been taken away to Egypt (v. 4). He is Jehoahaz, who came to the throne of Judah after the death in battle of King Josiah in 609BC. He reigned for only three months before Pharaoh Neco took him to Egypt as a captive, putting his older half-brother Jehoiakim on the throne (2 Kings 23:29–34). There is debate about the identity of the second lion cub, since two of Judah's last kings were taken as captives to Babylon (v. 9). One was Jehoiakim's son, Jehoiachin (2 Kings 24:15). The other was Zedekiah, Jehoiachin's uncle, whom Nebuchadnezzar put on the throne in his place (2 Kings 25:6–7). A key issue is how one understands the 'lioness' in the poem. Does it represent the nation of Judah or an actual queen mother? Since some stress seems to be put on the two cubs having the same mother, whose ambitions play a part in their coming to the throne, reference to an actual person seems likely. It is then significant that Jehoahaz and Zedekiah did have the same mother, Hamutal (2 Kings 23:31; 24:18). In a court where a king had more than one wife, there was scope for intrigue when an ambitious wife wanted to ensure that one of her sons gained the throne, as this would give her significant influence in the politics of the palace.

Plots and intrigues

If the two kings are Jehoahaz and Zedekiah, the poem takes on a particular significance. The episode of Jehoahaz was past history, and so a lament over it was appropriate, but at the time Ezekiel composed the lament, Zedekiah was still on the throne. The prophet, therefore, is looking forward to a future tragedy, declaring that Zedekiah's days are numbered. He will go the way of his brother. Moreover, the reference to the queen mother and her ambitions and schemes makes the poem an exposure of the futility of seeking salvation by means of political plotting and scheming. The book of Jeremiah makes it clear that the last years of Judah were marked by intrigues and plots, as a pro-Babylonian party and a pro-Egyptian party vied for control of national policy. Maybe Queen Hamutal was deeply involved in all this. Once again, the prophet is undermining false hopes. The imagery in verses 6–7 is probably ironic. As a Babylonian puppet, Zedekiah could not ravage other nations. The nation that is going to suffer at his hands is his own, as his (and his mother's?) policies lead it to disaster.

As Ezekiel composed his lament for the young lions of Judah, he did not know that eventually a 'Lion of the tribe of Judah' would come who would truly liberate God's people. He would not do it by tearing prey, devouring people and ravaging lands, but by dying for people like a sacrificial lamb (Revelation 5:5–6).

PRAYER

Lord, I pray for those in positions of power in the nation today. Keep them from getting involved in plots and intrigues to increase their power, and enable them to concentrate on using their power wisely and justly. Help them to curb their personal ambitions and to seek instead the good of the community.

A LAMENT *for a* VINE

The lament in Ezekiel 19 is presented as a single poem, but there is an abrupt change of imagery in verses 10–14, from lions to a vine. This may not have seemed so abrupt to the prophet's hearers. The combination of the images of lion, vine and sceptre is found in Jacob's blessing of Judah (Genesis 49:8–12). Also, Ezekiel has used the image of the vine to represent a king in chapter 17.

Here the vine represents the queen mother, just as she is the lioness in the previous allegory. The reference to the vine flourishing (v. 10b) may allude to the influence Queen Hamutal came to wield in the court in Jerusalem. The 'strongest stem' of verse 11 represents Zedekiah. In his time the vine is pulled up and left lying on the ground, exposed to the dry east wind from the desert. The vine and its strongest branch wither and are then burned. At the time this poem was composed, it was a warning of the disaster that lay ahead for Judah because of Zedekiah's decision to rebel against Babylon.

The end of the line

The word 'now' that introduces verses 13–14 may indicate that these verses are a later addition to the poem, written in the light of later events. Both biblical scholars and horticulturalists have noted that what is said here is impossible in reality. A vine that has been withered and burned cannot be transplanted. The prophet, no doubt, is using poetic licence to drive home his point. There is no hope for the future to be found in Zedekiah. With his line, at least, the Davidic monarchy comes to an end. As if by spontaneous combustion, fire breaks out of the transplanted vine, consuming its branches and fruit. There is no strong stem, no ruler, left. It may be that these verses were added by the prophet in response to some who sought at least a grain of hope in the continued existence of Zedekiah in exile in Babylon, even though blinded and imprisoned.

The closing words of verse 14, 'this is a lamentation, and it is used as a lamentation', read like an editorial comment. They make the point that what had been composed as a warning of impending dis-aster came to be used in the way a lament normally was, to grieve over the disaster once it had happened.

It would be possible to take verse 14 as implying that Ezekiel saw no future for the Davidic monarchy. With the failure of the policies of Queen Hamutal and her son King Zedekiah, even if the royal line survived physically in Babylon, it had no future in God's plans. However, the message of Ezekiel 17:22–24 runs counter to this. So, what is said here must be taken to mean that the line will not be continued through Zedekiah. In fact, his sons were killed before his eyes (2 Kings 25:7). Ezekiel's understanding of the role that the Davidic monarchy will play in the future of God's people becomes clearer in the later chapters of the book.

The true vine

From a Christian perspective, this tragic story of the self-destructive vine evokes Jesus' claim to be the true vine (John 15:1). He is the descendant of David through whom God's purpose of establishing a 'people of God' on earth will reach fruition.

Jesus uses the imagery of the vine in a rather different way than Ezekiel does. Whereas in Ezekiel the vine represents the rulers of God's people, Jesus uses it to represent the people of God. He is the main stem and his disciples are the branches. There is, none the less, an element of similarity in the use of the imagery by Ezekiel and Jesus. They both use the picture of withering and burning (Ezekiel 19:12; John 15:6). Ezekiel is countering false hopes—the result of relying on human aid rather than on God. Jesus warns against false complacency. Those who are truly part of the vine are those who 'abide' in him, who rely on him as their source of strength. What this means is spelled out in John 15:9–10: it implies an obedience to him that springs from our love relationship with him.

PRAYER

Lord Jesus, the True Vine, you have said, 'Those who abide in me and I in them bear much fruit, because apart from me you can do nothing.' Help me not to try to do things apart from you, but to learn daily what it means to abide in you, so that I may be fruitful for you.

FAILURE & FORGIVENESS

After several chapters of proverbs, parables and allegories, we return to the language of straightforward history. The date (v. 1) has no obvious meaning beyond marking the passage of time (see 1:2; 8:1). Once again the elders, the lay leaders, of the exilic community come to Ezekiel to seek a word from God. We are not told what their specific question was, but God refuses to answer it (v. 3). Instead, they are given a recital of Israel's history.

Three rebellious generations

The way the prophet retells Israel's history is reminiscent of chapter 18. Again he tells the story of three generations. Each is given the choice of obeying God's life-giving laws or disobeying them. The three generations presented in this historical 'case study' are those who lived in Egypt at the time of the Exodus (vv. 5–10), the first wilderness generation (vv. 11–17) and their children (vv. 18–26). Each generation's history follows a six-stage cycle.

- God spoke to them (vv. 5–6, 11, 18–19).
- He challenged them to an exclusive devotion (vv. 7, 12, 19–20).
- They rebelled against God (vv. 8a, 13a, 21a).
- As a result they provoked God's anger (vv. 8b, 13b, 21b).
- That anger was held back for the sake of the divine name (vv. 9, 14, 22).
- However, there was a limited act of judgment (vv. 10, 15–17, 23).

This way of telling the history highlights Israel's ingratitude and unfaithfulness towards God. God took a gracious initiative towards each generation—the promise of the Exodus (v. 6), the making of the Sinai covenant (v. 11), the renewal of that covenant after the apostasy of the golden calf (vv. 19–20). Yet each initiative was spurned and the people chose to disobey God's laws and go their own way. The history also makes clear God's mercy and forgiveness. He does not totally reject the rebels and wipe them out. Instead he bears with them and gives the next generation the opportunity of a new start.

The reason given for God's forbearance, the honour of his name in the sight of the nations, might seem rather self-seeking on God's part.

However, it is a reminder to the Israelites that they were not chosen by God for a special relationship with him because they deserved that relationship in any way. Therefore, they did not deserve any special consideration when they rebelled. Moreover, they were chosen because God wanted to bring blessing to the rest of the nations through them. Hence in his treatment of them God takes into account these nations, not wanting to put any further barriers in the way of their turning to him.

Facing up to failure

A sense of history played an essential role in Israelite religion. The story of the Exodus has been told at Passover right down to the present day. This was intended to remind the Israelites of God's goodness towards them and to encourage their continued commitment to the covenant with him. Any recollection of history runs the risk, however, of playing up the good parts and playing down the bad, of remembering the successes and forgetting the failures. Ezekiel wanted to remove any rosy view of Israel's history that would prevent his hearers from recognizing the desperateness of their situation as they faced God's anger, which was to be held back no longer, and so repenting and seeking forgiveness.

Reading this account of the Israelites' history, it is easy for us to think what a perverse and blind people they were, apparently incapable of learning from their mistakes. But are we really any different? In the life of faith, it is, of course, good to 'count our blessings', remembering the good things God has done for us. But we must beware the tendency to forget our past failures. Unless we recognize them and deal with them, we will not learn from them. Instead, we, like Israel, might perpetuate them time and again.

PRAYER

It is not easy to recall those past failures we have chosen to forget, so we need to echo the psalmist's prayer in Psalm 19:12–14.

'But who can detect their errors? Clear me from hidden faults. Keep back your servant also from proud thoughts; do not let them have dominion over me. Then I shall be blameless and innocent of great transgression. Let the words of my mouth and the meditation of my heart be acceptable to you, O Lord, my rock and my redeemer.'

A History *of* Horror

Ezekiel rounds off his narrative of the three generations of failure and rebellion with a brief account of Israel's occupation of Canaan (vv. 27–29). This is presented as a time of continued unfaithfulness to God as the Israelites got involved in the fertility religion of the Canaanites. The Hebrew of verse 29 uses a pun to express the eagerness with which they did this. It can be expressed in English by using the old verb 'to hie', which means 'to hasten': 'What is the high place to which you hie?' The prophet then asserts that the members of the present generation, including his audience, are continuing in the same way 'to this day'. That is why God refuses to listen to them and answer them (vv. 30–31).

An extraordinary claim

In verses 25–26 the prophet makes an extraordinary claim—that God gave to his people evil commandments that could not lead to life. This included the sacrifice of children, which was a practice among at least some of the Canaanite peoples (see, for example, 2 Kings 3:27). It was especially prevalent in Phoenicia and its colonies, and there are references to it being practised in Judah (2 Kings 16:3; 21:6; 23:10). The amazing thing is that in his retelling of the history of Israel Ezekiel identifies this horrifying practice with the commandment of God. What did he mean? There are three ways of understanding it, which are not mutually exclusive.

In the Old Testament there is a strong sense of God's providence. Nothing happens that does not somehow, however mysteriously, come under God's providence (see, for example, Isaiah 45:7). So, if Israel adopted the horrifying practice of child sacrifice, it must somehow have been related to God's purposes—which is not to say that this is what God wanted them to do.

This leads to a second strand found in the Old Testament, which is that if people insist on their own way, God may give them what they want, even though the outcome is bad for them (Psalm 81:11–12; 106:13–15). To some extent this is a counterpoint to the previous stress. It asserts that we are responsible for what we do and its consequences, and cannot blame them on God.

Thirdly, Ezekiel's words may imply that at least some people in Israel interpreted one of the commandments as sanctioning child sacrifice. If so, it would probably be Exodus 22:29: 'The firstborn of your sons you shall give to me.' Elsewhere in the Mosaic Law, however, it is made clear that this does not mean the sacrifice of children. The firstborn child was to be 'redeemed' (Exodus 34:20), presumably by an animal sacrifice (as at the Passover in Egypt). In Micah 6:7 the prophet depicts someone asking ironically whether God wants the sacrifice of firstborn children. Maybe some people, with their outlook moulded by involvement in Canaanite religion, tried to justify what they were doing by appeal to a commandment such as Exodus 22:29, taken out of the context of the covenant law as a whole.

Two wrong attitudes

These verses expose the horrifying possibilities that can flow from two wrong attitudes. The first is wilfulness. The choice put before each of the three generations was whether or not to align their wills with God's will. God willed good for his people. No doubt the people would have said that they wanted what was good, but they wanted to achieve it in their way, which was contrary to the divine will. As a result, Ezekiel's generation ended up in the privations of exile instead of in the land of milk and honey. The second wrong attitude is self-justification. Some Israelites were so concerned to justify adopting Canaanite practices that they twisted the meaning of God's law to support what they wanted to do.

Both of these attitudes are perennial temptations for God's people. Whenever we give way to them, we are not only in danger of becoming deaf to God, as happened to the Israelites depicted in Ezekiel's history lesson, but they can also lead to God's becoming deaf to us, as he was to Ezekiel's inquirers.

PRAYER

The highest, and hardest, prayer to pray sincerely is the one Jesus prayed in Gethsemane, 'Not my will but yours be done.' As a preparation for praying this, ask a friend whose judgment you trust in what ways you might have given in to wilfulness or sought to justify yourself wrongly. Bring these before God for his judgment and forgiveness before echoing Jesus' prayer.

PURGING *through* JUDGMENT

The cyclical pattern that Ezekiel has traced in Israel's history raises
the question of whether there is any way out of these 'vicious cycles'.
The prophet declares that there is, but it will require God to take
the initiative. Rebellion against God has become too ingrained in the
people for them to escape on their own.

A new exodus

The reason for Ezekiel's concentration, in his recital of history, on the
generations around the Exodus period becomes clear in verses 33–44.
He draws an analogy between the Exodus/wilderness generations
and his own. Once again the people stand at the end of a cycle of
rebellion. They are experiencing God's judgment in the form of exile
in Babylon and elsewhere. At this point the prophet brings a word of
hope. There will be a new exodus as God gathers together the people
who are scattered among the nations and brings them out of exile into
a new wilderness experience. This will not be a comfortable experience. The first wilderness experience had been a time of judgment
on those who lost faith in the God of the Exodus and rebelled against
him. They died in the wilderness and never saw the promised land.
The prophet warns that there will be a similar process again. In verse
37 he uses the picture of a shepherd counting the sheep and separat-
ing out those who are to go to slaughter as they pass one by one under
his staff. However, the challenge in verse 39 shows that this is not an
impersonal or automatic process. People are not sheep. God's 'staff'
is a challenge to people to make their choice. There can be no middle
way. They must either serve him wholeheartedly or they might as well
become wholehearted worshippers of pagan idols. This is reminiscent
of the challenge that Joshua gave to his generation: 'Choose this day
whom you will serve… but as for me and my household, we will serve
the Lord' (Joshua 24:15). For those who choose to repudiate the idols
and to serve the Lord, there will be a return to the promised land. The
worship of God will be re-established in its purity in Jerusalem so that
the holiness of God is portrayed as it should be before all the nations
(vv. 40–44). Here Ezekiel gives a glimpse of what will become an
extended vision in chapters 40—48.

God's faithfulness

The basis of this hope is not rooted in any way in what Israel deserves, but in God's faithfulness to his purposes. It is possible to understand verse 32 in two ways, as an expression either of what some people wished or of what they feared had happened to them. Either way, God makes it clear that it is impossible for them to become just 'like the nations'. He has chosen them and made them his people, and he is their king (v. 33). This has not been done just for their own good, but for the good of the nations—that they might come to know who is truly God (v. 41). God has not abandoned his purpose. This is why there will be a new exodus and wilderness experience, leading to a return to the promised land.

Being different

Although on the surface this passage may seem to stress the sovereign control of God over history—that his purpose will be achieved—there is a balance here that leaves no room for fatalism. The people are faced with the challenge of whether or not they are willing to embrace God's purpose and be part of it. To embrace it will mean being prepared to be, and to stay, different from the other nations. Behind verse 32 may well be the desire of the exiles to have their own temple in Babylon. The leaders could argue that it would be good for morale in the community. Perhaps the purpose of their visit to Ezekiel was to ask about this very plan. In the long run, though, it would have been disastrous. It would have encouraged people to feel at home in Babylon, to see themselves as immigrants in a new home, not exiles in a foreign land. Their distinctiveness, which was essential to their role in God's purposes, would have been lost.

MEDITATION

In Matthew 5:13 Jesus says that the lives of his disciples should be as distinctive as salt is in its flavour, and warns against the danger of losing this distinctiveness. Think prayerfully about how this should apply to the way you live.

FIRE & SWORD

The heading 'The word of the Lord came to me' shows that a new section begins here in verse 45. A series of oracles follows, each beginning with these words (20:45; 21:1, 8, 18; 22:1, 17, 23; 23:1). The first two oracles initially seem quite different, using the different images of a forest fire and of a sword. Nevertheless, they use similar ideas and terminology, and on closer consideration they obviously form a matching pair. In fact, the second interprets the first, after the prophet's hearers have complained that it is too obscure for them to understand (20:49).

An all-consuming fire

The first oracle links action with words. The prophet takes up a fixed stance, facing south, as he proclaims it. In verse 46 three different Hebrew words are used to refer to the south: *teman, darom, negeb*. The use of the third word, which is also the name of the desert region in southern Judah, no doubt helped to cause some confusion in the mind of his hearers, as we shall see. Ezekiel declares that God will kindle an all-consuming fire in the south. It will consume every tree, including the green trees that do not burn easily, as well as the dead, dried-up trees. It will cover the whole land from south to north, and not be put out. It will be so fierce that it will scorch the faces of the onlookers. Its dreadful all-consuming nature will make clear to people that this is a divinely kindled fire. Part of the puzzle for the hearers would have been the fact that what they naturally thought of as 'the *negeb*' was a desert, not a forest. Faced with their incomprehension, the prophet pleads with God to be allowed to make its meaning clearer to them (v. 49). The following oracle comes as a response to this prayer.

An unsheathed sword

In the second oracle God is depicted as a soldier brandishing his unsheathed sword menacingly while boasting about the havoc he will wreak with it. It is a terrible image, used to bring home the horror of what the Judean leaders have unleashed by their policy of rebellion against Babylon, despite prophetic warning against such action. Jeremiah in particular had consistently opposed this policy, and had warned about 'the foe from the north' that would bring disaster to Judah (Jeremiah 1:13–15). As Ezekiel address 'the south' from his position in Babylon, he is not speaking just of the southern deserts of Judah, but of the whole land. In fact, the three terms used in 20:46 are balanced by three in 21:2—Jerusalem, the sanctuaries, and the land of Israel. The fire is now replaced by the sword. Like the fire, it is all-consuming, striking down both the righteous and the wicked. It will go throughout the whole land from south to north, and it will not be sheathed again. It is now clear that both oracles are describing the destruction that will be wrought by the Babylonian invasion of Judah, and that this is depicted as the judgment of God on the nation. Once again the prophet combines actions with words as he shows bitter grief and anguish (v. 6). This is intended to bring home to his audience the horror of what the oracles depict. From the picture we get of Ezekiel, there is no reason to doubt that his expression of grief and anguish was more than play-acting. It was a genuine emotional response as he identified with his own nation. He was no prophet of doom who enjoyed proclaiming disaster to his hearers, however much they deserved it.

An unresolved tension

The indiscriminate nature of the judgment depicted in these oracles expresses a tragic reality. The choices of a nation and its leaders often have disastrous effects even for those who played no part in, or even opposed, those decisions. This realism stands in tension with what the prophet says about God recognizing and respecting individual responsibility (for example, ch. 18). This is an aspect of the tension between corporate and individual responsibility. Human individuality is real and creates a measure of freedom, but this does not mean that each person is a self-contained island. There is no clear resolution of this tension in the Bible. It is part of the reality in which we have to live responsibly before God.

PRAYER

Lord, I don't find this tension easy to live with. Sometimes life seems very unfair. Please help me not to use this as an excuse to do nothing, but to continue living responsibly before you.

The SHARPENED SWORD

The theme that links this oracle to the preceding one is the image of the sword as the instrument of God's judgment. The picture changes from that of a soldier boasting about what he will do with his sword to that of an armourer sharpening and polishing a sword and then handing it over to the warrior to use in battle. There are difficulties in the Hebrew of these verses, especially in verse 10b and verse 13, which lead to their being translated in different ways. Despite this, the general sense is clear. The opening words in verses 9b–10a are readily recognizable as Hebrew poetry and some scholars seek to restore a poetic form throughout the oracle, with the exception of verses 10b and 13.

Once again Ezekiel seems to have used a combination of actions and words. There are references to wailing (v. 12), slapping his thigh (v. 12, probably a gesture of grief and frustration), clapping his hands (v. 14, presumably a threatening gesture, as in 6:11) and brandishing a sword as if using it in battle (v. 16). Some commentators suggest that the prophet may well have been performing a traditional 'sword dance' as he uttered this oracle, its dramatic motions adding force to his chanted words.

God the warrior

The image of God as a warrior is one that was quite deeply imbedded in Hebrew thought, going back to the time of the Exodus (Exodus 15:3). For people experiencing injustice and oppression, as was the case with the Hebrew slaves in Egypt, the image of God as a warrior coming to defeat their oppressors and to set them free is clearly a powerful and comforting one. It is not surprising that at other times of national crisis the Israelites thought of God and God's help in such terms (for example, Judges 5:4–5; Habakkuk 3). There is an obvious danger in such imagery, though. It can lead to the false idea that God the warrior is always on our side. One of the surprising, indeed shocking, things about the preaching of the prophets is that, more often than not, they turn the 'warrior God' theme on its head. Instead of God being the warrior who fights for Israel or Judah, God is fighting against Israel. So, here in Ezekiel, the sharpened and burnished sword, flashing like lightning, is an instrument in God's hand which is directed not against Judah's enemies, but 'against my people… against all Israel's princes' (v. 12). No wonder the prophet wails and slaps his thigh!

We cannot help but speak of God in pictures drawn from our human experience. All such pictures have to be used with care. They are incomplete, drawing attention only to certain aspects of God. They may also carry connotations that, if we are not careful, can distort the picture. One problem with the 'warrior' picture is that often in human experience it seems as if 'might is right', so we seek to impose our subjective views or interests by force. What Israel had to learn the hard way was that God always uses his might to uphold what is objectively right. As a guide to what is right, God gave Israel the covenant Law. When Israel neglected the Law, or even wilfully departed from it, she forfeited any claim to have God fight for her. Instead, as the prophets warned, unless she changed her ways she would find that he was fighting against her.

Christ the warrior

The picture in Revelation 19:11–16 of Christ the warrior coming to establish justice and truth, itself based on an Old Testament passage (Isaiah 63:1–6), has been a source of hope to Christians when they have been oppressed or fighting against injustice. It is the imagery used in the old 'Battle Hymn of the Republic':

Mine eyes have seen the glory of the coming of the Lord,
He is trampling out the vintage where the grapes of wrath are stored;
He has loosed the fateful lightning of his terrible swift sword;
His truth is marching on.

If we have listened well to Ezekiel, we will take some time for self-examination and turning to God in repentance, seeking forgiveness, in order to ensure that the 'terrible swift sword' is not brandished against us.

PRAYER

Lord God, forgive me for so often assuming that you are
on my side instead of stopping to consider what is right
in your eyes. Please enable me to discern the truth
and justice for which you want me to fight.

The SWORD *of the* KING *of* BABYLON

The theme of the sword continues, and is developed further. In the previous oracle the sword was used as an image for the instrument of God's judgment in a general sense. Now the identity of that instrument is made specific. God's judgment is to be carried out by the king of Babylon.

At the crossroads

Once again the prophet uses a visual aid (vv. 19–20). He draws a road junction, either on a clay tablet or in the dust on the ground. It is a three-way junction, where the road from Babylon splits in two. One branch of the fork leads to Rabbah, capital of Ammon (now the site of modern Amman in Jordan) and the other to Jerusalem, the capital of Judah. The king of Babylon stands at the junction with his army, needing to decide which of these rebellious states should feel the might of his sword first (v. 21). In the ancient Near East, kings would normally seek guidance from their gods in situations like this (for example, 1 Samuel 23:2–4; 1 Kings 22:5–12). The king of Babylon is depicted making use of three different types of divination. The first is probably a form of drawing lots: marked arrows were put in a quiver, shaken and one drawn out. Teraphim were images of some kind, often of household gods. It is not clear how they were used in divination. Divination by examining the liver of an animal that had been sacrificed was very common in Babylon. Several clay models of livers used in teaching this form of divination have been excavated by archeologists. Presumably, three forms of divination are used to ensure a correct discernment of the divine will. The outcome is a decision to attack Judah and besiege Jerusalem, with all the misery that that will bring to the city (v. 22).

False hopes

This oracle seems to be another example of Ezekiel seeking to undermine any false hopes that his hearers might have. The fact that Judah was not standing alone in rebellion against Babylon, but was part of a coalition of small states, may have given some comfort to his hearers. If nothing else, they may have hoped that the Babylonian attack would be deflected away from Judah and against Ammon. There would then be at least a chance that the Babylonian army might be exhausted by its exertions against the Ammonites, and Judah might escape attack. The prophet declares this that is a vain hope. God will guide the Babylonians to attack Judah first, while their army is fresh.

Prophetic irony

The irony is that the pagan king, Nebuchadnezzar, so punctilious in using methods of divination of the sort forbidden in Israel (Deuteronomy 18:9–14), is the one who is acting as the agent of the God of Israel. By contrast, the king who was nominally the representative of the God of Israel and the ruler of God's chosen people, Zedekiah, is addressed as 'vile, wicked prince' (v. 25). This is because he has 'sworn solemn oaths' (v. 23) and committed 'transgressions' (v. 24). Behind these references is Zedekiah's infidelity to both his covenant with God and his oath of allegiance to Nebuchadnezzar (see the comment on Ezekiel 17:18–19, p. 94). As a result, God declares, things cannot remain as they are. The time for a final reckoning has come, and royal sovereignty will be taken away from Zedekiah. The second part of verse 27 echoes Jacob's blessing of Judah to which there were allusions in Ezekiel 19 (Genesis 49:10). Here there is clearly a word of hope, an indication that the Davidic monarchy will be restored, though not through Zedekiah's line.

The blindness of Zedekiah and his advisors to what was really happening is a warning to us. Right to the end, as the book of Jeremiah shows, they seem to have assumed that because they were God's chosen people, and Jerusalem, with the temple and the ark of the covenant, was God's city, all would be well. God would deliver them from Nebuchadnezzar's hand. They could not see that because of their sin they had forfeited God's protection and that God was working through Nebuchadnezzar and his false methods of divination.

PRAYER

Lord, please deliver me from the blindness that comes from assuming that you are at work in me and in the group of churches to which I belong. Let me be willing to see you at work in the wider world, even through those whom I think of as 'godless'.

The SWORD *against* AMMON

This short oracle brings to an end the series of oracles linked by the theme of the sword. It picks up on imagery and phrases found in the preceding oracles. Its opening in verse 28b echoes the opening of the sword song in verses 9b–10a. The second half of verse 29 is a slightly reworded version of verse 25, applying its words to the Ammonites instead of King Zedekiah of Judah. The reference to the sword finally being sheathed is a counterpoint to the statement in 21:5 about its being unsheathed. Finally, the imagery of fire looks back to the first oracle in the series in 20:45–49. All this raises the possibility that the oracle in 21:28–32 was composed after the others and as a complement to them. As we shall see, its content may indicate that it was composed after the fall of Jerusalem.

Ammon's punishment

Ammon corresponded to what is now the central part of the Hashemite kingdom of Jordan whose capital, Amman, covers the site of the capital of Ammon, Rabbah. It was one of the small kingdoms in the southern part of the fertile crescent which plotted together to rebel against their overlord, Babylon (Jeremiah 27:3). Baalis, the Ammonite king, seems to have taken a particularly hard stance against the Babylonians. After the fall of Jerusalem, Judah was incorporated into the Babylonian empire as one of its provinces. A man named Gedaliah, from one of the leading families of Judah, was appointed as governor, with his base at Mizpah. Baalis encouraged some nationalist Judeans to murder him (Jeremiah 40:13—41:3). This could be what lies behind the reference to 'their reproach' in verse 28. It is not easy to understand verse 29a, but it may well be a reference to the arguments the Ammonites used to encourage Judah and the other states to rebel against Babylon.

When Judah and Jerusalem fell, the Ammonites were spared for a while, and it seems likely that this oracle comes from that period. Ezekiel declares that this is only a delay of judgment, not a reprieve. Because of what Ammon has done, she too is going to face the sword of his judgment and the fire of his wrath. As a result, she will not be remembered any more (v. 32). In fact, unlike Judah, Ammon was eventually removed from the face of the map of the ancient Near East and never became an independent state again.

Babylon's punishment

The meaning of verses 30–31 is very unclear. Perhaps the most likely understanding is that they refer to Babylon, God's sword of judgment. With the destruction of Ammon its work would be done: it could be sheathed. Babylon itself, however, would have to face God's judgment. The fact that God had used its military might and expansionist policies did not render it immune from the judgment due to the way it had treated other nations. It too would have to face the punishment it deserved.

Justice, not favouritism

This short oracle adds an important element to the series of oracles of judgment. One aspect of the series as a whole is that it declares God's sovereignty in the realm of history. He can use a pagan king like Nebuchadnezzar to carry out his purposes. A great empire and local superpower like Babylon is like a sword in his hand, to wield as he pleases. In all this, his sovereignty is exercised with no hint of favouritism or unfairness. It is exercised according to the principles of justice. If his own people are wicked and rebellious, he will bring judgment upon them, even employing a pagan nation for this purpose. In doing this he is not being especially hard on them, as if in a fit of pique. Ammon, which had encouraged Judah to rebel and, like Judah, had broken its oath of loyalty to Babylon, is treated in the same way. Even the nation that God used as his instrument of destruction would have judgment meted out to it and be destroyed in its turn for the crimes it had committed. If this is so, we can conclude that, because God is concerned with justice, not favouritism, his activity in history is not limited to the history of his people, though it may be most easy to discern there.

PRAYER

If this conclusion is correct, it ought to spur us on to pray about the international events that feature in our news media. Make time to pray for some of them today.

A BLOODY CITY

Ezekiel 22 contains three prophetic oracles that have been combined to produce a sermon denouncing the corruption of Jerusalem and her inhabitants. They may originally have been delivered at different times and then been combined after the fall of Jerusalem (v. 31 may be speaking of it as a past event) in order to explain the destruction of the city. After its destruction, with the rosy view we often have of the past, people might have asked, 'Why didn't God save the city?' Ezekiel's words make clear that the real question is, 'How could a holy God have done anything but condemn the city?'

The case for the prosecution

In the first oracle the prophet is called by God to act as 'counsel for the prosecution', presenting the case against Jerusalem (vv. 1–2). It is a 'bloody city' in which 'abominable deeds' are done. What this means is spelled out in summary form in verses 3–5. Two broad classes of sin are presented here—bloodshed and idolatry. In the Old Testament the charge of 'shedding blood' often refers not just to murder but to general misrule and violent behaviour. Jerusalem is being indicted for a combination of social and religious sins.

A more detailed catalogue of sins is given in verses 6–12. The 'princes of Judah' are addressed because it is they, as the leaders of the nation, who were especially responsible for establishing and main-taining a properly ordered society. What is given is not a random col-lection of charges, but an accusation of having violated the covenant law. All the charges relate to laws that are found within a part of Leviticus that is sometimes called 'the Holiness Code' (Leviticus 18 to 27). Indeed, apart from the condemnation of excessive interest (which relates to Leviticus 25:36), they all concern laws found within Leviticus 18—20. The charges are wide-ranging. They cover the family, social justice, the temple cult, pagan worship, sexual matters, abuse of the legal system, and economic justice. Because these charges all relate to covenant laws, the indictment can be summed up in the words, 'You have forgotten me, says the Lord God' (v. 12). Ominously, this echoes Deuteronomy 8:11 and 19: 'Take care that you do not forget the Lord your God, by failing to keep his commandments… If you do forget the Lord your God and follow other gods to serve and worship them, I solemnly warn you today that you shall surely perish.' They had been warned! Punishment is now imminent.

Passing sentence

The judicial sentence that follows from the indictment is given in verses 13–16. It is announced with a clapping of the hands (apparently a threatening gesture, as in 6:11). The people will go into exile and be scattered among the nations. God will do this to purge the people of their sins and also to deal with their 'forgetting' him. Through it they will come to know him again. In order to achieve this, God is prepared to sacrifice his reputation in the eyes of the nations. Those nations will wonder what kind of God he is if his people can be driven out of their land and scattered, not realizing that their own God has done it to them as a punishment.

Religion and morality

In these verses, religious and moral sins are listed together and are both summed up under the rubric of 'forgetting' the Lord God. Religion and ethics are treated as interlinked. This is so throughout the Bible. The 'holiness' of God is not just an awesome 'religious aura', it is a moral passion. That is why the prophets see idolatry as leading inevitably to moral decline, and the apostle Paul agrees with them (Romans 1:18–32).

The link between religion and morals is clearly expressed in some of the Psalms. Psalm 24:3–6 is a 'gate' liturgy. When the worshippers arrive at the temple, they ask who may enter to worship there. The priest answers that it is those whose actions, attitudes and words are morally pure, and the worshippers have to affirm that this is true of them. In this way they are reminded that the worship of God in the sanctuary should be linked with moral living outside of it. The 'privatization' of religion and the divorcing of public morality from private behaviour in Western societies has eroded this link. From a Christian perspective, this is part of the reason for the moral confusion and decline in these societies.

MEDITATION

Would it be helpful to have a liturgy like Psalm 24:3–6 for use when arriving at church on Sundays?

A City of Dross

This second oracle has some conceptual links with those that come before and after it. Towards the end of the one before, it is said that God will scatter the people among the nations in order to purge them of their filthiness (22:15). In this oracle the idea of purging is expressed in terms of metal smelting. As a result, the idea of God 'gathering' the people for judgment (v. 19) becomes a counterpoint to that of him 'scattering' them in 22:15. Five metals are mentioned here—silver, bronze, iron, lead and tin (v. 18). They may be related to the five groups of people who are dealt with in the following oracle—princes, priests, officials, prophets and people of the land. The phrase 'the fire of my wrath' (v. 21) is repeated in 22:31.

The smelting furnace

The image of smelting metal in a furnace to purify it is used by other prophets as a metaphor for God's judgment, usually in a positive sense: the process of judgment will result in a purified people (Isaiah 1:21–31; 48:10; Malachi 3:2–3). Ezekiel, however, uses it in a negative sense. The process will produce nothing but slag, which serves no useful purpose. In the metaphor, Jerusalem becomes the smelter and the people are gathered into the city, as the raw material is poured into the smelter. Then, just as the furnace has to be raised to a high temperature to release the metal from its impurities, so God's wrath will be visited on the city. Instead of the process producing pure metal, it will simply prove that nothing worthwhile remains: the people are like worthless dross. In this sense the process will show that God's judgment was fully justified.

The tragedy here is that people were meant to be gathered into Jerusalem for quite a different purpose. People were meant to go there to meet with God and receive his blessing. That is why the psalmist says, 'I was glad when they said to me, "Let us go to the house of the Lord!" Our feet are standing within your gates, O Jerusalem' (Psalm 122:1–2). Some of the prophets had visions of people of all nations flocking there to learn about God and how he wanted them to live (Isaiah 2:2–4; Micah 4:1–4). In Zechariah's vision the quality of life of the Jews is such that it attracts people of other nations so that they plead for the privilege of going with them to Jerusalem to learn about their God (Zechariah 8:20–23). The use of this concept by Isaiah and Micah shows that it predates Ezekiel by over a century. It is probably alluded to in Ezekiel's reference to Jerusalem being set 'in the centre of the nations' (5:5). There is therefore something shocking and tragic about the use in this oracle of the idea of people being gathered to Jerusalem for judgment, and especially for one which has no positive outcome.

A refining process

For those who are willing to heed its message, the oracle contains a challenge to consider what we are doing with our lives. In every life there is the potential to produce both dross and valuable material. Seen from this perspective, the purpose of life can be seen as the removing of dross and the refining of what is good in us. Some New Testament writers make the point that if we face the problems and difficulties of life with God's help, they can have the effect of refining and strengthening our character (Romans 5:3–5; James 1:2–4; 2 Peter 1:3–8).

In 1 Corinthians 3:10–15 the apostle Paul uses fire as a metaphor for God's judgment in a way that is similar to its use by the Old Testament prophets. He warns his readers to be careful about the work they do for God, to ensure that it is worthwhile. The time will come when God will test it. Paul compares the test to fire, which burns up wood, hay and straw but leaves behind gold, silver and precious stones. Although we might tend to look at this metaphor in a negative way, as a warning against wasting our lives, it can be looked at positively. We can live our lives in such a way that what we are and what we do have a value that transcends this life, with eternal significance.

PRAYER

Lord, help me to live my life so that what I am and what I do can stand the test of your approval.

A CITY CONDEMNED

The first oracle of the three in Ezekiel 22 revealed the extent of Jerusalem's sins by the breadth of its catalogue of the covenant laws that had been broken. In this third oracle, the extent of her sins is expressed by a catalogue of the groups of people who have failed to carry out their proper responsibilities. There is considerable similarity between this oracle and a shorter one in Zephaniah 3:3–4. Since Zephaniah was active some time before Ezekiel, it may be that Ezekiel is taking up and expanding his words. On the other hand, both prophets may be making use of a traditional liturgy of condemnation.

One of the curses attached to breaking the covenant is the withholding of rain (Leviticus 26:19). This idea may lie behind verse 23. If so, the oracle may have been spoken after a period of drought. The lack of rain is given a double significance: it indicates the implementation of the covenant curse and also symbolizes the uncleanness of the land, like that of an unwashed person.

A failing society

Five groups of people have charges levelled against them.

- **The princes** should have cared for and protected the people, but have exploited them instead. They have behaved like hungry lions, treating the people as their prey. Instead of looking after vulnerable people, such as widows, they have made people into widows (v. 25).
- **The priests** were responsible for teaching the people the covenant law and for guarding the sanctity of worship. However, they have distorted the law and failed to maintain the distinction between holy and unholy, clean and unclean (v. 26). This distinction was more than a matter of arbitrary ritual rules. It was meant to signify and make real the distinctiveness of Israel as God's people. This is stated clearly in the part of the holiness code that lies behind the first oracle in this series: 'I am the Lord your God; I have separated you from the peoples. You shall therefore make a distinction between the clean animal and the unclean' (Leviticus 20:24–25).
- **The civic officials**, like the princes, are treating the people as prey instead of protecting them. They are concerned about what they can

gain by exploiting the people, not about what is good for the people (v. 27).

- **The prophets** should have been exposing the violations of the covenant and condemning the violators, but instead they are doing a whitewashing job. They are telling the corrupt leaders what they want to hear instead of declaring true words from God (v. 28).
- **The 'people of the land'** are probably the landowners. They have been exploiting the vulnerable people of society—the poor, the needy and the resident alien (v. 29).

These are the five sets of people who had the power and responsibility to establish a society on the basis of the covenant law. They have utterly failed to fulfil their responsibilities. Indeed, they have repudiated them.

Needed: a mediator

The desperate nature of the situation is brought home in verse 30. God has looked for just one person who could 'repair the wall and stand in the breach before me on behalf of the land'—that is, someone who could act effectively as a mediator, as Moses did after the incident of the golden calf (Psalm 106:23). But there was no one. Everyone was implicated in the sinfulness of the people. No one was able to deflect the wrath of God, which would therefore consume Jerusalem like a fire (v. 31).

This oracle brings out the responsibility of each group and profession that makes up a society. When one section of society fails in its responsibility, one of the others should step in to 'repair the wall and stand in the breach'. The princes could have called the priests to account for failing in their duties. On the basis of the law the priests could have called the princes or the landowners to account for their behaviour. The prophets could have condemned the blatant covenant-breaking that was going on. When none of these checks and balances is operating, a society is truly at the point of moral collapse.

PRAYER

There is plenty of evidence of moral collapse in our society today. It is tempting to feel that we can do nothing about it, but this passage challenges us to take up the role of mediator and to intercede for our society in prayer. Could you take on the responsibility to do this regularly for one group or profession?

A TALE *of* TWO CITIES

This chapter is taken up with another long allegory. It has similarities with the allegory about the foundling child in chapter 16, but this time concerns two sexually promiscuous women. They are sisters, named Oholah ('her tent') and Oholibah ('my tent is in her'). If the names have any significance other than the fact that they sound alike (like 'Tweedledum and Tweedledee'), the point may be that Oholibah refers to the presence of the temple, successor to the tent-shrine of the wilderness period, in Jerusalem (compare the name Oholibama, 'tent of the high place', found in Genesis 36:2, 5). These two sisters, we are told, represent the capital cities of Israel and Judah, Samaria and Jerusalem (v. 4).

From the beginning, in Egypt, these sisters prostituted themselves (v. 3). Ezekiel may be using allegorical licence here, referring to the unfaithfulness of the Hebrews to God during the wilderness period, especially the incident of the golden calf (Exodus 32) and the immorality with the Moabites (Numbers 25). Despite this behaviour God took them in marriage and had children by them (v. 4). They became his covenant people and he gave them the promised land.

Allegory and history

The story now jumps to the history of the kingdom of Israel after the division of the nation following Solomon's death (vv. 5–10). Behind the account of Oholah's wanton adultery with the Assyrians is the historical reality of the political actions of the later kings of Israel. From the time of Jehu onwards, they made, broke and remade alliances with Assyria as political expediency seemed to dictate. In the end, Israel's 'lovers' turned on her and destroyed her. From the prophet's point of view these political machinations involved unfaithfulness to God because behind them lay rejection of trust in God in favour of reliance on Assyrian might and wealth. Also, the price of an alliance with a superpower like Assyria would involve giving recognition to Assyria's gods in Israel's national shrines.

Oholibah is held to be more culpable than her sister. Far from learning from Oholah's disastrous experience, she outdid her in her lust, going after a series of lovers (v. 11–21). The history behind the allegory is fairly clear. Judah's relationship with Assyria began with Ahaz's appeal to Assyria for help against a threatened invasion by Pekah of Israel and Rezin of Damascus. Isaiah opposed this move (Isaiah 7), seeing it as motivated by lack of trust in God. Isaiah also opposed Hezekiah's willingness to consider an alliance with the Babylonian king, Merodach-Baladan (2 Kings 20:12–19). Hezekiah's son, Manasseh, was a loyal Assyrian vassal and his reign was a time of great apostasy as he encouraged various forms of pagan worship in Judah. When Assyria fell, Judah became a Babylonian vassal. Judah's final years were marked by vacillation between alliance with Babylon and with Egypt.

The allegory's message

The language of this allegory is even more sexually explicit and offensive than that of chapter 16. No doubt, as in that case, this reflects both the depth of Ezekiel's feeling about the sins of his compatriots and his sense that they were so deluded about their own state that shock tactics were needed to get through to them.

It is not only the language that causes us a problem today. It is also the implied attitude to women, in that guilt and blame for sexual misconduct is presented as primarily a female responsibility. While recognizing this, we must accept that the ability of figurative language to communicate its message is related to its cultural context. Ezekiel lived in a patriarchal culture in which women were not given the status that we as Christians would want to give them, following the way Jesus related to women. We would want to express the prophet's message differently. Even so, we must not let this prevent us from listening to his message and taking it to heart. He is insisting that spiritual adultery, the worship of false gods—be they idols of wood or stone, or ideologies such as materialism, capitalism or socialism—is a deadly serious matter. These false gods seem to offer 'salvation' from our present problems, but will only lead to disaster in one way or another.

MEDITATION

Think about the kind of allegory that you might write for our time and culture which would convey Ezekiel's message with as much power as his did in his own setting.

PROSTITUTION PUNISHED

The fate of Oholah has been described in the first part of the story. As Oholibah's fate is revealed in this passage, the veil of the allegory is gradually lifted. It becomes increasingly clear that it is the fate of the city of Jerusalem that is in view. The punishment that is going to befall Oholibah/Jerusalem is declared in four oracles, each beginning in Hebrew with the words, 'Thus says the Lord God' (vv. 22, 28, 32, 35). The general substance of the four oracles is very similar. The overall effect is to reinforce the finality of the divine judgment that is about to fall on the city.

Violent judgment

In 23:17 the prophet said that Oholibah's lust for her lovers turned to disgust—referring to the disenchantment with Babylon that led to the growth of a pro-Egyptian party within the Judean court. The message of the first oracle of judgment (vv. 22–27) is that these lovers from whom Jerusalem had turned in disgust will return to her. They will not do so in search of love, but only to unleash their violence on her. The very strength and military prowess that attracted her to them will now be used to assault her on every side (v. 24).

The Chaldeans, who are mentioned alongside the Babylonians in verse 23, were a group of tribes in southern Babylonia. It was their ruling dynasty that built up the so-called Neo-Babylonian empire, which toppled the Assyrians and eventually destroyed Judah. 'Pekod, Shoa and Koa' in this verse may be the names of Chaldean tribes. Whatever their literal meaning, the words may be there as a pun, since they sound like the Hebrew words for 'punish', 'cry for help' and 'shriek'. The facial disfigurement described in verse 25 is attested as both an Egyptian and a Mesopotamian form of punishment for rebellion. The aim of this severe punishment is to end Oholibah's lewd behaviour, and indeed to remove even the memory of her lovers from her.

A just judgment

The second oracle (vv. 28–31) repeats in a succinct way what has been said in the first. It emphasizes that although this punishment comes at the hands of human agents, it is indeed a divine judgment brought about by God. The way it is expressed also makes the point that it is a just judgment—the punishment fits the crime. The lovers whom Oholibah led on, and then turned from in disgust and hatred, will deal with her in hatred. What she is reaping is what her own behaviour has sown. Instead of learning from what happened to her sister, she has copied her behaviour and so will suffer a similar fate.

The cup of judgment

In verse 31 the image of drinking a cup is used to represent facing judgment. This is taken up and extended in the third oracle (vv. 32–34). While it is clear that this is a piece of Hebrew poetry, the text seems to be somewhat disordered, so that the exact pattern of the poem is not clear. It is a 'drinking song' and, like the 'sword song' in chapter 21, the prophet may be adapting a well-known song in order to convey his message. Again the point is made that since Oholibah has copied her sister's behaviour she will suffer the same punishment. She will have to drink the same 'cup of horror and desolation' and drain it to its very dregs.

The final oracle (v. 35) goes to the real heart of the matter. Oholibah had forgotten her true lover and turned her back on him in favour of prostituting herself. Now she must face the consequences. This verse repeats the connection we saw made in chapter 16 between forgetfulness and unfaithfulness.

The 'drinking song' here reminds us of Jesus' prayer in the Garden of Gethsemane, 'My Father, if it is possible, let this cup pass from me; yet not what I want but what you want' (Matthew 26:39). In spiritual terms, all humanity stands in Oholibah's shoes, having forgotten the one true God and gone after various idols in search of salvation. So all deserve to drink Oholah's cup. However, on the cross Jesus drained that cup for us, as his terrible cry, 'My God, my God, why have you forsaken me?' (Matthew 27:46) shows. As a result we can receive forgiveness and not face the punishment of God-forsakenness.

PRAYER

Thank you, Lord Jesus, for draining that cup for me. Help me never to forget what you have done, but to show my gratitude by living as your faithful disciple.

The TWO SISTERS REVISITED

Having got to the point where the story of the two sisters seems to have reached its end, it is a bit surprising to find another set of indictments followed by a final verdict. At first sight this section seems to add little to what has gone before. In particular, verses 40–45 summarize what has been said in 23:5–17. So why is it here? One reason may be to bring together what has been said about the two sisters in a recapitulation. Since 23:11 Oholah has receded into the background as the prophet has concentrated on the story and fate of Oholibah/Jerusalem. In addition, this section acts as a conclusion to both chapters 22 and 23. It opens with the rhetorical question used in 22:2, as Ezekiel is once again called upon to act as the 'counsel for the prosecution', in this case to indict the two sisters (v. 36). The threefold charge of adultery, bloodshed and child sacrifice (v. 37) picks up the charge of bloodshed which was prominent in chapter 22 but has not so far been levelled at the two sisters, and adds the charge of child sacrifice. The result is a comprehensive indictment, combining the political crimes which are the theme of 23:1–35 with a reminder of the social and religious crimes mentioned in chapter 22.

A double indictment

Child sacrifice was practised by some of Judah's kings, Ahaz (2 Kings 16:3) and Manasseh (2 Kings 21:6). The prevalence of the charge of child sacrifice in Ezekiel (see also 16:20–21, 36; 20:25–26) and Jeremiah (19:4–6) suggests that it was actually used in the final crisis period of Judah's history. Perhaps there is a parallel in the story of the king of Moab sacrificing his firstborn son when in a desperate military situation (2 Kings 3:26–27). The indictment of the two sisters is doubly shocking. Not only have they practised child sacrifice and other forms of idolatry, but they have compounded the offence by continuing to worship in the sanctuary of the God of Israel (vv. 38–39), as if their unfaithfulness to him did not matter, or might even have been approved by him.

'Profaning the sabbath' (v. 39) is also a repeated charge in Ezekiel (see 20:12–13; 22:8, 26), found too in Jeremiah (17:19–27), suggesting that laxity in this regard was another feature of the closing years of Judah. The significance of this charge is indicated in Ezekiel 20:12: 'I gave them my sabbaths, as a sign between me and them, so that they might know that I the Lord sanctify them.' The sabbath feasts were unique to Israel, not shared with the other peoples around them. Keeping them was a reminder of Israel's covenant with the Lord, so the neglect of them was another aspect of breaking the covenant.

Part of the force of the allegory of the two sisters arises from the fact that the Hebrew word commonly translated as 'covenant' can be used to describe (a) the covenant relationship with God; (b) political alliances; and (c) marriage. In each case the essence of the covenant is to be found in faithfulness. When faithfulness breaks down in one area of life, it is likely to do so in others. In the case of Israel and Judah, the practice of ritual prostitution in the fertility religions of her neighbours, which expressed unfaithfulness to the covenant, resulted in lax sexual morality in society.

A word of warning

The final announcement of punishment (vv. 46–49) conjures up the image of a besieged city. Some commentators see verse 48 as a moralizing comment (probably added by a later editor of the book) which rather gratuitously blames women alone for sexual misconduct, but it is more likely that it should be taken within the context of the allegory. The 'women' here might be other cities or nations or, more likely, the verse is intended as a warning to future generations of the covenant people. They were to learn from the lesson of the fall of Samaria and Jerusalem.

PRAYER

Think about 'covenant' relationships in your life—with God, your family, at work and in the church. In some the 'covenant' has been made explicit—baptismal promises, marriage vows, church membership declarations, a job contract. What does 'faithfulness' mean in each case? Are you living it out as you should? A prayer of confession and rededication might be appropriate in some cases. Or maybe you've never thought of some of these relationships in covenant terms before and need to ponder that idea prayerfully.

The ALLEGORY of the POT

We now reach a major turning point in Ezekiel's ministry, to which everything since his call has been leading. For nearly five years he has proclaimed a message centred on the fate that is to befall Jerusalem. He began his ministry by acting out the siege of the city and the devastation that would follow from it. He has consistently exposed the sinfulness of Judah and Jerusalem, which made them ripe for God's judgment. He has continually undermined any false hopes of deliverance apart from a radical repentance and return to God. Initially his message was probably greeted with indifference and disbelief. As time went on and news came of the deteriorating situation in Judah, his words may have begun to seem more convincing. Now, as a way of supporting the veracity of his message, he is commanded to write down the date of the beginning of the siege of Jerusalem, before the exiles have had any news of it—though they were no doubt expecting it to happen. The date (v. 1) is 15 January 588BC by our reckoning. The verb Ezekiel uses for 'laid siege' (v. 2) means 'to lean, rest on' and is used in ritual contexts of a person offering an animal sacrifice, resting a hand on its head (Leviticus 1:4; 3:2).

The cook's song

To mark the occasion, the prophet utters a song (vv. 3–5). Like the songs of the sword and the cup, this one too may be based on a popular song, an occupational work-song. The cook sings of filling the pot with water, adding the joints of meat that are to be cooked in it, preparing the fire and cooking the meat on it. In the ancient world, most people could not afford to eat meat often. The most common occasions for meat-eating would be when the meal was associated with an animal sacrifice (for example, Leviticus 7:11–18). So there may be sacrificial overtones to the image, corresponding to those of the verb used for 'laid siege'.

On its own, this work-song may not have conveyed much to Ezekiel's audience, unless they remembered the boast of the officials reported earlier: 'This city is the pot, and we are the meat' (11:3). In that case it may have been an assertion of their sense of security, but in two variations on the theme of the song, each beginning 'Woe to the bloody city', the prophet develops the idea of Jerusalem as a cooking pot in a very different way.

A double meaning

The first variation (vv. 6–8) uses the image of a 'filthy' or 'rusty' pot. It is not clear whether the word used does mean 'rust' or refers to some other kind of filth, perhaps the remains of burnt-on food. In any case, this filth renders the food inedible and the cook empties it out of the pot on to the ground. Here again, sacrificial concepts come into play. Apparently we are to think of the discarded food as still containing blood from the meat. It is poured out on to bare rock, so that the blood remains uncovered. Because blood symbolized life, it had tremendous ritual importance: it was always to be poured out on the ground and covered with earth, except when used in a ritual way (Leviticus 17:13). Blood left exposed would provoke the wrath of God. This reminded people of the value to God of life, both animal and human. In the allegory of the pot, the uncovered blood stands for all the 'bloodshed', social injustice and violence, that has gone on in Jerusalem. It has provoked God's judgment on the city.

In the second variation (vv. 9–14) the pot is put on the fire and heated until it glows red-hot to burn off the filth. In the process, everything in the pot is burned up. This leads to the prophet's last words about God's judgment on Jerusalem: 'I will not refrain, I will not spare, I will not relent. According to your ways and your doings I will judge you, says the Lord God' (v. 14). It is to be total and final.

MEDITATION

*The image of the 'rust' or 'filth' that has built up in the pot and rendered it useless is a reminder of how sin can build up in our lives unless we take care to deal with it promptly and effectively.
Ponder Jesus' words in Mark 9:43–48 about taking drastic action to remove causes of sin from our lives.*

The DEATH *of* EZEKIEL'S WIFE

We have seen that Ezekiel often acted out his message, so that in a sense the man became the message. Here we find that even the death of his wife becomes part of his message. We do not know the exact circumstances of her death. Perhaps she was sick and the prophet realized that her end was near. All we know is that her death came fairly suddenly (v. 16). One morning the prophet announced that she was going to die, and in the evening she died (v. 18). Faced with this tragedy, the prophet did not carry out the mourning rituals that were customary in his culture. There were no loud lamentations and tears, no dressing in sackcloth and ashes, no covering of the lower part of the face and going barefoot, and he did not take part in a funeral meal.

Too shocked to mourn

When Ezekiel did not mourn his wife's death in the expected way, the people were disconcerted. They asked him for an explanation (v. 19). What they got was another declaration about the doom of Jerusalem. Just as his wife was the delight of Ezekiel's eyes, so the temple in Jerusalem was the pride and delight of the Judeans. Yet it was going to be destroyed. Moreover, the children whom the exiles had left behind in Judah would be massacred (v. 21). When the news of all this disaster reached the exiles, the shock and grief would be too great to be expressed in conventional ways: only inward grief would be possible (v. 23b). They would behave as Ezekiel had done.

The closing verses of this passage (vv. 25–27) are not easy to understand in detail, for two reasons. Firstly, they seem to say that news of the fall of Jerusalem will reach the prophet on the day it happens, brought by someone who has escaped it. It may be that verses 25–26 simply collapse the time span between the event itself and the report of it reaching Ezekiel. Alternatively, 'they' in verse 25 may mean the exiles—the arrival of the news is the taking away from them of 'their stronghold' as all their false hopes are finally smashed beyond any possibility of recovery.

Secondly, there is the reference to Ezekiel's dumbness in verse 27. We have discussed another reference to the prophet's dumbness in

3:22–27 (see pp. 36–37), suggesting some possible ways of understanding it. Is verse 27 a reference to the same dumbness, or is it about something different? Some think it refers to a complete silence that stretched from the death of Ezekiel's wife to the arrival of the news of Jerusalem's downfall. Although there are some oracles that are dated during this period (26:1; 29:1; 31:1), these may have been written rather than spoken.

A costly calling

The description of Ezekiel's wife as the delight of his eyes (v. 16) leaves no doubt that he would have been deeply shocked by her death. The demand not to mourn openly might therefore seem an intolerable one. However, we must not get this out of proportion. What God asked of Ezekiel was not unique. He was a priest, and priests in general lived with restrictions on the public expression of mourning, except in the case of closest relatives, in order to avoid becoming ritually unclean (Leviticus 21). Moreover, the restriction on public mourning was not a command not to grieve, but a command to do so in private and to refrain from the visible forms of grieving normal in the culture. Of course Ezekiel would have found this difficult. He would have drawn comfort from being able to express and share his grief with other people. That he was deprived of this comfort is one of many examples of what it cost to be a prophet in ancient Israel and Judah.

The calling to proclaim God's word is never an easy or comfortable one. It cannot be fulfilled faithfully and effectively unless the messenger to some extent becomes the message: the messenger has first to feel something of what God feels in order to be able to proclaim the message as God's word. But the messenger must also be able to empathize with the hearers in order to know how to communicate the word effectively. That is why the ultimate communication of God's word had to be in the form of the word becoming flesh.

PRAYER

Pray for those you know who have the responsibility of proclaiming God's word regularly, that God will sustain them in their costly task.

A PROPHECY *against* AMMON

Chapters 25—32, with their prophecies against seven foreign nations, form a self-contained unit that interrupts the 'storyline' of Ezekiel. Chapter 24 ends by clearly foreshadowing the destruction of Jerusalem in 586BC, and this is announced as having happened in chapter 33. So what is the purpose of these chapters, and why are they put here?

Two questions answered

In terms of the structure of the book, they provide a dramatic interlude, creating a sense of tension as the reader waits for the dreadful news, foreshadowed in chapter 24, to become a reality. But they also have an important place in the overall message of the book. The final fall of Jerusalem and destruction of the temple raised sharply the two questions, 'Is the God of Israel really in control of events? If so, has he finally abandoned his people?' Both needed answering before there could be any hope for the future for Ezekiel's audience.

The prophecies against the nations answer both these questions. Firstly, they assert that the God of Israel is sovereign over all the nations of the world, not just Israel and Judah. The nations' destinies are in his hand. The destruction of Jerusalem and the temple is not a result of his weakness, but of his judgment on his people, and he is able to use other nations as agents of that judgment. Secondly, in many cases the reason given for proclaiming judgment on the other nations is the way they have treated Israel and Judah, so showing God's continuing concern for his chosen people. These two truths, God's universal sovereignty and his continuing concern for his people, are important bases for the messages of salvation and restoration that form a large part of Ezekiel 34—48.

Ammon's sin

As already mentioned, the Ammonites lived to the north-east of Judah, in territory that is now part of modern Jordan. Their capital, Rabbah, was near the modern Jordanian capital, Amman. The kingdom of Ammon came into being at about the same time as the Israelites settled in the promised land (around 1200BC). There was periodic friction between the two peoples, sometimes breaking out into open warfare. After the fall of Jerusalem in 586BC the Ammonite king, Baalis, had made the situation worse by instigating an attempted coup against Gedaliah, the Babylonian-appointed governor of Judah (Jeremiah 40:14). However, the crime of Ammon cited here is not some specific political act in either the recent or the distant past, such as this one or the one that provoked King David's wrath (2 Samuel 10). Rather, it is their malicious delight over the fate of Judah at the hands of the Babylonians. They are depicted as gloating with glee at the destruction of the temple and the nation (v. 3), and dancing with delight when it all happened (v. 6). The prophet declares that, as a consequence, the land of Ammon will be invaded by the nomadic Arabs from the fringes of the Arabian desert. The capital city will become a place of pasture for the invaders' herds of camels, and the surrounding territory a place for their flocks of sheep and goats. The nation will cease to exist.

Ammon's crime was the absence of compassion, compounded by their malicious glee. Their delight over the destruction of the temple may also have implied contempt for the God of Israel. While taking delight in Judah's downfall, the Ammonites failed to learn anything from the crises taking place around them. They did not stop to seek to understand the reasons for Judah's downfall, part of which was their attempt to play off Egypt against Babylon in a bid for independence. The Ammonites tried to join in the game of power politics in order to gain advantage for themselves. In supporting Ishmael against Gedaliah, they probably hoped to gain some control over him and Judah should his coup succeed. They themselves were destined to end up victims of this grasping for power and territory.

MEDITATION AND PRAYER

To take delight when others suffer because of their sinfulness and rebellion against God is to fail to recognize that God's sovereignty extends not only over them, but also over ourselves. That failure makes us blind to the need to examine our own life before God. Take some time examining your life, asking God to help you to recognize and root out any rebellion towards him or wrong attitudes towards other people.

Prophecies *against* Moab, Edom & Philistia

Together with Ammon, these three nations encircled Judah on her eastern, southern and western borders. Initially they all seem to have joined in the plot to rebel against Babylon, but when Judah was invaded none of them came to her aid. Instead, they took advantage of her plight in various ways.

Moab

Moab (vv. 8–11) emerged as a kingdom at about the same time as Israel and Ammon. It lay to the south of Ammon and east of the Dead Sea. Moab was conquered by David (2 Samuel 8:2). It seems to have regained its independence when Israel and Judah split apart, but later, Omri of Israel reconquered it. The Moabite Stone, now in the *Louvre* in Paris, tells us this and how the nation won back its freedom from Omri's son Ahab (see 2 Kings 3:4–5). This oracle does not condemn the Moabites for any particular action, but for their attitude towards Judah, expressed in the saying, 'Judah is like all the other nations' (v. 8). There could be two things implied here. The first is derision of Judah's claim to special status because of her covenant with God. The second is that her God is no different from those of other nations, and in fact clearly does not have the power to protect her. Because of this derision of Judah and her God, Moab, like Ammon, would fall to invaders from the Arabian desert. This is what did eventually happen.

Edom

Edom (vv. 12–14) was located to the south of Moab and east of the Dead Sea. Its territory stretched south to the Gulf of Aqaba. Much of it was semi-desert, but it controlled valuable trade routes. It became a nation state earlier than its neighbours. The brief statement in verse 12 that 'Edom acted revengefully against the house of Judah' is filled out in more detail in the prophecy of Obadiah. There Edom is accused of aiding and abetting the Babylonians, looting Judah, killing some fugitives and handing others over. The Judeans' strong sense of outrage at Edom's behaviour is expressed in Psalm 137:7–9 and Lamentations

4:21–22. Because of this revengeful attitude, God will execute vengeance on Edom, using his own people to do so. Its territories will be laid waste from north to south ('Teman to Dedan', v. 13).

Philistia

The Philistines (vv. 15–17) settled on the coastal plain to the west and south of Judah at about the time the Israelites were settling in Canaan. They had migrated from the islands and coastlands of the eastern Mediterranean. The Cherethites (meaning 'Cretans') were one of their sub-groups. There was intermittent warfare between the two peoples until David defeated the Philistines, but they retained their identity and became independent again after Solomon's death and the division of the kingdom. They too are condemned for taking revenge against Judah in her time of disaster. As a result God will 'cut off' (*karat*) the 'Cherethites' (*keret*). The Cherethites are clearly used to represent all the Philistines because their name allows this word-play.

The prophecies against Ammon, Moab and Philistia end with the phrase, 'Then they shall know that I am the Lord.' There is a variant form of the phrase at the end of the prophecy against Edom. This is a statement of the universal sovereignty of the God of Israel. It is amazing that a Judean prophet should make this assertion at a time when Judah had just suffered a crushing defeat and the temple in Jerusalem had been destroyed. Normally such a catastrophe would be taken to show the weakness of that nation's God. Since the mid-eighth century, Israelite and Judean prophets had been warning the people that they were breaking the covenant with God and that as a result the covenant curses would come into operation. The ultimate curse was defeat by her enemies and exile from the land. Therefore, when this happened first to Israel and then to Judah, the prophets saw these events as a vindication of their God and his control of history, not evidence of his weakness. None the less, it must have taken considerable faith to hang on to this insight through the crisis of Judah's downfall.

PRAYER

Lord God, it is sometimes difficult to hold on to belief in your universal sovereignty today in the face of what is going on in the world. Help me to go on praying and working for the time when all will see that 'the kingdom of this world has become the kingdom of our Lord and of his Messiah' (Revelation 11:15).

PROPHECIES *against* TYRE

The city state of Tyre lay on the Mediterranean coast, in what is now Lebanon, about 100 miles north-west of Jerusalem. In Ezekiel's day it was the most prosperous and powerful of the Phoenician cities. It consisted of two parts, a city on a small offshore island (about a mile long and half a mile wide) and suburbs on the mainland. Its main asset was a pair of excellent harbours. The Phoenicians were great seafarers, rivalling the Greeks in commerce, colonization and exploration. Relationships with Israel and Judah were generally good. These kingdoms controlled overland trade routes along which goods were transported to and from Phoenicia, and it was in the interests of both parties to keep the trade flowing. Hiram, king of Tyre, supplied Solomon with materials and skilled labour for his building projects. He also helped Solomon to develop trade along the Red Sea. Ahab's queen, Jezebel, was a Tyrian princess. Her attempts to impose Baal-worship in Israel led to her murder by Jehu in a coup, and this must have soured relationships with Tyre for a while. The Tyrians were involved in plotting the rebellion against the Babylonians. Although they did not take active steps to help Judah, Tyre was besieged by Nebuchadnezzar once he had dealt with Judah.

Ezekiel's seven prophecies against Tyre fall into three groups, each ending with the same phrase about Tyre's end (26:21; 27:36; 28:19). The first four oracles are each fairly brief and similar in form to those in chapter 25. The other three are of a very different kind. The date in 26:1 probably refers to all of the first four oracles. It is incomplete, lacking the month, which suggests some copying error in transmission of the text. It places the oracles at about the time of Jerusalem's downfall, as their content also suggests.

Gloating over gain

The first oracle (vv. 1–6) castigates Tyre for gloating over Jerusalem's destruction since it removed a hindrance to the Phoenician city's commercial enterprises. The reference may be to the taxes that Judah levied on merchants carrying goods on the trade routes to and from Tyre. Judgment on Tyre is described by an image that is particularly appropriate for that city. Nations will come against it like the waves of the sea breaking on a rock. The defences in which it has put so much confidence (the Assyrians had not breached them) will be shattered and the city scraped off its island, leaving only bare rock (the Hebrew name for Tyre, tsor, means 'rock'). Its suburbs ('daughters') on the mainland will be overrun and the inhabitants killed.

In the second oracle (vv. 7–14), King Nebuchadnezzar of Babylon (Ezekiel uses an alternative spelling of the name) is named as the one who will lead the assault against Tyre. The attack is described using the conventional language of siege warfare, which ignores the peculiar problems of an assault on the island part of the city state. The attackers will breach the defences, kill the inhabitants and plunder the city's wealth. It will become a bare rock on which fishermen dry their nets. In this oracle no reason is given for the destruction of the city. Maybe the naming of Nebuchadnezzar as its agent implies that it is because of Tyre's role in encouraging Judah on the disastrous course of rebellion against Babylon and her failure to come to Judah's aid when Nebuchadnezzar besieged Jerusalem.

Avarice

Throughout its history, the city of Tyre got involved in the political intrigues that went on among the powers, great and small, of the eastern Mediterranean world. No doubt its commercial importance and wealth gave it considerable influence politically. Its gloating over the commercial advantage of Judah's downfall shows the corrosive effect of avarice. What matters to Tyre is not the disaster that has befallen a political ally, but the commercial opportunity it creates. Any thought about the loss of life, or the pain and suffering that has happened, is lost in greedy anticipation of increased wealth. As a result, Tyre's avarice is going to cause its downfall.

It is not only commercial tycoons who need to heed and learn the lesson of Tyre's judgment. The apostle Paul warns that 'the love of money is a root of all kinds of evil' (1 Timothy 6:10), and Jesus warned his disciples, 'You cannot serve God and wealth' (Matthew 6:24).

MEDITATION

'There is great gain in godliness combined with contentment; for we brought nothing into the world, so that we can take nothing out of it; but if we have food and clothing, we will be content with these.'

1 Timothy 6:6–8

TYRE'S FUNERAL

The third of this set of four fairly brief oracles against Tyre describes the impact its fall will have on its maritime trading partners (vv. 15–18). The prophet paints a picture of the funeral of the island of Tyre. The princes of the island and coastal states of the Mediterranean world have gathered together. In accordance with the mourning rituals of the time, they leave their thrones, take off their regal finery, and sit on the ground beside the corpse, trembling and wailing. The prophet puts a lament into their mouths. They remember Tyre's renown and power, which had enabled it to impose its will on others. Now they are awestruck and dismayed by the destruction of the city. It may be that the downfall of such a great city was seen as a warning of what could happen to any one of them.

In the fourth oracle (vv. 19–21) the prophet weaves together several different strands of imagery. This may originally have been an independent oracle but, placed after the funeral lament, the imagery of the sea closing over the city to engulf it evokes a maritime funeral (v. 19). The corpse of the deceased is weighted down and dropped into the sea after the funeral words have been spoken. In this case it is not just a human corpse, but an entire city that is to be dropped into the depths of the sea, never to be seen again.

'The deep' and 'the Pit'

The sea of verse 19 is no ordinary ocean. It is described as 'the deep' (*tehom* in Hebrew) and 'the great waters'. The word *tehom* is used in Genesis 1:2 of the formless waters that existed at the beginning of God's creative activity. So here Ezekiel is drawing on imagery that was widespread in the mythology of the ancient Near East—that of the primeval waters. The cosmos was thought of as being created in a 'space' within the waters. In the biblical flood story, it is these primeval waters that return to inundate the earth in a great act of divine judgment—a kind of 'uncreation'. In verse 19 the destruction of Tyre is depicted in a similar way. The city is not just destroyed, it is 'uncreated'. That is one reason why it will 'never be found again' (v. 21).

There is another strand of mythological imagery in verse 20.

Behind it is the visualization of the universe as a three-storey building. The earth is the middle storey, with the heavenly world above it and an underworld below, where the dead go. Various terms are used for the underworld in Hebrew, including the one used here by Ezekiel, 'the Pit'. This term is often used with negative connotations: God 'hides his face' from those in the Pit (Psalm 143:7); his wrath is on them (Psalm 88:6–7). Once again the imagery carries the idea of Tyre suffering divine judgment, and the picture of the city being made to descend into 'the Pit' prepares the way for the statement in verse 21 that although people may search for it, they will never find it.

So, in striking picture-language the prophet speaks of the downfall of Tyre. The city becomes a corpse, and worse: it is 'uncreated', it descends to 'the Pit' and no trace is left of it. The theme of these two oracles seems to be the great reversal that is involved in the downfall of Tyre. A city that was universally renowned disappears from the face of the earth, demonstrating the transience and hollowness of fame based on wealth and power. This is why the other rulers tremble at its downfall. It brings home to them the insecurity of their own position and power.

A warning to the wealthy

The Bible contains several warnings against thinking that we can find our security in material wealth. The apostle Paul warns the wealthy not to set their hopes for the future on 'the uncertainty of riches' but on 'God who richly provides us with everything for our enjoyment' (1 Timothy 6:17). Jesus told the parable of the rich man who prospered materially and thought that as a result his future was assured. But God said to him, 'You fool! This very night your life is being demanded of you' (Luke 12:20).

PRAYER

Lord, thank you for the measure of material security I have.
Help me to remember that it is transient, and that true security
can only be found in your eternal love for me.

The GOOD SHIP *TYRE*

This chapter contains a beautiful and powerful poem, written in the style of a lament, concerning a ship and its eventual shipwreck. The poetry is interrupted by a passage in prose (vv. 10–25a) which describes the ship's crew and the extent of its trading activity. There is no explicit mention of divine judgment in the poem, or anything to connect the fate of the ship with the destruction of Jerusalem. However, it can be seen as a development of the oracles in 26:15–21. It picks up the imagery of the sea engulfing Tyre, though now it is in the form of a shipwreck rather than a burial at sea. It can also be seen as expanding on what has been said briefly in those oracles about the power of Tyre and the impact of its destruction.

The ship, its crew and cargo

The first poetic section (vv. 3b–9) describes the good ship *Tyre*. The description justifies the opening statement, 'I am perfect in beauty.' The ship is made of the finest materials. The main planks are made out of fir trees from Hermon, the mast is the trunk of a cedar from Lebanon, and the oars are made of oak from Bashan. The decking is made of pine from Cyprus, inlaid with ivory. Fine Egyptian linen is used for the sail and the deck is covered with an awning made of embroidered cloth from Elishah (possibly another name for Cyprus). The crew of rowers, navigators and craftsmen able to do necessary repairs are recruited from the other Phoenician cities. This shows the superiority of the Tyrians in that they can afford to hire the best seamen and craftsmen from the other cities.

Even if the prose section is a secondary addition to the poem, as some scholars suggest, it is not a gratuitous one. By elaborating on Tyre's fame and influence among the nations, it heightens the glory described in the first part of the poem, and this in turn makes the disaster described in the second part all the more dramatic. In verses 10–11 the trained soldiers who form the ship's marines are described. They come from far-flung places—Persia, Asia Minor (Lud is probably Lydia) and north Africa (Put) as well as other Phoenician cities. Their painted shields and helmets hung on the sides of the ship add to its beauty.

The list of trading partners with their wares seems to be organized in geographical groups, beginning in the western Mediterranean. Tarshish is probably Tartessus in north-east Spain. It was a source of mineral ore. The phrase 'ships of Tarshish' (v. 25), which occurs a number of times elsewhere in the Old Testament, seems to mean ocean-going vessels capable of sailing the length of the Mediterranean with a heavy cargo such as metal ore. The places listed in verses 12–15 encompass Greece, Asia Minor and the islands of the eastern Mediterranean. In verses 16–19 the list moves north through the fertile crescent, from Edom through Judah and Israel to Syria. Next come places in the Arabian peninsular (vv. 20–22), and finally Mesopotamia (vv. 23–24). The wide geographical coverage and the diversity and quality of the merchandise builds up a picture of Tyre as a very successful and prosperous trading power.

Being the best

In all this description there is no hint of criticism, no rebuke of the claim to perfect beauty in verse 3b. This absence of criticism makes an important point. There is nothing wrong in striving for and achieving excellence. Indeed the poem celebrates it. The Tyrians had sought to excel at what they did—building seaworthy ships, sailing them well, engaging in international trade—and they had been successful. What matters is the motivation for that striving, and what is done with the result when it is achieved. We can strive to be the best because of the fame and fortune it will bring us. If so, we will probably trample on other people on the way, and on reaching our goal will probably go on trampling them. On the other hand, we can strive to be the best because we want to honour God, who gave us our gifts and abilities, and to serve him through serving other people to the best of our ability.

MEDITATION

*'Whatever is true, whatever is honourable, whatever is just,
whatever is pure, whatever is pleasing, whatever is commendable,
if there is any excellence and if there is anything worthy of praise,
think about these things.'*

Philippians 4:8

The WRECK of the TYRE

The ship metaphor, having receded somewhat in the prose section, revives with the return to poetry. The heavily laden vessel leaves the harbour but has not got very far out to sea when it is struck by an east wind and sinks (v. 26). It is lost with all hands and all its cargo (v. 27). Hearing of the loss, those on board the ships still in the harbour gather on the shore to bewail the tragedy. They perform the usual mourning rites of wearing sackcloth and ashes and lamenting loudly. The sense of tragedy is enhanced by having a lament within a lament as they express their grief (vv. 32b–36). In it we hear of the people and kings of the coastlands being appalled by the disaster (v. 35), while merchants hiss or whistle in amazement and consternation (v. 36a).

It is striking that in this lament there is only a passing mention of the loss of the crew (v. 34b). What is really bemoaned is the loss of a ship that provided people with the means to satisfy their desires and to enrich themselves (v. 33).

The two themes found in the oracles of chapter 26 are implicit in this poem. The fact that the main burden of the lament within the lament is the loss of merchandise and wealth raises the issue of avarice. This is also implied in verse 25b, with the suggestion that the ship was overloaded, presumably in the desire to maximize profit from the voyage. The fine ship was therefore vulnerable to a storm.

A false sense of security

The second theme, that of a false sense of security, is also suggested by verse 25b, taken in the light of what has gone before. Here is a ship built of the finest materials, served by a skilful crew, including experienced navigators, and so they risk overloading it. As a result it is top-heavy and, when hit by the east wind, sinks so rapidly that no one can escape. If there is any particular significance in the east wind, it may be that this is the direction from which disaster is going to hit the city of Tyre—Nebuchadnezzar of Babylon. More to the point, though, is the reminder that, in the ocean storm, there is a power that transcends human control. The recognition of this is probably behind the fear of the kings and the merchants. However well-built the ship, however skilled and experienced the crew, there are times when a storm is more than human beings can cope with. This, of course, is a metaphor for the power of God. Because God is the Creator, he can use the powers of nature to do his will: 'You make the winds your messengers, fire and flame your ministers' (Psalm 104:4). But this means that although storms are beyond human control, God can control them: 'You rule the raging of the sea; when its waves rise, you still them' (Psalm 89:9). Once again we are reminded that it is only in God that we can find true security.

True security

The story of the wreck of the *Tyre* has a counterpoint in the Gospel story of the storm on Lake Galilee (Matthew 8:23–27). Here too, a group of experienced sailors find themselves being overwhelmed by a storm. Maybe they are slow to wake Jesus, thinking that they can cope. Almost too late ('the boat was being swamped') they wake him up. To their utter amazement, at his command the wind and the waves calm down. They cannot understand how a human being can act with the authority of the Creator and control the wind and the sea. Nevertheless, they discover that the true source of security is trust in Jesus.

Down through the centuries, Christians have rightly seen in this story a lesson about coping with life. To weather the storms of life and prevent shipwreck, we must avoid over-confidence in our own ability to deal with whatever may confront us and put our trust in Jesus to guide us through life and to bring us safely through its stormy periods.

PRAYER

Lord, I am sorry that, like the disciples, I am sometimes slow to admit my need of your help. Please forgive me for that. Help me to have a sober estimate of my ability to cope and a greater willingness to seek help from you when things get difficult, so that I am not driven to my wits' end.

The PRIDE *of the* PRINCE OF TYRE

This satirical poem is addressed to 'the prince of Tyre' who, as the ruler of the city, is a kind of embodiment of it. In Ezekiel's time, the ruler of the city was Ittobaal II. However, there is nothing in the poem to indicate that a particular person is in mind. It could apply to any arrogant ruler. Although it is very different in form from the allegory that precedes it, there is some continuity in the reference to Tyre as being 'in the heart of the seas' (v. 2).

Excessive pride

The prince of Tyre is not condemned for any crime against Judah but for an offence against God—his claim to divine status. He is accused of the sin of hubris, an excessive pride. This is expressed in his claim to the status and position of a god: 'I am a god; I sit in the seat of the gods' (v. 2). The basis of the prince's pride is his wisdom and his wealth (v. 5). The reality of these qualities is not disputed, though there may be a touch of sarcasm in the statement, 'You are indeed wiser than Daniel' (v. 3). The name is better read as 'Danel' and refers to the legendary hero who has already been mentioned in Ezekiel 14:14, 20. We know of him through the 14th century BC Canaanite texts excavated at Ras Shamra (the site of the ancient city of Ugarit) in northern Syria. In these texts he is a king who is renowned for his wise administration of justice. In the ancient Near East, wisdom was not primarily academic intelligence, but the ability to cope successfully with the demands of life. As such, it could be put to either good or bad ends. Thus Jonadab uses his wisdom to devise a plan whereby Amnon's evil designs on his half-sister may be accomplished (2 Samuel 13:3–5), while Solomon uses his to administer justice wisely (1 Kings 3:28). The prince of Tyre has used his wisdom to amass wealth for himself. Again, of itself, wealth is neither good nor bad: what matters is how it is used. There is an implied criticism here in the frequent use of the possessive pronoun 'your'—'for yourself', 'your' treasuries, 'your' wealth (v. 4). The wealth has been amassed for selfish ends, not used for the good of others.

The hollowness of the prince's proud boast to be a god will be exposed when the Lord God brings against him 'the most terrible of the nations', the Babylonians (v. 7; see 30:10–11). Their swords will cut the prince's wisdom and splendour down to size. When he dies a violent death at their hands, his mortality will prove that he is no god. His rightful place 'in the heart of the seas' will be shown to be not 'the seat of the gods' but 'the Pit', the abode of the dead (v. 8). Here there is a clear echo of what has been said of the city of Tyre itself in 26:19–20.

True wisdom

This picture of the proud prince of Tyre is a widely applicable condemnation of the sin of human pride, which is often expressed in the assertion that we can run our own lives without reference to God. In that sense there is a strong human tendency to claim to be a god. This poem exposes a form of 'vicious circle' in which the deployment of wisdom leads to success and prosperity, the amassing of wealth. This encourages pride, which then distorts the wisdom and the use of the wealth. The way out of this vicious circle is to heed the biblical injunction that 'the fear of the Lord is the beginning of wisdom' (Psalm 111:10). When wisdom itself is rooted in the fear and reverence of the Lord, the possibility of hubris emerging from the accomplishments it achieves will be prohibited. Someone whose starting point is 'the fear of the Lord' will not be able to go on and claim, 'I am a god'.

PRAYER

'If any of you is lacking in wisdom, ask God, who gives to all generously and ungrudgingly, and it will be given you'

James 1:5

Lord God, life is full of challenging and difficult situations. Please give me the wisdom I need in order to cope successfully with its demands; and please give me the grace always to use that wisdom in an attitude of reverence towards you.

EXPULSION *from* EDEN

The Bible presents hubris, in the form of the desire to be like God, as the archetypal sin. In the story of the garden of Eden in Genesis, the serpent tempts Eve to disobey God with the words, 'When you eat of it your eyes will be opened, and you will be like God, knowing good and evil' (Genesis 3:5). In this lament over the king of Tyre the prophet combines elements of the Genesis story with other, seemingly Canaanite, traditions about the primeval paradise. There are echoes of Genesis in the location of the paradise ('in Eden, the garden of God', v. 13) and the guardian cherub who drives the king out of the garden (v. 16). The reference to the paradise being 'on the holy mountain of God' (v. 14) is probably drawn from the Canaanite idea of the seat of the gods being on a high mountain. Although precious stones are mentioned in connection with Eden in Genesis 2:12, the presentation of paradise as a mineral garden may reflect Canaanite ideas.

The primeval man

In the Christian tradition this chapter, together with Isaiah 14, has been used to construct an account of the fall of 'Lucifer' as an explanation for the origin of Satan as a rebellious, fallen angel. However, this ignores the metaphorical nature of these chapters. The prophet is taking imagery that was deeply rooted in the culture of his time and place, in order to depict the hubris of the king of Tyre. It is an imaginative portrait of 'the first man', just as Ezekiel 27 is an imaginative portrait of a great merchant ship. In neither case is the portrait meant to be taken literally.

The king of Tyre is depicted as the primeval man in 'the garden of God' in Eden. He was 'full of wisdom and perfect in beauty' (v. 12). There on 'the holy mountain of God' with a guardian cherub, his life began in blamelessness. However, as in Genesis 2—3, he sinned: 'iniquity' was found in him (v. 15). But here is no explanation of how this sin came about, no account of a tempter at work. The essence of the 'iniquity' is identified as pride (v. 17). It is a characteristic of absolute monarchs that they tend to bolster their position by ruthless exercise of their power and extravagant display of their wealth. This is the accusation against the king of Tyre (vv. 16–17). Because of Tyre's position, its sin was expressed primarily through his trading activities. Trade in itself is not evil, but in this case it became the instrument of unchecked avarice as the king sought to increase his 'beauty' further. His wisdom was corrupted as it was turned towards this one end. As a result, he was cast out of the garden, driven out by the guardian cherub. Indeed, the judgment goes further than that. The fire of God destroys the king (v. 18). The fall and destruction of such a magnificent creature appals all who know of it (v. 19).

The new Adam

The way Ezekiel uses the story of the primeval fall of human beings makes clear its universal applicability. Pride, leading to greed and violence expressed in various ways, is all too obvious in human history, written large in the behaviour of prominent people and, less obviously, observed in the personal experience of the ordinary person. These sins mar all attempts to create our own 'paradises' on earth. The situation may seem hopeless, but the remedy for it is to be found in yet another version of the garden of Eden story, one developed by the apostle Paul. In Romans 5 he presents Adam as the representative of all human beings. Like him we are all guilty of disobedience against God. As a result, we deserve condemnation and death. However, Jesus Christ has come as a new Adam. He too was a perfect human being but, unlike Adam, he did not disobey God. Rather, he lived a life of perfect obedience to God, culminating in his death on the cross. As a result, God now offers us forgiveness, a right relationship with himself and eternal life—all as a free gift.

PRAYER

'When I survey the wondrous cross,
on which the Prince of glory died,
my richest gain I count but loss,
and pour contempt on all my pride.

Forbid it, Lord, that I should boast,
save in the death of Christ my God:
all the vain things that charm me most,
I sacrifice them to his blood.'

Isaac Watts (1674–1748)

SORROW *for* SIDON, JOY *for* JACOB

The oracle against Sidon (vv. 20–23) concludes the series of oracles against Israel's immediate ring of six neighbours—Ammon, Moab, Edom, Philistia, Tyre and Sidon. The following oracles against Egypt (Ezekiel 29—32) bring the total number of nations addressed to the 'complete' number of seven. Because the oracle against Sidon closes the ring of neighbouring states, it is followed by some words addressed to Israel which indicate the eventual consequences for them of God's judgment of their neighbours (vv. 24–26).

Judgment on Sidon

Sidon was some 25 miles north of Tyre on the Mediterranean coast and, with it, was one of the four principal Phoenician cities (Arvad and Gebal being the other two). Its more exposed position made it more vulnerable to attack than Tyre, and it was captured by the Assyrian ruler Esarhaddon.

In Ezekiel's day Sidon was less prosperous and powerful than Tyre. It was a member of the coalition that plotted against Nebuchadnezzar (Jeremiah 27:3). Its king was eventually deported to Babylon along with other rebellious rulers, including Jehoiachin of Judah. However, the city itself seems not to have suffered much destruction. Eventually it was able to take over the lead role from Tyre.

Although the oracle against Sidon clearly proclaims God's judgment on the city, no explicit reason is given. This is unlike the oracles against Israel's other neighbours. Maybe Sidon's part in plotting the rebellion, and so in that sense contributing to Judah's downfall, was sufficient reason for her inclusion in judgment. The form that the judgment will take is expressed in very general terms—pestilence, bloodshed, the sword. All this could refer to the city being besieged (as disease often broke out in a city during siege) and captured in war. The aim of the judgment, as in all these oracles, is expressed in the phrase, 'Then they will know that I am the Lord' (v. 23).

Hope for Israel

The words addressed to Israel fall into two parts. The first (v. 24) speaks of the beneficial effects for Judah of the judgment on her neighbours. She will no longer have to suffer insults, derision and attacks from them. This will be no cause for pride on Judah's part, because it is not her doing but entirely the result of God's control of international events. Therefore it should lead her to a fresh recognition of, and commitment to, God.

The oracle in verses 25–26 probably comes from a late period in Ezekiel's ministry, when he was delivering words of hope, and was placed here when the book was put together in its present form, in order to provide the centrepoint of the collection of oracles against foreign nations. It contains a reminder of God's original purpose in choosing first Abraham (Genesis 18:18) and then Israel (Exodus 19:6)—that through them the nations might recognize who God is. As we have seen, this is frequently repeated to be the purpose of the judgment on the nations spoken of in this collection of oracles. This purpose has been jeopardized by the need to punish Judah by the destruction of Jerusalem and the temple, and the exiling of the nation from its land. The oracle therefore gives great comfort to God's people with its promise of a reversal of the scattering of the exile and a return of the people to the promised land. Moreover, there is a note of permanence injected into the promise by the mention of building houses and planting vineyards. This oracle ends with a formula that is slightly, but significantly, different from the oracles addressed to the other nations, 'Then they will know that I am the Lord *their God*'. This implies not just a return to the land but also a restoration of the special covenant relationship with between God and Israel.

In times of crisis it is easy for our perspective to become very narrow. We concentrate on what is happening to us and ignore everything else. As a result, we get things out of perspective. The placing of the words 'to the house of Israel' in the middle of the section of oracles against other nations is a reminder that God's purposes embrace all nations and that those he chooses as his people are meant to play their part in that wider purpose.

MEDITATION

Jesus reaffirmed God's purpose that through his people
all nations should come to recognize who God is.
How can you be involved in this?

The DEATH *of* DRAGON EGYPT

Ezekiel 29—32 contains seven oracles against Egypt, paralleling the seven oracles against Tyre. Each begins with the formula, 'The word of the Lord came to me' and, with the exception of the third (30:1–19), is dated. Apart from the second (29:17–21), the oracles are in chronological order. The significance of the dates is not clear, particularly since there is still disagreement over whether Jerusalem fell to the Babylonians in August 587 or 586BC.

The first of the oracles is dated in January 587BC, about a year after the siege of Jerusalem had begun. It begins with a word of judgment on Pharaoh, expressed in Hebrew poetry (vv. 3–6a). This is followed by two articles of indictment (vv. 6b–9a, 9b–12) which give reasons for the judgment. The oracle is rounded off by a promise of partial restoration for Egypt (vv. 13–16).

A great dragon

In the poem, Pharaoh is depicted as a great dragon lurking in the waters of the Nile delta. There are two strands to this imagery. One is the role that the dragon plays in ancient Near Eastern mythology. It is one of the symbols of the forces of chaos that had to be overcome before the world could be created. This imagery occurs in Hebrew poetry both in the prophets (Isaiah 51:9) and in the Psalms (89:10). As the great dragon, Pharaoh is an embodiment of those evil forces that threaten the stability of the created order.

The other strand of imagery is that of the Nile crocodile, which was considered a sacred animal in some Egyptian cults and was associated with the Pharaoh. In an Egyptian text, the god Amon-Re says to Pharaoh Thutmoses III, 'I cause them to see your majesty as a crocodile.' God's judgment on Pharaoh is depicted in terms of a crocodile hunt. The great beast is caught with hooks (presumably baited) and pulled out of the water on to dry land. In view of what follows, the fish sticking to its scales probably represent the nations allied to Egypt. The crocodile is left as carrion exposed in the open field to be eaten by scavenging birds and animals. Leaving corpses exposed like this was a way of dishonouring them.

A broken reed

The first indictment (vv. 6b–9a) describes Egypt as an unreliable crutch or walking-stick. Like the weak papyrus reed of the Nile, it breaks, injuring the user. As far as Egypt was concerned, the smaller states of the southern fertile crescent were of interest because they acted as a buffer between her and the Mesopotamian powers. She was therefore always ready to offer them support against Assyria or Babylon. More than once in Judah's history, Egypt encouraged Judah to rebel against one of these powers, promising military assistance, only to prove unable to fulfil the promise. Egypt had encouraged Zedekiah to rebel against Babylon, and early in the siege an Egyptian army did try to come to Judah's aid, only to be defeated by the Babylonians. The respite it gave to Jerusalem was only temporary (Jeremiah 37:3–10). Ezekiel may have uttered this oracle at about that time in order to combat false hopes raised when the news of an Egyptian army coming to Judah's aid reached the exiles.

Delusions of grandeur

The second indictment (vv. 9b–12) concerns Pharaoh's divine pretensions, expressed in the saying, 'The Nile is mine, and I made it' (v. 9b). In this form of the saying, he is claiming creative powers, an attribute of deity. In verse 3 the Hebrew says literally, 'The Nile is mine, I made myself'. This echoes the claim of the sun-god Amon-Re, with whom the Pharaoh was associated, to be self-begotten. As a result of these claims, Egypt will be desolated for a generation (40 years) and the population scattered. The grace of God is seen in the promise of restoration, though it is said that Egypt will never regain its former power and status.

The other side of the indictment of Egypt as a broken reed is the folly of Judah in relying on such military alliances instead of on God. Isaiah summed this up well over a century before Ezekiel: 'Alas for those who go down to Egypt for help and who rely on horses... but do not look to the Holy One of Israel or consult the Lord!' (Isaiah 31:1).

MEDITATION

'Trust in the Lord with all your heart, and do not rely on your own insight. In all your ways acknowledge him, and he will make straight your paths.'

Proverbs 3:5–6

66

EGYPT *in* EXCHANGE *for* TYRE

This second oracle in the series about Egypt is the latest-dated oracle in the whole book of Ezekiel. The date in verse 17 shows that it was delivered in the spring of the year 571BC, just over 16 years after the first oracle in this series. For most of the intervening years, Nebuchadnezzar's forces had been besieging Tyre. The siege, which the Jewish historian Josephus tells us lasted 13 years, ended some time in 573BC. It was a success for Nebuchadnezzar in that the king of Tyre became his vassal and paid tribute to him. However, the island portion of Tyre was not sacked and the Babylonians never captured the treasure of Tyre. It is unclear whether this was because it was evacuated by ship to some safe haven, or because it was spent on the defence of the city. A long, unrewarding siege like this would have caused Nebuchadnezzar problems. Soldiers were not paid well in the ancient world, and expected to be able to supplement their pay from the spoils of war. When they were deprived of these spoils for long periods, the morale and the discipline of the army suffered. Moreover, a considerable portion of the Babylonian army were mercenaries, for whom capturing booty was a major reason for fighting. When it was not forthcoming, they would start looking for another army to join.

God's unwitting workers

The unrewarding nature of the siege of Tyre is picked up explicitly in the oracle. The *Torah* contains laws about the prompt and fair payment of workers (for example, Deuteronomy 24:14–15). The God of Israel, the prophet declares, will stand by his own laws. The oracle contains the rather amazing statement by God about Nebuchadnezzar and his army, that 'they worked for me' (v. 20). God will behave fairly even to those who are carrying out his purposes unwittingly! There will be an adequate reward for the Babylonians, which will come from the plunder of Egypt. So, although the oracle is about the Babylonians, it is in fact addressed to Egypt. It warns her of the specific form that the judgment spoken of in the previous oracle will take. Quite what did happen in terms of a Babylonian invasion of Egypt, we do not know. Few Babylonian records from the later years of Nebuchadnezzar's reign have yet come to light. A fragmentary text attests an expedition against Egypt in the 37th year of his reign (568/7BC), about the time when there was upheaval in Egypt associated with the deposition of Pharaoh Hophra and the usurpation of the throne by Amasis II. It has been suggested that Amasis bought off the invading Babylonians by paying massive tribute, but this is supposition.

Unfulfilled prophecy

For the modern reader, this oracle raises the question of how we should understand the seemingly predictive element in the oracles of the Hebrew prophets. In Ezekiel 26:12 there was a promise of rich booty from Tyre for the Babylonians. When this does not prove true, the prophet does not seem to be concerned about the issue of unfulfilled prophecy, but rather about the issue of the justice of God towards his 'labourers'. Moreover, nothing is said in this oracle about the warning in Ezekiel 26:4–5 that the island city of Tyre would be annihilated and become an uninhabited rock. There was no mention of exactly when this annihilation would happen (this was, in fact, the outcome of Alexander the Great's attack on Tyre in 332BC), but the fact that the warning in 26:4–5 was followed by an oracle naming Nebuchadnezzar (26:7) could be taken to imply that he would bring it about. The implication is that in ancient Israel prophecy was understood in an open-ended rather than a literalistic way. Through the prophets, God expresses his intentions, but does so looking for a human response. In his sovereignty he is free to take that response into account and modify either his intentions or how they are worked out—the most obvious example being the revoking of the destruction of Nineveh in the story of Jonah.

The closing verse of the oracle (v. 21) is a reminder that God is not just playing at power politics but is concerned with his chosen people and fulfilling his purposes through them.

PRAYER

This oracle contains an unexpected reminder of God's concern for the just treatment of workers (v. 20). Think of some recent or current examples of this issue and pray about them.

The DAY *of* JUDGMENT *for* EGYPT

The third oracle against Egypt is, in fact, a composite of four oracular sayings. Each begins with the phrase, 'Thus says the Lord (God)' (vv. 2, 6, 10, 13). The overall message is the same as that of the first oracle against Egypt (29:1–16), but now it is spelled out in more detail. There is also another significant change. Like many of Ezekiel's oracles of judgment, it is set in the form of a lament. As we have noted before, the use of this form, which is associated with funerals and mourning, gives added emotional impact to the message. Lamenting the dead before the funeral, as it were, also adds a sense of the certainty of the impending judgment.

The day of the Lord

The position of the third oracle in the sequence is probably determined by the verbal link of the word 'day' in Ezekiel 29:21 and 30:2. In 30:2b–4 the 'day' is identified as 'the day of the Lord'. The earliest known reference to 'the day of the Lord' is in Amos 5:18–20. The fact that the prophet can use the concept without needing to explain it shows that by the mid-eighth century it was already a well-established one. In the oracles of the Hebrew prophets 'the day of the Lord' is the moment of his judgment upon his enemies. The judgment is often expressed, as here in Ezekiel, by the use of battle imagery. This suggests that the origin of the concept lies in the 'holy wars' associated with the settlement in Canaan. In these the Israelites believed that the Lord intervened to give them victory because they were carrying out his judgment on the sins of the Canaanites. From this may have developed the idea of a final great day of judgment on all those opposed to God. However, 'the day of the Lord' seems to have been thought of as marking not the end of the world but the end of one world order (in which most nations defy God and do not recognize Israel's true status) and the beginning of another (in which all the nations recognize the sovereignty of God exercised on earth through Israel).

The 'day' foreshadowed

An act of judgment such as the one depicted here in verse 4 is a foreshadowing of the final, universal judgment. In this case the judgment encompasses the nations around Egypt, which were in some kind of alliance with her. The phrase 'the people of the land that is in league' (v. 5) could be an allusion to Israel (taking 'league' as the covenant with God), but it is more likely that it refers to nations in league with Israel. 'Put' refers to the region around modern Tripoli. 'Lud' in the Old Testament normally refers to Lydia in Asia Minor, but here it may designate colonies of Lydian mercenaries in Egypt.

The second component of the oracle (vv. 6–9) reinforces what has been said in verse 5—that the judgment includes those nations who have given support to Egypt. Its language echoes that of Ezekiel 29:9b–12.

In the third component of the oracle (vv. 10–12), the nature of the judgment is made more specific, in two ways. Firstly, Nebuchadnezzar is named as God's agent who will conquer Egypt. Secondly, God himself will dry up the Nile, on which Egypt's existence depends. This is a riposte to Pharaoh's claim in Ezekiel 29:3, 9 to be the creator and controller of the Nile. These two forms of judgment show that God is in control of both history and nature.

The final component (vv. 13–19) makes the completeness of the judgment clear by piling up the names of the cities that will experience it. There is no discernible order in the list.

The theme of 'the day of the Lord' as a final great day of judgment continues in the New Testament. But there is a new aspect to it—the return of the risen Jesus in glory. Jesus told parables that stress the importance of being prepared for judgment (for example, Matthew 25), and, in a doxology that is often used at the end of church services, Jude assures us that we can be prepared for it if we rely on God as the one 'who is able to keep you from falling, and to make you stand without blemish before the presence of his glory with rejoicing' (Jude 24).

PRAYER

Lord, make me ready, and keep me ready, to greet your coming in glory with rejoicing and not with fear.

PHARAOH'S BROKEN ARM

This short oracle is dated to the spring of 587BC, during the later stages of the siege of Jerusalem. In the previous year Hophra had become Pharaoh of Egypt and, in response to Judah's plight, had sent an army to help her. Nebuchadnezzar abandoned the siege of Jerusalem in order to deal with this threat (Jeremiah 37:1–10). The Egyptian army was defeated and the siege resumed. Although it is about Egypt, this oracle is clearly addressed to those Judean exiles whose hopes had been raised by Hophra's action, and who still clung to the hope that he would intervene a second time with more success.

Pharaoh's arm

The imagery of the oracle, even though only metaphorical, is unpleasant. Once again the prophet is having to use 'shock tactics' to break through the self-delusion of some of his audience. Behind the imagery is the use of 'the arm' as a metaphor for agency and power. Moreover, at least some Pharaohs adopted the title 'strong-armed man'. In this oracle the initial breaking of Pharaoh's arm is clearly the defeat of Hophra's army by the Babylonians in 588BC. Of course it is possible to lose a battle but still win the war, so some Judeans must have hoped that this would be only a temporary setback for Egypt. Maybe the arm could be healed; maybe Hophra could regroup and rearm his forces and defeat the Babylonians. The prophet declares that this has not happened and will not happen. Indeed, to drive the point home and to remove any lingering trace of hope, Ezekiel asserts that God will break the broken arm again, as well as the sound arm. As a result, Pharaoh will be unable to wield a sword and will be left groaning helplessly before Nebuchadnezzar, whose arms God will strengthen.

The arm of the Lord

A constant theme of the Hebrew prophets is that the folly of seeking deliverance through reliance on the arms of other nations (usually the regional superpowers of Egypt, Assyria and Babylon) is a besetting sin of Israel and Judah. They fail to recognize that the only sure source of help is 'the arm of the Lord', despite the fact that it is something of a refrain in the Old Testament that Israel came into being when God brought his people out of Egypt 'by a mighty hand and an out-stretched arm' (Deuteronomy 4:34). In the worship of the temple, God was praised in terms such as, 'You have a mighty arm; strong is your hand, high your right hand' (Psalm 89:13). Ezekiel's imagery probably has its roots in the traditional language of laments used in the temple. In one of these, the psalmist calls on God to help the poor, the needy and the powerless, crying out, 'Break the arm of the wicked and evildoers; seek out their wickedness until you find none' (Psalm 10:15). If it is folly to rely on human arms instead of God's arm for deliverance, it is double folly to rely on them for deliverance from the instrument of God's judgment. Yet this is just what Zedekiah of Judah was trying to do when he appealed to Egypt to support him against Nebuchadnezzar.

Although the use of the metaphor of God's arm in the Old Testament is often associated with military imagery and the destruction of the wicked as the counterpart to the deliverance of the righteous and the oppressed, this is not always the case. At times it is used to express God's loving care and protection. There is the picture of God the shepherd who 'will gather the lambs in his arms' (Isaiah 40:11) and God the parent of whom it is said, 'Underneath are the everlast-ing arms' (Deuteronomy 33:27, RSV), and who says of Israel, 'I took them up in my arms' (Hosea 11:3). Most amazing of all is the revela-tion of 'the arm of the Lord' in Isaiah 52:13—53:12. In fact, it is so amazing that the prophet expresses doubt that anyone will be-lieve it! (Isaiah 53:1). This is because God's arm, his power, is revealed in one who suffers willingly for others so that through his suffering their sins will be dealt with and they will be made whole. The New Testament equivalent of this is the repeated assertion in John's Gospel that God's 'glory' is revealed by Jesus' death on the cross.

PRAYER

Lord God, help me to find my ultimate security in your
everlasting arms, and nowhere else.

The FALL *of the* CEDAR TREE

The fifth oracle against Egypt has three parts. It begins with an allegorical poem comparing Egypt to a magnificent cedar of Lebanon (vv. 1–9, RSV, which, probably correctly, takes the mention of 'Assyria' in verse 3 to be the result of a scribe miscopyng the Hebrew word for 'I will liken you to'). There are then two prose sections—an indictment and announcement of judgment (vv. 10–14) followed by a description of the nation's descent to the underworld and the effects this will have (vv. 15–19). The oracle is dated barely a couple of months after the previous one. Once again, its purpose is to undermine any hope of deliverance for Judah from Egypt.

The 'world tree'

The cedar of Lebanon was the tallest and most impressive tree known to the people of the ancient Near East. Ezekiel's description of it includes motifs from the mythical image of the 'world tree' which is found in many cultures. Its roots go down to the subterranean primeval 'deep' (the same word as is used in Genesis 1:2) from which it draws nourishment not available to other trees. It is greater and more beautiful than the trees in the garden of Eden. The poem depicts its rich foliage, its wide-spreading branches and its great height. It gives shelter to birds that nest in it and provides shade for all kinds of animals. The reference to the nourishing rivers and streams that flow around may be an allusion to the situation in the Nile delta, and the poet departs from the allegory to speak of the protection Egypt gave to the nations allied to her (v. 6c). The poem effectively evokes the splendour and power of ancient Egypt. It is purely descriptive, with no hint of criticism of the splendid tree. Indeed, its magnificence is attributed to what God has done for it (v. 9).

God's lumberjacks

It is not until the start of the first prose section that the criticism comes (v. 10). As with Tyre (Ezekiel 27—28), magnificence leads to pride, and pride to downfall. Since the beauty of the tree was due to God, not the tree's own effort, the pride is doubly culpable. God therefore gives the tree over to destruction by 'a mighty one of the nations' (Nebuchadnezzar) and 'the most terrible of nations' (the Babylonians) (see 30:10–11). They are God's chosen lumberjacks to chop down this great tree. The mighty and magnificent tree will fall to earth with its great branches lying broken in the valleys and watercourses. This will be a lesson to all the other great trees about the danger of pride, and a reminder of their own mortality. Again, at the end of verse 14, the allegory recedes and the reference is clearly to the rulers of the other nations.

The mention of mortality leads into the third section of the oracle (vv. 15–18), in which the allegory becomes rather forced. The fall of the tree does not stop when it hits the ground. It will go down to the underworld—Sheol, or the Pit. Here it will be dishonoured, lying with the uncircumcised (a disgrace for the ancient Egyptians, who practised circumcision) and those slain in battle (who were often left unburied). However, this part of the oracle is concerned not with the situation in the underworld, but with the effects on other nations of the tree's descent into it. The cosmic springs that its roots seemed to release (v. 4) will be stopped, and gloom will descend on all the trees of Lebanon. Once again the allegory recedes in verses 16a and 17b. The nations that were allied to Egypt will be terrified by its downfall. The fact that such a powerful nation could fall is a warning to them of the precariousness of their own position. They will share a similar fate one day.

Selfish pride

In the oracles against Tyre, the prophet has already exposed the danger of pride arising from success. It is not success itself that is wrong, but one's attitude to it and how it is used. For Egypt, like Tyre, it became the cause of self-centred pride. This oracle, more than those against Tyre, brings out the responsibility of successful nations for others who also benefit from that success: the birds and animals that found shelter in the tree inevitably suffered from its downfall. This is one reason why those privileged by a degree of success should accept it with humility and use it carefully. Instead of resulting in selfish pride, success can be used to benefit others.

MEDITATION

'Pride goes before destruction, and a haughty spirit before a fall.'

Proverbs 16:18

LAMENT *for a* DEAD DRAGON

The sixth oracle against Egypt is dated to March 585BC, which is some months after the destruction of Jerusalem. News of Jerusalem's fall would have had time to reach the exiles. In essence the oracle repeats what the previous ones have said: the Egyptian Pharaoh will be killed by the king of Babylon and the country devastated. After the fall of Jerusalem, a considerable number of Judeans fled to Egypt and established communities there. Some Jews began to think of Egypt as the base from which a rebirth of Judean life might come about. However, both Jeremiah (chs. 24; 44) and Ezekiel declared that this was a false hope. The rebirth was to come from those in Babylon who had accepted and experienced God's judgment.

This oracle is described as a lament, but only verse 2 is in the strict lament metre. It is followed by two sections (vv. 3–10, 11–15) in which there are only traces of the lament metre. Finally there is a rubric enjoining the chanting of the lament.

Destroying the dragon

Verse 2 contrasts Pharaoh's own image of himself as 'a lion among nations' with the reality. He is a dragon (*tannin*, the same word as in Ezekiel 29:3, and again the crocodile is probably in mind) lurking in the waters of the Nile delta, muddying and fouling them. Verse 2 is followed by an allegorical poem with a prose finale, which describes the hunting and killing of the dragon. There are echoes of 29:3–5, but this time the hunting is done with nets, not baited hooks. The great beast is caught, hauled out of the waters and dumped on the dry land as food for scavenging birds and animals. In verses 5–8, the language takes on apocalyptic tones. The dragon is so huge that its flesh covers the mountains and its blood fills the valleys. Cosmic disturbances accompany its death. The water-courses filled with blood and the darkening of the sun, moon and stars are reminiscent of the plagues in Egypt (Exodus 7:14–24; 10:21–23). The prose finale (vv. 9–10) speaks of the nations and their kings being appalled at the destruction of the dragon, fearing for their own lives.

In verses 11–15 the king of Babylon is identified as the agent of divine judgment on Egypt. The land will be denuded of its human and animal population. This will allow the waters that had been muddied and fouled by the dragon to become clear and tranquil again. The closing verse (v. 16) enjoins the chanting of the lament by mourners from all the nations associated with Egypt. This gives a sense of finality to the oracle, as if the events depicted in it have already taken place.

Chaos and order

Ezekiel's audience of Babylonian exiles would have recognized in this oracle an echo and adaptation of the Babylonian creation story, *Enuma Elish*, which was read and enacted each year in Babylon during the great New Year festival. It describes the emergence of an ordered world from the primeval waters of chaos in terms of a great battle. In this battle, the young champion of the gods, Marduk (the god of the city of Babylon), slays the leader of the forces of chaos, Tiamat, who takes the form of a great sea-monster. Marduk is then able to establish an ordered world. In Ezekiel's poem, Egypt plays the role of the monster Tiamat, and the Babylonian king, quite appropriately, plays the role of Marduk. In this case, however, both Egypt and Babylon are subject to the control of the one true God—the Lord the God of Israel.

When this background is realized, the oracle takes on new depth. The ancient creation stories were not really concerned with the origin of matter but with the establishment of order. The judgment of Egypt is therefore portrayed here as part of the establishment of world order out of the chaos caused by Judah's rebellion. This puts the prophet's preoccupation with judgment in a new light. All God's acts of judgment have the positive purpose of defeating the forces of evil, with the aim of establishing God's good order in the world.

PRAYER

*Lord God, all too often chaos does seem to be rampant
in the world. Genocide, civil war, economic exploitation,
epidemic disease and natural disasters fill our news media.
Please act to restrain the forces of chaos and to establish your just
order. Show your people what part we should play in this,
and give us the courage to do as you ask.*

WELCOME *to the* UNDERWORLD

The exact date of this final oracle in the series against Egypt is unclear. The Hebrew text lacks the number of the month. The early Greek translation of the Hebrew Bible, the Septuagint, has 'the first month', but some scholars think that the month intended was the same as in the previous oracle, the twelfth month. Whatever its date, the oracle forms an appropriate climax both to the oracles against Egypt and the whole collection of oracles against foreign nations. It depicts Egypt going to its final resting place in the underworld, joining other formerly powerful nations whose earthly glory has passed.

The underworld

In the Old Testament, the underworld, called Sheol or the Pit, is the abode of the dead. It is a place where people survive as a weak shadow of their earthly selves (Isaiah 14:10), cut off from God: 'For in death there is no remembrance of you; in Sheol who can give you praise?' (Psalm 6:5). It is characterized by darkness and forgetfulness (Psalm 88:12; Ecclesiastes 9:5–6).

Ezekiel is told to 'wail' over the Egyptian multitudes and to send them down to the netherworld. The picture seems to be of a kind of funeral procession; perhaps a parody of the elaborate funeral processions of the Pharaohs is intended. The Egyptians are accompanied by the official mourners spoken of in 32:16, 'the daughters of the majestic nations'. As they enter the underworld, the chiefs of the nations already there greet them, wondering at the fact that Egypt has come to join them. Even more than that, Egypt has been consigned to the most dishonourable place in the underworld, where the uncircumcised and those slain by the sword lie. Here 'uncircumcised' seems to have the ring of 'barbarian'. As noted already, those 'slain by the sword' probably means those who have not had a proper burial and so have been dishonoured in death.

Six nations are mentioned as welcoming Egypt to the Pit. The reason for this particular list of powers is not clear. Assyria was a superpower for over a century until the fall of Nineveh to the Medes and Babylonians in 612BC. Elam, east of Assyria, was a major power until defeated by the Assyrian Emperor Ashurbanipal. Meshech and Tubal were kingdoms in

Asia Minor (Phrygia and Cilicia). They are named as trading partners of Tyre (27:13). All these are said to have 'spread terror in the land of the living'. Edom and Sidon were lesser powers, mentioned perhaps because they lay to the south and north of the land of Israel. Nothing is said of Edom spreading terror, though Sidon is said to have caused terror by her might. Pharaoh is reconciled to his fate in the sense that he sees himself joining these other former spreaders of terror.

Transient power and pomp

This oracle is a striking presentation of the transient nature of human power and pomp. Nations that at one time stride arrogantly across the world, flaunting their military might and material wealth, all pass from the scene eventually. Some, like Egypt and Assyria, are remembered by their monuments and some recollections of their achievements. Others pass from history leaving little or no trace. There is also an indictment of human militarism and the futility of war in the catchphrase 'slain by the sword', which is repeated twelve times in these few verses.

Growing understanding

We also see here a movement towards the fuller understanding of life beyond death that emerges late in the Old Testament period. Earlier references to Sheol and the Pit seem not to make any differentiation between the positions of their occupants. Here, places of greater or lesser honour are indicated, although the basis for differentiation is un-clear. A few of the psalmists have a sense that their relationship with God is so real that it must surely survive even death, though what that may mean is not clear (for example, Psalm 49:15; 73:21–23). It is not until Daniel 12:1–3 that we find a clear picture of the resurrection of the dead, with rewards and punishment for the righteous and the wicked.

MEDITATION

In a well-known hymn, John Newton contrasts the transience
of human pomp and power with the 'lasting treasure'
that results from serving God obediently:

'Saviour, since of Zion's city I through grace a member am,
let the world deride or pity, I will glory in your name:
fading is the worldling's pleasure, all his boasted pomp and show;
solid joys and lasting treasure none but Zion's children know.'

The PARABLE *of the* WATCHMAN

Ezekiel 33 marks the turning point in Ezekiel's ministry and in the structure of his book. With regard to the story of his ministry, this chapter takes us back to chapter 24, with the prophet struck dumb and awaiting news of the destruction of Jerusalem—a wait of some two years. The prophecies against the nations in chapters 25—32 provide a tension-filled interlude. Some of them relate directly to this period, but their primary purpose within the book as we now have it is to encourage the reader to reflect more deeply on the destruction of Jerusalem and its wider implications for the nations around Israel. The 'storyline' is resumed in 33:21–22, but first there is a reflection on Ezekiel's role and ministry, which picks up some themes from the first part of the book.

The parable

In verses 1–9 the metaphor of a watchman, which was used in the account of Ezekiel's call and commissioning in 3:16–21, is expanded into a parable. The picture is of an ancient Near Eastern city with its surrounding fields and villages. The city is the safe stronghold for the surrounding area. In a time of crisis a watchman is appointed to stand at some high point on its ramparts to keep a lookout for any signs of trouble. When he sees danger on the horizon it is his responsibility to sound the alarm so that those outside the city have time to return to it and those within have time to prepare for battle. The parable stresses that it is the watchman's responsibility to sound the alarm, but it is the citizen's responsibility to listen and to take appropriate action.

In chapter 3 the metaphor of the watchman was presented as a personal message to the prophet. No doubt it was intended to encourage him to take his task seriously. The parable here, though, is to be made a public proclamation (vv. 2, 7), so shifting the emphasis more towards the responsibility of those who hear his message. One reason for this must be the destruction of Jerusalem. The parable is placed before the report of the arrival of the news, but if Ezekiel was silent between his wife's death and its arrival, the parable would not have been spoken in public until after the news came. One effect of the news, of course, was to vindicate the prophet for his four-and-a-half years or so of exposing the people's sins and proclaiming God's judgment. He had fulfilled his task as a watchman faithfully, although the Judeans had not listened and acted appropriately. In that sense the parable marks the close of one phase of his ministry. But it is only one phase. His ministry is not over. In verses 7–9 his commissioning as a watchman is repeated, not terminated. The people now face a new crisis. How are they going to respond to the devastating reality of the destruction of Jerusalem and the temple and the prospect of an indefinite period in exile in Babylon? Where are they going to find any hope for the future? God has more to say to his people, which is why Ezekiel's freedom to speak to them is going to return. Perhaps after the experience of the past they will now be more ready to listen and to act.

Individual and corporate responsibility

The parable brings into focus the issue of the balance between individual and corporate responsibility which extends across all forms of Christian ministry, whether ordained or non-ordained. Each of us is responsible to God only for our own actions and the fulfilment of our own responsibilities. However, because these actions and responsibilities inevitably affect the lives of other people to some extent, individual responsibility always has a corporate dimension. It is this that makes the responsibility of ministry in any form so awesome. It is one thing to know that you stand or fall by your own actions; it is quite another to know that others may stand or fall by those same actions. But while we must take this seriously, the parable reminds us that we must not take it too far. Those whom we serve by our ministry are responsible for how they receive and respond to it.

PRAYER

Think of two or three people you know who have some form of Christian ministry. Pray that they will be able to keep the right balance between taking their responsibility seriously and being wrongly burdened or discouraged by people's responses.

The MESSAGE of the WATCHMAN

Some of the exiles in Babylon seem to have responded to the news of Jerusalem's destruction with despair (v. 10). Since the news vindicated Ezekiel's prophecies of judgment on Judah, it vindicated the basis on which they were made—the sinfulness of the nation. At least the people were now recognizing the true root of their problem. But if what had happened was indeed God's judgment on them, did that mean that God had now given up on them? Was the nation as good as dead, never to live again?

Hope for the wicked

The prophet's answer is to some extent a briefer version of the lengthy argument set out in chapter 18. The first thing the prophet makes clear is that God does not desire the death of anyone, not even the wicked. Therefore, there is always hope for the wicked if they are willing to turn their backs on their wicked ways and seek God (v. 11). Ezekiel then states a general principle—that the possibility of 'turning', of redirecting one's life, is always open. There is no accumulation of good deeds on which someone can rely if they decide to turn and do evil, and there is no accumulation of sin that will be held against someone who turns from evil to do good (v. 12).

This statement is expanded in a more concrete form in verses 13–16 with two brief 'case studies'. Although they are presented as two matching cases, the length of the second shows that the prophet's main concern is to drive home the truth that there is real hope for the wicked. That is the message relevant to the situation of his hearers. The prophet is saying that neither God's salvation nor his judgment is an automatic process that operates regardless of human actions. God responds to actual human behaviour. What matters is the present orientation of one's life, which can be changed. So it is not too late to turn and be saved.

Ezekiel's hearers seem to find this message too good to be true. They claim that it is unjust, preferring a 'balance sheet' view of justice. There are two errors in this. The first is well expressed by the psalmist: 'Do not enter into judgment with your servant; for no one living is righteous before you' (Psalm 143:2)—or, as the apostle Paul put it, 'All have sinned and fall short of the glory of God' (Romans 3:23). If one wants to talk about 'balance sheets', the standard set by the holy God is not 51 per cent on the 'good' side of the ledger but 100 per cent. The second error is related to the first. It is that God's concern is not with an abstract administration of justice, but that people should live in a right relationship with him and with one another. To make this possible, strict justice has to be tempered with mercy. Because no one who turns to God is perfect, that relationship has to begin on the basis of forgiveness, not of credit balances. A true 'turning' to God includes a recognition of one's sinfulness and therefore of the need for forgiveness. God's declared willingness to accept those who turn to him, to forgive, is the only ground of hope for the future.

Rebirth

It was the ground of hope for the individual Judean exile, but it was also the ground of hope for the rebirth of the nation. As long as Jerusalem remained unconquered, the Judeans, whether in Judah or in exile, assumed that the future of the nation rested with those in Judah. With the city destroyed, the temple a ruin and the king in chains in Babylon, what was to be the basis on which the nation could be re-established? With whom did its future lie? The implication of this message from the watchman is that it lay with those who, recognizing their wickedness and that of the nation, made the decision to turn from their past ways, back to their God.

The message that Ezekiel brought to his compatriots is one that brings hope to God's people whenever they find themselves in a situation where past failure tempts them to despair. A genuine turning back to God to receive his forgiveness opens up a new future through a restored relationship with him.

MEDITATION

'If anyone is in Christ, there is a new creation: everything old has passed away; see, everything has become new!'

2 Corinthians 5:17

The FALL *of* JERUSALEM

The account of the arrival of the news of the fall of Jerusalem makes a clear link back to Ezekiel 24:25–27, where the arrival of the news is foreshadowed. The messenger is described by a Hebrew word meaning 'a survivor'. Elsewhere in Ezekiel it refers to a deportee (6:8–10; 14:22), and that is probably what it means here. It is unlikely that a stray fugitive would head for Babylon, the home of their conquerors, several months' travel away over some difficult territory.

The date given in the text corresponds to mid-January 585BC. Since it is difficult to understand why news of the disaster should take some 17 months to reach the exiles, most commentators assume that a small copying error has occurred and emend the text to read 'the eleventh year' instead of the 'the twelfth year'. Since it took Ezra four months to travel from Babylon to Jerusalem (Ezra 7:9; 8:31), this gives a reasonable time lapse of about five months between the event and the news reaching Ezekiel.

With the arrival of the news, Ezekiel's dumbness, whatever its nature and its length, came to an end (v. 22), as predicted at the beginning of the siege (24:27). This symbolically marks a new beginning, both for his ministry and for his hearers, which raises the question, 'Are they ready for it?' It is evidence of the people's stubbornness, their unwillingness to accept what they find unpalatable, that the prophet has to begin the new phase of his ministry in the same vein as the previous one—dispelling false hopes and calling for obedient acceptance of God's word.

Land-grabbing

The first oracle (vv. 23–29) is addressed to those left in the devastated land of Judah. After the first deportation, some of those who remained had taken over land owned by the deportees, arguing that in effect the exiles had been expelled from God's people and so had forfeited the right to the land (11:15). A similar land-grabbing took place after the second deportation. The justification given for it is not absolutely clear (v. 24). It is probably more than simply an argument about the weight of numbers: 'If Abraham could do it on his own, how much more can we who are many.' Some theological basis seems to be needed. Isaiah 51:2 provides a clue: 'Look to Abraham your father and to Sarah who bore you; for he was but one when I called him, but I blessed him and made him many.' Those who appealed to Abraham were claiming that as 'the many' left in the land, they were the ones inheriting the blessing and so were the rightful owners of the land. This land-grabbing, and the attitude that went with it, was a source of tension and trouble decades later when the exiles began to return to Judah. Ezekiel's response is to declare that those appealing to the promise to Abraham had no right to do so. He was a righteous person, and they are not. Ezekiel describes them, in somewhat stereotypical terms, as violators of both the ritual and the moral demands of the covenant (vv. 25–26). As a result, they will continue to experience the three classic forms of the covenant curses, to which he has referred in several of his earlier oracles of judgment—the sword, wild animals and disease (v. 27). The land will become truly desolate (vv. 28–29).

Hearing and doing

The fall of Jerusalem vindicated Ezekiel's earlier prophecies and so it is not surprising that his fellow exiles flocked to hear what he had to say once his dumbness ended. However, God warns him not to be taken in by this new popularity (vv. 30–33). They are treating him as an entertainer, like a singer of love songs. Just as listening to love songs does not necessarily lead people to behave in a loving way, so they will not necessarily heed what he says and act accordingly. This is where the message of the parable of the watchman fits in, with its vitally important reminder of the responsibility that lies with the hearers of the prophet's words. The same responsibility faces us as we read the Bible. 'But be doers of the word, and not merely hearers who deceive themselves… those who look into the perfect law, the law of liberty, and persevere, being not hearers who forget but doers who act—they will be blessed in their doing' (James 1:22, 25).

PRAYER

Land ownership is again a cause of terror in the Middle East. Palestinians see Israeli settlers as 'land-grabbers'. The Israelis believe that the land is rightfully theirs. Pray for those who are trying to find a just and reasonable solution to this problem.

The DELINQUENT SHEPHERDS

This chapter contains a collection of oracles introduced by the formula 'Thus says the Lord God' (vv. 2, 10, 11, 17, 20) and united by the theme of shepherding. In the ancient Near East, shepherding was a well-established metaphor for governing a people. In the third millennium BC the Sumerians applied it to both kings and gods, and it appears quite often in royal inscriptions. For the Israelites, it gained added significance from the fact that their greatest king, David, was originally a shepherd.

Failed shepherds

Ezekiel's first two oracles (vv. 2–10) are addressed to 'the shepherds of Israel', meaning the kings who ruled throughout the history of the kingdoms of Israel and Judah, but perhaps having in mind particularly the later kings of Judah. Shepherds ought to care for their flock by protecting it from danger outside and from divisions within, by leading it to good pasture and clean water, and taking special care of those weakened by illness or injury. The shepherds of Israel are condemned for failing in their duty. They have exploited the sheep for their own ends. Instead of feeding the sheep, they have eaten them. Instead of caring for them, they have clothed themselves in their skins. As a result, the flock has been scattered and has become the prey of wild animals. These retrospective oracles make clear that the rulers of Judah bore considerable responsibility for the downfall of the nation and the exile.

God as shepherd

The oracle in verses 11–16 shifts the perspective to the future. Theologically the true king of Israel had always been God. The earthly kings ruled in his name as his representatives. That is why the metaphor of shepherd is applied appropriately to God in Psalm 23. God now vows to search for his scattered sheep himself and to bring them back to 'the mountains of Israel' (vv. 13–14). There they will be safe and find rich pasture and ample water. God will care for the injured and the weak. Translations differ over whether he will 'watch over' or 'destroy' the fat and the strong (v. 16). The Hebrew text says 'destroy' but only a slight emendment changes it to 'watch over'. In either case, taken with the final statement, 'I will feed them with justice', the idea seems to be that God will look after the interests of the weak against the strong.

Leaders as shepherds

In the New Testament the metaphor of the shepherd is taken up and applied to church leaders. Peter is charged by Jesus to 'feed my lambs' and 'tend my sheep' (John 21:15–17). In the first letter of Peter, church elders are exhorted to 'tend the flock of God that is in your charge' willingly and eagerly, without looking for 'sordid gain'. They are to be good examples to the flock, remembering that they are answerable to 'the chief shepherd' (1 Peter 5:1–4). This metaphor, drawn from an agricultural society, might seem out of place in modern urban and industrial society. Indeed in some churches it is being pushed out in favour of other models of church leadership, such as manager or team leader. There is a danger, as one writer (Leith Anderson) puts it, of a shift towards regarding church leaders as 'ranchers' overseeing a sheep-producing enterprise rather than as 'shepherds' caring for the sheep. It is a danger because the element of personal care inherent in the shepherd metaphor is an essential component of the biblical concept of leadership. This has made its mark on the secular world as well as the Church. In all kinds of secular organizations from schools to big businesses, there is recognition of the need for 'pastoral care', even if the root of this term in the shepherd metaphor has been forgotten. Leadership that lacks any pastoral dimension soon becomes impersonal, and risks becoming dehumanizing for those under it. Perhaps there is a particular danger that political leaders will see themselves as 'ranchers' rather than 'shepherds'. This is why they ought to keep closely in touch with the needs of those who elected them.

The statement by God, 'I myself will be the shepherd of my sheep' (v. 15), marks an important change in Ezekiel's oracles. Up until now God has appeared in his oracles primarily in the role of judge and executioner. The pastoral metaphor presupposes God's love and care for his people. With it the future begins to look brighter.

PRAYER

In 1 Timothy 2:2 we are urged to pray for 'kings and all who are in high positions, so that we may lead a quiet and peaceable life in all godliness and dignity'. If you don't do so already, pray regularly for those leaders, both secular and Christian, who affect your life.

The GOOD SHEPHERD

Having addressed the shepherds, God now addresses the flock. Although the rulers bore a heavy responsibility for the disaster that had overtaken the nation, the people themselves were not free from blame. In the pastoral metaphor the stronger animals are condemned on two counts. Firstly, they have used their strength to push other animals aside and get to the best pasture and water first (v. 18). This selfish behaviour is compounded by the second thing for which they are condemned. They have trampled down the uneaten grass so that it is inedible, and they have stirred up the mud in the water after they have drunk from it, so that it is unfit to drink (vv. 18–19). The background to this is no doubt the behaviour of the wealthier and more powerful members of the community before the exile, but it has obvious relevance to the land-grabbing that went on in Judah after the fall of Jerusalem. God declares that he will judge between the powerful and the weak, and protect the weak.

Tender but tough

Pictures of shepherds usually put the emphasis on the tenderness involved in caring for the flock—rescuing a stray sheep from a perilous situation, carrying an injured animal in his arms, bottle-feeding a newborn lamb. However, a shepherd needs toughness too, both to protect the sheep from wild animals and to protect the weak in the flock from the strong. The apostle Paul made this point to the elders of the Ephesian church, warning them that 'savage wolves will come in among you, not sparing the flock. Some even from your own group will come distorting the truth in order to entice the disciples to follow them' (Acts 20:29–30).

'My servant David'

The need for justice and protection leads to God's announcement that he will set over his flock 'my servant David' as their shepherd (v. 23). This is a re-affirmation of the Davidic covenant. The covenant might have been thought to have lapsed when Jerusalem fell and King Zedekiah was taken into captivity. However, the author of the book of Kings clearly found a basis of hope in the fact that King Jehoiachin was freed from prison in Babylon in 561BC (2 Kings 25:27–30). The Davidic line could continue through him. This oracle in Ezekiel is very general and non-specific, but it gives assurance that God has not forgotten his promise to David and it promises that the nation still has a future. There are some interesting nuances in verse 24. It is made clear that the Davidic shepherd is God's servant. He is called a 'prince', not 'king', and he is a prince 'among' the people. All this is surely meant to safeguard God's role as the chief shepherd, the real king.

The final section (vv. 25–31) paints a picture of a world in which God's rule is truly established. It is closely related to the blessings of the covenant set out in Leviticus 26:3–13. There is freedom from wild animals, adequate rainfall (showers, not damaging storms), fruitfulness in the land, security and freedom from oppression. All this is summed up in the promise of 'a covenant of peace' (v. 25). In the Old Testament, peace is not just the absence of hostility. It stands for a positive state of order and harmony, based on justice.

The good shepherd

The metaphor of God as the good shepherd is carried over into the New Testament. It lies behind Jesus' parable of the lost sheep (Luke 15:3–7), and we find Jesus sending his disciples to 'the lost sheep of the house of Israel' (Matthew 10:6; 15:24). The good shepherd discourse in John 10:1–18 is clearly based on this chapter in Ezekiel, presenting Jesus as the one whom God has sent to gather together the scattered sheep. The implication is that he is the one who fulfils the promise about 'my servant David' and who inaugurates the covenant of peace. It also adds something not explicit in Ezekiel: the good shepherd lays down his life for the sheep. This idea, though, may be hinted at in the term 'servant', if it is linked with the figure of the suffering servant of the Lord in Isaiah 40—55.

MEDITATION

'They will hunger no more, and thirst no more; the sun will not strike them, nor any scorching heat; for the Lamb at the centre of the throne will be their shepherd, and he will guide them to springs of the water of life, and God will wipe away every tear from their eyes.'

Revelation 7:16–17

DESOLATION *for* MOUNT SEIR

At first sight, this oracle of judgment on the land of Edom seems out of place here. It would seem to belong better among the oracles against the foreign nations in chapters 25—32, which do in fact include a short oracle against Edom (25:12–14). However, on more careful consideration the reason for including the oracle among Ezekiel's prophecies of hope for the future becomes clear. The restoration of Israel after the disaster of 586BC would require a new leadership (most naturally thought of in terms of a restoration of the Davidic monarchy) and a return to the land. The question of the leadership has been dealt with in the previous chapter. Restoration to the land raises the practical problem that some of it has been occupied by other people, in particular the Edomites. It is this issue that is now addressed, and this is why the oracle against Mount Seir is paired with the one that follows it, addressed to 'the mountains of Israel'. Another reason why this oracle occurs here may be the words of the Edomites quoted in verse 10, which treat Israel and Judah as two distinct countries and territories. Although, following Solomon's death, the two nations (sometimes referred to as Israel and Judah, but quite often as Ephraim and Judah) were divided politically, in the Old Testament they are always regarded as a single entity theologically. Together they are God's covenant people Israel. Their reunification is the subject of the oracle in 37:15–28.

Edom and Israel

Mount Seir was the central mountain of the territory of Edom (see Genesis 36:8–9), and here it stands for the whole country. According to Genesis 36:9, the Edomites were the descendants of Esau, the twin brother of Jacob, who was the ancestor of the Israelites. The stories in Genesis 25:19–34 and 27:1–45 depict growing enmity between the brothers from the time they were in the womb. Although there was a reconciliation of sorts between them (Genesis 33:1–17), the relationship between the nations of Edom and Israel was not smooth. When the Israelites asked permission to pass through Edomite territory on the way to the promised land, they were refused it and opposed by an Edomite army (Numbers 20:14–21). Later David conquered Edom and garrisoned the land (2 Samuel 8:14). The Edomites eventually rebelled against King Jehoram of Judah and regained their independence (2 Kings 8:20). After the fall of Jerusalem, the land of Judah was in ruins and had no strong effective central government. The Edomites took advantage of this to break out of their homeland to the south-east of the Dead Sea and to take possession of land in southern Judah.

Enmity, anger and envy

The oracle against Mount Seir begins with a declaration of God's coming judgment upon the nation (vv. 1–4). Edom will become a desolate wasteland with its cities in ruins. Two reasons are given for this. The first is that the Edomites have 'cherished an ancient enmity' against the Israelites (v. 5). Even at the time of Israel's greatest need, they were motivated by their hatred and did nothing to help. Indeed the implication is that they joined the Babylonians in slaughtering some of the Judean population (v. 5). Having been guilty, either directly or by condoning it, of the slaughter of so many people, Edom will herself suffer the slaughter of much of her population. The second reason for judgment is the 'anger and envy' (v. 11) which led the Edomites to rejoice over the collapse of Judah because it gave them the opportunity to grab some of her land. Having rejoiced over the desolation of Judah, Edom will be desolated.

This oracle provides a concrete example of the importance of a principle that Jesus expresses in the Sermon on the Mount, when he says that anger is as serious as murder, and lust as serious as adultery (Matthew 5:21–28). Our inner thoughts and attitudes are as important as our outward deeds, because the one leads to the other. It was because they had 'cherished an ancient enmity' and its associated anger and envy that the Edomites responded as they did when disaster struck Judah. As a result, they faced God's judgment —and note how it is made clear that they will reap what they sowed.

MEDITATION

One way of avoiding behaviour like the Edomites' is to heed the following advice: 'Be angry but do not sin; do not let the sun go down on your anger' (Ephesians 4:26). Do you need to take this advice seriously?

HOPE *for the* MOUNTAINS *of* ISRAEL

This oracle is a counterpart to the previous one, as the reference to
Edom in verse 5 makes clear. The message of doom for Mount Seir is
the prelude to the message of hope for the mountains of Israel. This
oracle is also a counterpart to one addressed to the mountains of
Israel earlier in Ezekiel's ministry (6:1–7). In that prophecy Ezekiel
warned of the coming desolation of the mountains of Israel. Now he
sees beyond desolation to new hope for the land.

God's land

The oracle falls into two parts. The first (vv. 1–7) declares God's
coming judgment on the nations that have looked with glee on the
desolation of Judah and taken advantage of it. Only Edom is mentioned by name, but others acted in similar ways. The Philistines, for
example, took the opportunity to encroach on the western borders of
Judah. God gives two reasons for his wrath against these nations. One
is the insults and suffering that they have heaped on Judah (vv. 3, 4b,
6b). The other is that they have presumed to take for themselves land
that belonged to the Lord God ('my land', v. 5). From a theological
perspective the land of Israel never belonged to the Israelites, but to
their God, whose tenants they were. This is expressed in Leviticus
25:23: 'The land shall not be sold in perpetuity, for the land is mine;
with me you are but aliens and tenants.' The people were reminded
of this by the institution of the year of Jubilee, which is the subject of
Leviticus 25.

It was because the land was seen as the special possession of God,
given as a gift to Israel, that it had such significance for Ezekiel
and his contemporaries. The disaster of 586BC could be seen by the
surrounding nations as evidence of the weakness of Israel's God—
that he was unable to keep control of his land. No doubt some
Judeans were tempted to think like this too. Others may have con-
cluded that the loss of the land was evidence that God had given up
on them and driven them out, and that therefore they were no longer
God's covenant people. The possession and use of the land was a
central theme in the Sinai covenant. However, this oracle counters
both these conclusions. The promise of the visitation of God's wrath

on the nations because they have dared to take possession of 'my land' is an assertion that God is still in control of it and of who possesses it. The second part of the oracle (vv. 8–15), with its promise of the restoration of the Israelites to the land, addresses the second conclusion.

God's love

It is the second part of the oracle that is the counterpart to Ezekiel 6:1–7. The earlier prophecy was one of desolation and ruin; this one promises restoration and prosperity. This change of message has been made possible because God's judgment has fallen on Judah and some, at least, of the people have come to recognize that it was their rebellion and sinful ways that were the cause of it. Now God's grace and love will make a new beginning possible. The promise is addressed to 'the mountains', and the terms in which it is expressed carry a double echo. There are echoes of the creation story in the references to the land being tilled and fruitful and the people and animals multiplying. There are also echoes of the promise to Abraham in Genesis 12:1–3, that God would give him a land in which his descendants would grow numerous and that the nations would recognize that they were blessed by God. The 'double echo' reminds us that God's plan of salvation, initiated by the call of Abraham, is the restoration of his creation.

This oracle reminds us that God's purposes in creation and salvation give us hope in the possibility of restoration beyond the disasters which we may bring into our lives by our own sinfulness. For this to be so, we, like Ezekiel's hearers, must be ready to admit the justice of God's judgment and to accept that it is God's grace and love that give us a new start and hope for the future.

PRAYER

Lord, I thank you for your grace and love, expressed in your commitment to your purposes and your people despite our sinfulness, and for the hope that this gives in the midst of desolation.

A NEW HEART & SPIRIT

This section forms the core of Ezekiel's words of hope. It consists of four sections. The first (vv. 16–21) explains why the Israelites were cast out of the land. This is followed by a promise of restoration (vv. 22–32). Finally, there are two short oracles which enlarge upon the promise of return to the land, dealing with the rebuilding of the cities (vv. 33–36) and the repopulating of the land (vv. 37–38).

The purpose of Israel's existence

When Israel came into being as a covenant people at Sinai, God's purpose was that 'you shall be for me a priestly kingdom and a holy nation' (Exodus 19:6), which implies that the nation was both to protect God's holiness and to demonstrate it to other nations. Israel singularly failed to do this. Using language drawn from his priestly background, the prophet declares that the people have defiled the land that was intended to be holy. As in his earlier oracles, he sums up their sins as bloodshed (violence) and idolatry. God had to cast them out of the land because they had defiled it. However, this created a new affront to God. The very fact of their being in exile caused the nations to cast slurs not just on them but on their God, because he did not seem up to looking after his people. As a result, they had not only defiled the land, they had profaned his name.

The promise of restoration is a statement of God's answer to the problem of Israel's failure to live up to her purpose for existence. God will take the initiative and act, not because Israel deserves to be restored, but so that his holiness might be recognized and receive the respect due to it (vv. 22–23). There will be several stages to the restoration. God will gather the scattered exiles together and return them to the land (v. 24). He will forgive and remove their sins (v. 25: again Ezekiel uses priestly imagery). Then, in response to the possible objection that this is not enough since even after such forgiveness in the past the people have fallen back into sin, God promises a radical inward transformation of the people (vv. 26–28). To understand what this involves, we need to remember that in Hebrew thought, the heart is not the seat of the emotions (that is located in the 'bowels') but of the thinking, willing and decision-making processes. What is being promised here is a kind of 'mind transplant'. The people's whole attitude to God, themselves and life will be transformed. Along with this will go a new dynamic, a new power for living, expressed both in terms of a new (human) spirit and the giving of God's Spirit. As a result, the people will be able to live in obedience to God's laws in the promised land. God will restore the land so that it does provide for all their needs. Faced with this undeserved goodness of God towards them, the people will be humbled. They will recognize their past sinfulness and be ashamed of their failure to live up to their calling.

Renewal through Jesus

Jesus may well have had this passage of Ezekiel in mind when he spoke to Nicodemus of the need to be 'born of water and the Spirit' if one is to enter the kingdom of God (John 3:5). Christians see the ultimate fulfilment of Ezekiel's promise of forgiveness and renewal in the forgiveness of our sins through the sacrificial death of Jesus and the inner renewal that is brought about in us by the work of the Holy Spirit. The Christian's 'homeland', though, is not a geographical entity, but the fellowship of the Church.

God's holy name

God's concern for his 'holy name' above all else might seem strange to us. However, it becomes understandable when we realize that in the Old Testament, God's 'name' is the expression of God's personality, of who God is. God's 'holiness' stands for God's 'otherness'—all that makes him God and not a creature. So, if God were not concerned with preserving the 'holiness' of his 'great name', he would be encouraging or condoning idolatry, the human worship of something less than the true God. This is not only an affront to God, but is harmful for humans who were created in the image of God and only find their full humanness by living in a proper relationship to their Creator.

MEDITATION

Jesus taught us to pray 'Our Father in heaven, hallowed be your name'. How can you protect and demonstrate God's holiness by the way you live?

NEW LIFE *from* DRY BONES

In essence this vision repeats the message of the previous section, but it does so in a vivid and memorable way that makes it probably the best-known part of Ezekiel. It was a vivid experience for the prophet himself. It is one of four visionary experiences introduced by the phrase 'The hand of the Lord came upon me', which seem to have involved a sense of physical translocation (3:22; 8:1; 37:1; 40:1). On this occasion Ezekiel felt himself taken to a valley full of sun-bleached bones. Perhaps it was a battlefield on which the dead had been left unburied. His reply to the question, 'Mortal, can these bones live?' (v. 3) is ambiguous. Some commentators see it as a respectful way of saying, 'No, you know that they cannot.' Others take it as a recognition that although humanly speaking it is impossible, God's power is unlimited. Whatever the prophet's thoughts or feelings about the matter, he obeys God's command to prophesy to the dry bones (v. 7). Amazingly, the bones come together to form skeletons, and then sinews and flesh cover the skeletons. The result is a multitude of lifeless corpses, like an army that has been struck down by some mysterious force. The prophet is then commanded to prophesy to the wind or breath (it is the same word in Hebrew) to come and give life to these corpses (v. 9). The result is a vast army of living people.

We saw that there were echoes of the creation story in Ezekiel 36:1–15. There is another echo of it in this vision. The two-stage process by which these bones are turned into an army of living beings is reminiscent of God forming Adam out of the dust of the ground and then breathing into him the breath of life (Genesis 2:7).

A resurrected nation

Although this is one of the best-known passages of Ezekiel, it is often misunderstood. From early Christian times, both Christian and rabbinical commentators have tended to read it in terms of the bodily resurrection. We have seen earlier in Ezekiel, especially in 32:17–32, that at this period the people viewed life after death only as a shadowy existence in Sheol. There is no hint of belief in resurrection until later in the Old Testament, in Daniel 12:1–3. Also, here Ezekiel is given an explanation of the vision (vv. 11–14) which clearly applies it to the restoration of the nation of Israel, not to the resurrection of individuals after death. The vision was given in response to the exiles' complaint that they were like dried-up bones, helpless and hopeless (v. 11). As the message of the vision is applied to this sense of despair, the imagery changes from that of a deserted battlefield to that of a graveyard (vv. 12–13). This intensifies the message. The exiles might feel that the nation is as good as 'dead and buried', but God is going to restore it to life in its own land.

God's Spirit

A key term in this passage is the Hebrew word *ruach*. It occurs ten times, though this is obscured in English translations because they represent different facets of its meaning by using the three words 'spirit', 'breath' and 'wind'. It is the 'spirit' of the Lord that transports Ezekiel to the death valley of his vision (v. 1). He is commanded to prophesy so that the life-giving 'breath' will come from the four 'winds' (v. 9). In the explanation of the vision, we are told that it is because God will put his 'spirit' in the people that the nation will be restored (v. 14). Once again, as in all the oracles of hope and restoration, the emphasis is on God's initiative and God's power, apart from which there is no realistic hope.

In the New Testament, this hope is both universalized and individualized by the bodily resurrection of Jesus from the dead. As the apostle Paul puts it, 'If the Spirit of him who raised Jesus from the dead dwells in you, he who raised Christ from the dead will give life to your mortal bodies also through his Spirit that dwells in you' (Romans 8:11). This promise is available to everyone, not just the Judean exiles, and it is a promise of bodily resurrection for individuals, not just a picture of a restored nation.

PRAYER

Lord God, thank you for raising Jesus from the dust of death and breathing new life into the graveyard of this world. Help me to live out this newness of life day by day.

REUNIFICATION

This passage, which concludes the section of prophecies concerning Israel's new future, asserts the unity of Israel as God's people (vv. 15–23) and sees it in terms of Israel as one nation under a single Davidic ruler (vv. 24–28).

A prophetic action

Once again the prophet begins by acting out the message. He takes two sticks and inscribes names on them (v. 16). One represents the southern kingdom of Judah (which included the tribe of Benjamin, 1 Kings 12:21) and the other the northern kingdom, which is referred to in the Old Testament by various names. Here it is given the name 'Joseph'. The two tribes named after Joseph's sons, Ephraim and Manasseh, settled in the central hill-country of Canaan (some of Manasseh remained east of the Jordan) and became the dominant tribes in the northern kingdom. Of these two tribes, Ephraim was the stronger, and the northern kingdom is often called 'Ephraim'.

Ezekiel takes the two sticks and holds them together in his hand, concealing the join between them, so that they appear to be one stick. When the people ask what this means, he replies with an oracle declaring that God is going to gather the people of Israel from among the nations and make them one nation again in their own land, under one king. Moreover, God will cleanse them of their sins, particularly idolatry, so that they are again united in worshipping one God.

Historically, after settling in Canaan, Israel was a fully unified entity for only a short period under David and Solomon (the figures in 1 Kings 2:11 and 11:42 make it 73 years). The northern kingdom was destroyed by the Assyrians in 722BC, nearly a century and a half before Ezekiel's prophecy. For this reason, Ezekiel's hearers, concerned as they were with their own fate and that of Judah, may well have been somewhat surprised by the message. However, the theological reality of Israel as a single covenant people of God is pervasive in the Old Testament, not least in the prophets (for example, Hosea 1:11; Isaiah 11:12–13; Jeremiah 3:18). Ezekiel himself never loses sight of it: it is clear in his historical surveys in chapters 16 and 20.

As we shall see, this unity is an important element of Israel's witness to the nations.

A visionary statement

The concluding section (vv. 24–28) draws together all the themes of chapters 34—37: a restored people living in the promised land under a single Davidic king and bound to God by an everlasting covenant, with a new temple as the symbol of God's presence among them. Israel will then be the witness that she should be to the nations. As well as drawing these themes together, the closing verses of this oracle prepare the way for the great vision of the restored land centred around the new temple in chapters 40—48.

Even in Ezekiel's day it must have been hard to know how to understand this oracle. The northern kingdom was long gone and most of its inhabitants had probably become absorbed into other cultures. How could both Joseph and Judah be restored to the land and reunited? Probably the prophecy was never intended to be taken literally. It is a visionary statement about the eventual coming to fruition of God's purposes, and an assurance that all God's people will somehow have a part in this.

For the Christian, this purpose is now seen to include the people of the new covenant established by the sacrificial death of Jesus (Hebrews 9:15). Jesus proclaimed the coming of the kingdom of God (Mark 1:15), with himself as the Messiah (Mark 8:29) descended from David (Mark 11:9–10). The unity of the Church is something for which Jesus prayed, seeing it as an important aspect of the Church's witness to him and his mission (John 17:21–23). Although the Church has failed in this as sadly as Israel did in the Old Testament, we should not accept that failure with resignation. Ezekiel's vision of the reunification of the people of God as something that God intends to achieve should give us the hope and motivation to go on praying and working for it to become a reality.

PRAYER

Lord God, make the vision you gave to Ezekiel a reality.
Make your divided people one in your hand, united under the
lordship of your Son, so that your loving purpose for the world
to know you, the one true God, and him whom you sent,
Jesus Christ, might be fulfilled.

PROPHECIES CONCERNING GOG

Ezekiel 38—39 is among the most difficult and most contested parts of the book. Opinions are divided about the origin and purpose of these chapters. Numerous suggestions have been put forward as to who 'Gog of the land of Magog' might be. We do not have space here to survey all the different opinions, and so I shall tentatively put forward one approach to understanding these chapters.

A coherent narrative

The chapters are made up of seven sayings, each introduced by the formula, 'Thus says the Lord God' (38:1–9, 10–13, 14–16, 17–23; 39:1–16, 17–24, 25–29). These are not independent oracles put together haphazardly. There is a coherent narrative:

* An enemy will attack the land of Israel from the north.
* The invasion will lead to a final war in which God fights for Israel.
* This conflict will be accompanied by earthquakes and other convulsions.
* Following the enemy's defeat, their weapons will be burned as fuel.
* There will be a great sacrificial banquet.

Each element of this narrative can be found in the writings of other prophets, as 38:17 suggests, but here they are put together in a particular way.

It seems strange that this narrative should come after the oracles of hope and restoration of chapters 34—37. In some ways it would seem to fit better after the oracles against the nations, as a prelude to the oracles of hope. However, what is said of Gog and his allies in verses 1–6 may give the clue to the purpose of the narrative and why it occurs here in the book of Ezekiel.

A symbolic narrative

None of the attempts to identify Gog with a particular historical figure are convincing, nor are the attempts to identify 'the land of Magog'. It is just possible that the words which the NRSV translates as 'chief prince' (v. 2) could mean 'prince of Ros', but there is no mention elsewhere in the Bible of a place called 'Ros'. The suggestion that it refers to Russia has no basis in Hebrew ('Russia' seems to be derived from a Norse word). If Gog is 'chief prince' of Meshech and Tubal, he is the leader of a group of seven nations (surely a significant number), since five others are mentioned in verses 5–6. All of these names, except Persia, are found in the 'table of the nations' in Genesis 10, and most have been mentioned earlier in Ezekiel, in the oracles against the nations. The geographical spread of these countries is significant. Meshech, Tubal and Gomer are located in Asia Minor, to the north-west of Israel. Beth-togarmah is usually placed in the foothills of the Caucasus, to the north-east. Persia lies to the east and Ethiopia (Cush in Hebrew) to the south. Put refers to an area in north Africa to the south-west of Israel. Therefore, these seven nations can be seen as forming a ring around Israel, more or less on the horizon of the known world. So what we have in these chapters is probably an archetypal, symbolic depiction of the opposition of the nations to God's people. However, the nations are entirely under God's control (v. 4) and their defeat, which is due to his intervention, will prove this fact to Israel and the nations (39:21–22).

Placed where they are, these chapters address any fears about Israel's safety following the restoration promised in chapters 34—37. They give the assurance that God is in control of history and that no one will be able to stop his people from having the future he has planned for them. This is not an open-ended guarantee that God will preserve any partic-ular political expression of his people: the Judean state that emerged after the return from exile was eventually brought to an end by the Romans in AD70. It is an assurance that God will preserve his people as an entity in whatever form he wants.

Romans 8:35–39 stands as a Christian counterpart to this assur-ance: 'Who will separate us from the love of Christ? Will hardship, or distress, or persecution, or famine, or nakedness, or peril, or sword? … No, in all these things we are more than conquerors through him who loved us. For I am convinced that neither death, nor life, nor angels, nor rulers, nor things present, nor things to come, nor powers, nor height, nor depth, nor anything else in all creation, will be able to separate us from the love of God in Christ Jesus our Lord.'

MEDITATION

What causes you to be anxious or fearful? Can you relate these worries to the catalogue that Paul gives in Romans 8:35–39? Then thank God that they cannot separate you from his love!

The INVASION *by* GOG

In the first of the oracles that form the account of Gog's invasion (vv. 10–13), he is depicted as making up his own mind to campaign against Israel. He is motivated by the country's defencelessness and prosperity. That it offers rich plunder is made clear by the chorus of nations on the sidelines. Their rhetorical questions addressed to Gog (v. 13) seem to express a desire to share in the anticipated loot.

The second oracle (vv. 14–16) presents Gog's decision in a different light. As Gog and his associated hordes mount their campaign, advancing from the north, they might think that they are simply carrying out their own plans. However, in reality they are carrying out God's plan (v. 16). It is all happening in order to establish his holiness in the eyes of all the nations.

A difficult question

The meaning and significance of verse 17 is much debated. Two issues are involved. First, many scholars think it implies that the days of the great prophets lie some way in the past, and that this oracle is a later addition to the collection. This is possible. However, several of the prophets, from Amos in the mid-eighth century to Jeremiah in the late seventh century, warned of an invasion from the north as one form that God's punishment would take, so it would not be out of place for Ezekiel to refer to such a prophecy as being made in 'former days'. Second, does the question expect an answer 'Yes' or 'No'? Although many scholars assume that the answer intended is 'Yes', this is problematic. After all, the enemy spoken of in the earlier prophecies was an agent of God's judgment on his people. This is not so with Gog. Moreover, those prophecies were fulfilled by the Assyrians' destruction of the northern kingdom of Israel and the Babylonians' destruction of Judah. So it seems that the answer should be 'No'. But then, why ask the question? There is no hint that Gog sees himself as God's agent of judgment.

A significant question

The significance of the question is that it highlights the difference between the situation addressed by the former prophets and the one envisaged here. In the past, Israel and Judah had relied wrongly on God to deliver them from their enemies. They had presumed on the covenant relationship even though they were flouting the covenant laws. They had a false sense of security. Now, however, as a purified, forgiven and restored nation, Israel truly is secure (vv. 11, 14) even though, physically speaking, she seems defenceless. She is secure because her relationship with God is right. Her deliverance by God from this great horde will demonstrate God's greatness to all the nations.

The contrast between 'then' and 'now' is also made by the reference to Israel living 'at the centre (literally, 'navel') of the world' (v. 12b). This echoes Ezekiel 5:5. The earlier passage emphasizes Israel's failure to be a positive witness to the nations in the centre of whom she has been placed. Now, however, her central position means that the deliverance will be seen by all as a witness to God's power.

A cosmic battle

The third oracle (vv. 17–23) describes the defeat of Gog's army. This is clearly due to an act of God, not human action. The forces of nature are turned against Gog—earthquake, plague, storm and volcanic activity. These forces inspire such panic among Gog's hordes that they turn their weapons on one another. The language and imagery here are reminiscent of the old stories of the 'wars of the Lord' (for example, Judges 5:20–21; 7:22; 1 Samuel 14:20), and this is a clue to the meaning of this prophecy.

Israel always believed that her God was supreme and that one day his rule of justice and peace would be established over all nations. Psalm 46:8–11 expresses this belief. However, Israel's history showed that opposition to God is not easily overcome. There is a battle going on between the forces of good and evil which is not limited to the plane of human history—it has another dimension. In the end there must be a final 'cosmic battle' to destroy evil and establish God's rule over all. In the New Testament, Ezekiel's 'last battle' is seen as the final event of a campaign in which the crucial victory is won at the cross (Colossians 2:13–15).

PRAYER

Lord God, hasten the day when we can say, 'The kingdom of the world has become the kingdom of our Lord and of his Messiah' (Revelation 11:15).

The DESTRUCTION of GOG

This chapter begins with a reminder that, far from being the master of his own destiny, Gog has been a puppet in the hands of God. It was God who brought him out from the north and led him to destruction upon the mountains of Israel (vv. 1–6). There is some repetition here of what has been said in chapter 38, but a note is added that Gog's homeland, Magog, and those of his allies will suffer the fire of God's wrath. The destruction of Gog is the ultimate, longed-for vindication of God's holy name (vv. 7–8).

An end to all war

Although the story of Israel is filled with war and bloodshed, it is worth noting that war is not glorified in the Old Testament. Indeed there is a longing for the day when there will be no more war.

> *For all the boots of the tramping warriors*
> *and all the garments rolled in blood*
> *shall be burned as fuel for the fire.*
> *For a child has been born for us, a son given to us;*
> *authority rests upon his shoulders; and he is named*
> *Wonderful Counsellor, Mighty God,*
> *Everlasting Father, Prince of Peace.* (Isaiah 9:5–6)

> *They shall beat their swords into ploughshares,*
> *and their spears into pruning hooks;*
> *nation shall not lift up sword against nation,*
> *neither shall they learn war any more.* (Micah 4:3)

> *Come, behold the works of the Lord;*
> *see what desolations he has brought on the earth.*
> *He makes wars cease to the end of the earth;*
> *he breaks the bow, and shatters the spear;*
> *he burns the shields with fire.* (Psalm 46:8–9)

Ezekiel's prophecy is a particularly vivid way of expressing that hope.
The victory is totally God's. Israel appears on the scene simply to despoil the despoilers (vv. 9–10) and to bury their corpses

(vv. 11–16). The magnitude of the victory is expressed by the amount of weaponry recovered (seven years' worth of fuel), the time taken to bury the dead (seven months) and the fact that the buried corpses block a whole valley. Great care is taken to bury all the remains of the horde in order to purify the land. The summons to the birds and the animals to feast on the corpses (vv. 17–20) does not follow on chronologically from verses 1–16 but expands on the note in verses 4b–5 that Gog's army will fall in the open field and be the prey of carrion eaters.

An end to all evil

The destruction of Gog is like the final act of a play that makes sense of the whole drama. The demonstration of God's power will prove that Israel went into captivity as an act of judgment on their sin, not because their God could not defend them (vv. 21–24).

Down the centuries, some Christians have tried to identify Gog with specific foes: the Goths in the fourth century, the Arab armies in the seventh century, the Mongols in the thirteenth century and the Russians in the twentieth, to name only a selection. These interpretations were mistaken in seeing Ezekiel 38—39 as a coded message for those living in 'the last days' (a phrase not used in these chapters). They were right, however, in finding in these chapters a word of encouragement for God's people when they are faced with overwhelming forces of evil. Ezekiel's vision expresses the conviction that, even then, God is in control. His purposes will eventually triumph. This will mean the ultimate destruction of all that is evil and will result in the ultimate security of those who trust in him.

The last paragraph (vv. 25–29) is a summary of the message of chapters 34—39 and not of chapters 38—39 alone. It repeats the promise of restoration and forgiveness and a secure existence in their land. Most important of all is the promise of a new relationship with God: 'I will never again hide my face from them, when I pour out my spirit upon the house of Israel, says the Lord God.'

PRAYER

O God, we live in a world that is still torn apart by war.
We pray that you will give success to those who work for peace,
so that wars may come to an end. We ask this in the name of
the Prince of Peace, our Lord Jesus Christ.

A VISION *of the* FUTURE

In Ezekiel 40—48 the prophet describes a long and detailed vision of
the restored Israel. A heavenly being takes him on a guided tour
of the temple. He is given detailed instructions for the temple personnel, the offerings and the religious festivals. He is also given
instructions for 'the prince', the ruler of the land. There is a description of the river of life flowing from the temple. The vision ends with
details of the tribal territories and the new Jerusalem. Although the
vision is a self-contained unit, it is also an integral part of the book
of Ezekiel. It forms a counterpart to the vision of the temple in
Jerusalem reported in chapters 8—11. In particular, the departure of
God's glory from the temple and city, reported in 11:22–23, is
matched by the report of its return in 43:1–5.

Four different interpretations

Traditionally, four main views have been held about the interpretation
of the vision.

The *literal prophetic* interpretation sees the vision as a blueprint for
what should be done when the exiles return to Judah. This could be
applied to the vision of the temple itself, although a good deal of
imagination would need to be applied to the description given in
order to build an actual structure along the lines indicated. However,
the impracticality of the siting (on a very high mountain, v. 2), the
unreality of the tribal boundaries and the impossible source and
course of the river of life all stand against such a literal interpretation.

The *literal futurist* view has been popularized by the Scofield
Reference Bible, which takes the vision to refer to a rebuilding of the
temple and re-establishment of the priesthood and sacrifices in 'the
last days'. The indications of a non-literal meaning listed above mili-
tate against this view too, unless one envisages a miraculous reorder-
ing of the geography of Palestine. Also, from a Christian perspective,
it is hard to understand the re-establishment of the temple and its
worship after the atoning work of Christ on the cross, which the
writer of Hebrews sees as having fulfilled, and so made obsolete, the
Old Testament pattern of worship.

The *symbolic Christian* interpretation holds that the vision has its fulfilment symbolically in the Christian Church. Temple imagery is certainly used of the Church in the New Testament (for example, 1 Corinthians 3:16; 1 Peter 2:5). However, it cannot be said that Ezekiel had this consciously in mind, and, while the temple is central to his vision, it is part of a larger vision of the restored land and nation that is not readily amenable to a symbolic Christian interpretation.

The *symbolic apocalyptic* view sees in Ezekiel, and especially in these chapters, a movement from classical Hebrew prophecy towards what is called 'apocalyptic'. One of the common features of apocalyptic literature is the description of visionary experiences, often including an 'interpreting angel'. The visions are full of symbolic imagery, which is not meant to be taken literally. There is often a symbolic use of numbers, and it is notable how many of the numbers in Ezekiel 40 to 48 are multiples of five.

A symbolic apocalyptic vision

In what follows, we shall basically follow the symbolic apocalyptic approach. The double dating of the vision echoes the double dating at the beginning of the book, and may explain the significance of the number five in the vision. The 25th year of Ezekiel's exile (v. 1) corresponds to 573BC, and this fits with its being 14 years after the destruction of Jerusalem and the temple. The significance in the figure of 25 (5 x 5) years may well be that it is half of a jubilee period. The year of jubilee was the year of release from slavery and debt and the time when ancestral land was returned to its owners. It came after seven cycles of sabbatical years, that is after 7 x 7 years, and so was the 50th (5 x 10) year. As halfway to a jubilee, the 25th year could be seen as marking a turning point in the fortunes of the exiled community. In addition, the tenth day of the first month lies in the period of preparation for the Passover, the festival celebrating the end of the Hebrews' enslavement in Egypt. So, the dating suggests that this is a vision about a new future for God's people once they have been freed from the oppression of evil.

MEDITATION

By faith, Abraham 'looked forward to the city that has
foundations, whose architect and builder is God' (Hebrews 11:10).
Do you share that vision?

The OUTER COURT

Ezekiel is taken on a tour of the temple by a heavenly guide carrying a measuring rod, six cubits (about three metres) long, and a linen cord (40:3). The cord was probably marked off in rod lengths for making the longer measurements. The presence of the guide is an indication that this is a vision of heavenly realities that a human mind cannot grasp properly on its own.

Details of the outer court

The detailed measurements may make the description of the outer court confusing. The purpose of the detail is to make the point that this is a carefully planned and well-proportioned structure (note the frequency of measurements of 5, 10, 25, 50 and 100 cubits). Putting the detail to one side, the overall picture is clear. The whole temple area was enclosed in a massive wall about six cubits thick and six cubits high (v. 5). There were three gates, one each in the middle of the east, north and south sides of the enclosure. The gates were identical in plan. Seven steps led up to the gate (v. 22). Within the gatehouse there was a passage flanked on each side by three guardrooms (vv. 7, 10, 'recesses') and leading to a vestibule. The pilasters (square columns projecting from the wall) flanking the exit from the vestibule into the outer court were decorated with palm trees (v. 26). Around the inside of the outer court wall there were thirty chambers (v. 17), presumably five on either side of each of the three gates.

In the ancient Near East, temples were usually built with the entrance to the sanctuary facing east. Ezekiel begins his tour by entering the east gate of the outer wall, and so would have been facing the front of the sanctuary. As we shall see, this was separated from the outer court by an inner court. The distance between the gate into the outer court and the gate into the inner court was one hundred cubits (v. 19).

Protecting God's holiness

The purpose of this concentric structure with its sizable courts as 'buffer zones', and the massive protecting wall with its impressive gates, is to make clear the holiness of God and also the importance of protecting it. This, of course, has been a theme throughout the book of Ezekiel. The reason the people were driven into exile was that they had polluted the land by bloodshed (violence) and idolatry. The vision of chapters 8—11 showed how this pollution had penetrated even the temple in Jerusalem, with the result that God's glory was withdrawn from it. In the new temple, the symbolism of the wall, the gates and the courts emphasizes that this must not be allowed to happen again.

Many Western people today find the idea of holy places, or sacred enclosures, rather strange. This is partly because 'holiness' has come to be understood primarily in terms of moral categories, and these are clearly not readily applicable to objects and places. However, in the Bible, in both Testaments, while holiness includes morality, its meaning is wider. It sums up all that makes God uniquely God. It is sometimes defined as the 'otherness' of God—what makes God different and separate from any other being. The spatial separation of the inner sanctuary of the temple, the 'holy of holies', from the 'ordinary world' outside was a way of impressing on people that God is different from human beings, and that Israel's God was different from other gods.

Of course there are dangers in this kind of 'physical' imagery of holiness. It can lead to a ritualistic view of holiness that divorces it from everyday life. On the other hand, the loss of the imagery, and the consequent narrowing of the understanding of holiness, can bring its own dangers. In 1 Corinthians 6:19 the apostle Paul uses temple imagery when appealing for sexual purity: 'Do you not know that your body is a temple of the Holy Spirit within you, which you have from God?' The power of this appeal rests partly on his readers' sense of a temple as a 'sacred space' which should not be violated by bringing into it anything that would profane it. Here the wider dimension of holiness supports the narrower, moral dimension. It is not surprising that when we lose the wider dimension, it becomes harder to hold on to the moral dimension. Perhaps even more importantly, we need to consider whether a narrowing of our concept of holiness diminishes our concept of God.

MEDITATION

Are there ways in which we can symbolize the 'otherness' of God appropriately in our churches today?

The INNER COURT

(*Refer to figure 1, page 230, while reading this section.*) Ezekiel enters the inner court by its southern gate. This court was on a higher level than the outer one, with eight steps up to the gate. No wall is mentioned and, although many commentators assume there was one, none may have been needed. Depending on the height of each step, the inner court was elevated by about one-and-a-half to three metres. This height difference would have made encroachment on it difficult other than through the gateways. The absence of a wall would have allowed people in the outer court to observe the offering of sacrifices within the inner court.

Details of the inner court

The gatehouses of the inner court are identical to those in the outer wall, except that the vestibule is on the outer end, facing the outer court (vv. 28–31). Measured from the inner threshold of the gates, the inner court is a square of one hundred cubits in size. This leaves a surround of fifty cubits (the depth of the gates). At least some of this space is taken up with chambers (vv. 44–47). Although the Hebrew text of verse 44a says, 'There were chambers for the singers', a small alteration in the Hebrew gives, 'There were two chambers', which is how the early Greek translators read it. This makes more sense in the light of what follows. By the north gate there were rooms for the priests responsible for the day-to-day running of the temple, and by the south gate there were rooms for the priests who officiated at the altar. Only priests descended from Zadok could officiate at the altar. Their status will be described further, later in these chapters. The altar itself was in the centre of the inner court, opposite the doors to the sanctuary.

In verses 38–43 there are details of the provisions for the slaughter of sacrificial animals and preparation of their flesh for presentation on the altar. These details are not absolutely clear. The implication is that all the slaughtering and preparation was done at the north gate. According to 46:2, the prince's offering was to be prepared at the east gate, but this may be a special case. The exact siting of the tables is uncertain. It is not clear from verses 40–42 whether they were all on one side or other of the vestibule, or whether some were inside it and others outside. There were twelve tables, eight used for slaughtering and preparing the sacrifices, and four holding the knives and other instruments required for this.

Sacrifice and worship

This description makes clear the importance of the sacrificial aspect of Israel's worship. Careful provision is made for it to be carried out properly in terms of equipment and specialized personnel. The place where the sacrifices take place is protected by the raised level of the inner court and its massive gates. The altar is placed before the entrance to the sanctuary. Only three offerings are explicitly mentioned—the burnt offering, the sin offering and the guilt offering (v. 39). The burnt offering was essentially an act of homage to God. The whole animal was burnt on the altar (Leviticus 1). The sin and guilt offerings were made in order to atone for inadvertent sins against God or humans (Leviticus 4—6). It is significant that before the exile, judging by the narratives in the Old Testament, the most usual offering was none of these, but 'the sacrifice of well-being' (Leviticus 3), which had a very different character. In this offering, part of the animal was burnt on the altar and the rest cooked and eaten by the worshippers and priests, presumably to signify, and to strengthen, fellowship between God and people. Following the experience of the exile, there was a much greater awareness of sin, the harm it does, and the need to deal with it effectively.

As the letter to the Hebrews points out, this sacrificial system was 'only a shadow of the good things to come' because 'it can never, by the same sacrifices that are continually offered year after year, make perfect those who approach' (Hebrews 10:1). What the sacrifices foreshadowed was what Jesus achieved: 'We have been sanctified through the offering of the body of Jesus Christ once for all... For by a single offering he has perfected for all time those who are sanctified' (Hebrews 10:10, 14).

PRAYER

Lord God, I thank you that Christ has done all that is
necessary for my salvation by giving himself as a sin offering.
Help me, in response, to live my life as an offering of
thanksgiving in his service.

The NEW TEMPLE

(*Refer to figure 2, page 231, while reading this section.*) Ezekiel is now taken to inspect the temple proper. It stands on a platform raised above the inner court. Like Solomon's temple, it has three rooms. First, there is a vestibule measuring twelve cubits by twenty cubits (40:48–49). This leads into an outer sanctuary or nave, measuring twenty cubits by forty cubits (41:1–2) and then the inner sanctuary, or 'most holy place', which is a square of twenty cubits (41:3–4). No height measurements are given. The increasing holiness of each space is indicated by the successively narrower entrances—fourteen, ten and six cubits respectively.

Ezekiel does not enter the 'most holy place'; his angelic guide enters it alone (vv. 3–4). In Solomon's temple, only the high priest could enter it, and then only once a year on the Day of Atonement.

The inside of all three rooms is panelled with wood, covered with carvings of palm trees and two-headed cherubim (vv. 15b–20). At the top of the walls there are windows in recessed frames. In front of the doors to the most holy place is a wooden structure which Ezekiel calls 'something resembling an altar' and which his guide calls 'the table that stands before the Lord' (vv. 21–22). This corresponds to the table on which 'the bread of the Presence' was placed in Solomon's temple (1 Kings 7:48).

Around the north, south and east sides of the temple are three storeys of rooms, thirty in each storey, reached by entrances on the north and south sides (v. 11) and stairways (v. 7). The side-walls of the temple are stepped so that the successive tiers of rooms can rest on them and not be actually attached to the walls (v. 6), which might be thought to violate the sanctity of the temple. Presumably these are storage rooms. At the back of the temple, on its west side, stands a large building, ninety by seventy cubits. Nothing is said of its purpose.

Significant measurements

The significance of the measurements given in verses 13–15a is that the temple proper, with its associated 'yard' or open area on either side, formed a one-hundred-cubit square, and the same is true of the large building to the west of it plus the 'yard' between it and the temple. In front of the temple there is the one-hundred-cubit square of the inner court. A concern for symmetry and precision is evident in the plan of the temple and its surrounds.

The transcendence of God

As well as the symbolism of increasing holiness as the most holy place is approached, there is another piece of symbolism in the structure of the layout of the temple and its courts. The approach to the temple involves an ascent—seven steps up to the gates of the outer court (40:22, 26), eight up to the gates of the inner court (40:31) and then ten up to the vestibule of the temple (40:49). It is probably no coincidence that the total number of steps from the 'outside world' to the temple is twenty-five. This 'going up' is a reminder of the transcendence of God, that God is not limited to this world. This is emphasized by the very location of the whole temple complex 'upon a very high mountain' (40:2). This description is not true of the physical Mount Zion, which is overlooked by the Mount of Olives. However, in the ancient Near East the gods were thought of as living on a very high mountain in the north. This is echoed in Psalm 48:2 when Mount Zion is described as 'beautiful in elevation... in the far north'. When speaking of the establishment of God's rule in 'the last days' the prophets speak of the temple, the symbol of God's presence on earth, as being 'established as the highest of the mountains' (Isaiah 2:2).

The geography and structure of the temple in Ezekiel's vision seeks to express the truth that God is indeed present in this world, and especially with his people. But at the same time it expresses the truth that God's presence is not something to be treated casually. This is both because God is holy and because God cannot be confined to this world, let alone any structure or community within it.

MEDITATION

'Will God indeed dwell on the earth? Even heaven and the highest heaven cannot contain you, much less this house that I have built.'

1 Kings 8:27

'Do you not know that you are God's temple and that God's Spirit dwells in you?'

1 Corinthians 3:16

The PRIESTS' ROOMS

The prophet is now taken to see buildings on the north and south sides of the temple, separated from it by the temple yard (fig. 1). These buildings face the side-rooms that abut the walls of the temple (41:5–11). The buildings on the north side are described more fully because those on the south are an exact copy of them. Because the Hebrew text is rather obscure, it is not easy to understand the architectural details fully.

The buildings on each side consist of two blocks, separated by a passage ten cubits wide. The block nearest the temple is one hundred cubits long. It is unclear whether this is aligned with the temple itself, or offset somewhat towards the west. There is another building between those described here and the west wall of the whole complex but its size is not given (46:19–20). The block on the other side of the passage is only fifty cubits long, but a fifty-cubit-long wall extends from it, paralleling the other building. It is not clear whether both blocks of buildings, or only the outer one, form a stepped structure of three storeys, each storey being narrower than the one below it. It is also unclear whether verse 9 means that the outer block can be entered from the outer court or simply that the passage allows entry from the nearby gatehouse between the courts.

The uses of the priests' rooms

These buildings have a threefold function.

- They contain dining-rooms where the priests eat the portion of the offerings allotted to them. To some extent this was simply the way the priests were provided for, since they had no land of their own to farm (44:28–30). However, the eating of the sin and guilt offerings seems to have had a special significance as part of the process of removing the offerer's sins (Leviticus 6:24—7:6).
- They contain rooms for storing the portions of the offerings that belonged to the priests.
- They include changing-rooms, because the clothes worn by the priests in the inner court had to be exchanged for different clothes before they went back to the outer court of the temple complex. This protected the greater holiness of the inner court.

Finally, Ezekiel's guide measures the overall external dimensions of the temple complex. It is a five-hundred-cubit square, which, like most of the smaller measurements, is a multiple of five. Everything fits together to produce a perfectly symmetrical shape. The closing comment (v. 20) is a reminder that the wall separates the 'holy' from the 'common'.

Holy, clean and unclean

The worldview of the Old Testament divided reality into three spheres—the holy, the common or clean, and the unclean. Uncleanness is a difficult concept to understand. Sometimes it is contracted in a quasi-physical way by contact with certain things, animals or people. Sometimes it is the result of moral failure. There was a variety of rituals, ranging from washing in clean water to costly animal sacrifices, to remove uncleanness. The normal status of God's people was common or clean, while certain rituals rendered particular objects and people (the Levites within Israel) holy, fit for service in the temple.

This threefold division had an educative purpose. It impressed on the Israelites that they were to live differently from other people, as a witness to the nations of the different character of their God. However, there is a fine balance to be struck between doing this in an open and welcoming way and falling into an 'holier-than-thou' exclusivity. In Herod's temple there were separate courts for Priests, Israelite men, Israelite women and Gentiles. A stone barrier separated the Court of the Gentiles from the others, and it bore plaques forbidding Gentiles to cross it on pain of death. Paul had this barrier in mind when he wrote to the Gentiles in Ephesus, 'In Christ Jesus you who once were far off have been brought near by the blood of Christ. For he is our peace; in his flesh he has made both groups into one and has broken down the dividing wall, that is, the hostility between us' (Ephesians 2:13–14). Paul realized that in Christ other barriers disappear as well: 'There is no longer Jew or Greek, there is no longer slave or free, there is no longer male and female; for all of you are one in Christ Jesus' (Galatians 3:28).

PRAYER

Lord Jesus, help me to live differently in the way you did,
a way that attracted 'sinners' towards the love of a holy God
rather than repelling them.

The GLORY RETURNS

The return of the glory of the Lord to the new temple is the high point
of chapters 40—48. The prophet sees it as a vision within a vision
(v. 3). His three visions of the glory of God sum up the message of the
book. The vision beside the Chebar (chs. 1—3) assured Ezekiel that
the God of Israel is the God of all the world and that he had not abandoned the exiles in Babylon. The vision of the glory leaving the temple
and Jerusalem (chs. 8—11) made clear that the people's idolatry and
other sins were the cause of the destruction of the city and the temple.
Finally, in this vision he is assured that there is a future for a forgiven
and cleansed nation, among whom God will dwell for ever (37:26–28).

God returns

In his earlier vision, Ezekiel had seen the glory of God leaving
Jerusalem by the east gate and moving to the east. As he sees it
returning from the east, he is awestruck and falls on his face (vv. 2–3).
The Spirit lifts him up and takes him to the inner court, where he
hears God addressing him from the temple. What God says is reassuring: 'This is the place of my throne and the place for the soles
of my feet' (v. 7). It echoes the symbolism of the (now lost) ark of
the covenant and the cherubim associated with it. In the ancient
Near East, the steps up to a throne were usually flanked by 'throne
guardians', statues of protective deities, often symbolized as animals
(for example, 1 Kings 10:18–20). The cherubim associated with the
ark could be seen as guardians of God's invisible, heavenly throne.
Important documents, such as international treaties, were often kept
in a receptacle under the throne, like the tablets of the Law in the ark.

Once again there is a balancing of symbolism. The vision of the
chariot-throne speaks of the omnipresence of God in the world. This
is balanced by the symbolism of the 'most holy place' in the temple
as a place where God 'touches earth' in a special way. It is important
to hold on to both truths, that God is present and active everywhere
and at all times, but that there are times and places where we meet
God in a special way. The danger is that either we think of God's
presence as so 'diffuse' that it means little, or that we think we can
'capture' God in particular places or experiences for our own ends.

God's glory

In the Old Testament the glory of God is often depicted in terms of shining light. This symbolizes what the word means—that which humans can discern about God. For the New Testament writers this is now to be seen in Jesus: 'And the Word became flesh and lived among us, and we have seen his glory, the glory as of a father's only son, full of grace and truth… No one has ever seen God. It is God the only Son, who is close to the Father's heart, who has made him known' (John 1:14, 18). The language used in John 1:14 evokes the image of the glory of God dwelling in the temple in the midst of God's people. The claim being made is that Jesus shows what God is like because, in Jesus, God 'touched earth' in a unique way. This claim is repeated in John 2:19–21 when Jesus is spoken of as the temple.

God's holiness

The vision within a vision ends with a command to write down the vision of the new temple and to make it known to the people (vv. 10–12). This command was to impress on them the importance of recognizing and protecting God's holiness, and it applied particularly to the kings of the nation. Solomon's temple was really part of a wider palace complex and was too easily seen as a royal shrine of the kingdom rather than as the throne of the Great King, the God of Israel. This led to the danger of presuming that God, or at least God's power, was at the disposal of the king, rather than the recognition that the king was God's servant, to be at his disposal. In the future, God must be given his true place.

Church history warns us that it is all too easy to repeat the error of the Judean kings. We too can assume that God is on our side and that therefore he will bless and support all we do. Instead of this, we should be seeking to ensure that we are on God's side, discerning and obeying his will.

MEDITATION

'Long ago God spoke to our ancestors in many and various ways
by the prophets, but in these last days he has spoken to us by a Son…
He is the reflection of God's glory and the exact imprint
of God's very being.'

Hebrews 1:1–3

The NEW ALTAR

The fact that after the return of the glory of the Lord the prophet's vision continues with further descriptions of parts of the temple complex, as well as some detailed regulations concerning the temple's use, might seem something of an anti-climax. However, the point seems to be that until the return of the glory of the Lord, what Ezekiel has described is a splendid but empty building. With God's presence now in it, it is time for instructions on its proper use. At the heart of the temple complex, geographically and in terms of its ritual, is the altar. It is therefore appropriate that the prophet now describes the altar and the ritual for bringing it into use (see figure IV).

The structure of the altar

The altar would have been a stone structure. It stood on a base that was eighteen cubits square with a rim around it—perhaps to collect and channel away blood (v. 13). On the base were three further layers, each two cubits shorter than the one below, resulting in a stepped structure. The lowest layer was two cubits high (v. 14a), and each of the others four cubits high (vv. 14b–15), giving a structure that was eleven cubits high, including the base. The top layer, the altar hearth, was twelve cubits square (v. 16). There were four horns projecting from the four corners of the hearth (v. 15). It was reached by a flight of steps on the altar's east side, so that the officiating priest would be facing the temple (v. 17).

The purification of the altar

Ezekiel is given an elaborate and lengthy procedure that is to be followed for a week in order to 'purify' the altar, to move it into the realm of holy things (vv. 18–27). No doubt at least part of the reason for this was to impress on the minds of the worshippers that the altar was a very special part of the temple complex. It stood for the restoration and maintenance of the relationship with God, and this was not something that could be treated casually. It is an extraordinary privilege for sinners to have a means of seeking forgiveness and entering into a relationship with the holy God.

Sacrifice and obedience

Like all religious activities, sacrifice can degenerate into the routine performance of a ritual devoid of any inner meaning. The pre-exilic prophets from Amos to Jeremiah accused the people of Israel and Judah of having let this happen. Many of the people were punctilious in making the offerings (Amos 4:4–5) but they were relying on the acts themselves and ignoring the fact that they meant nothing to God unless offered in the right spirit. The evidence that they were not being offered in the right spirit was the people's failure to obey the covenant law in their daily life. This showed that, whatever their motivation might be, they were not concerned primarily with pleasing God. Therefore all their sacrifices and associated worship were abhorrent to God (Amos 5:21–24). The sacrifices were meant to express an attitude of humble obedience to God that permeated the whole of life. The material sacrifice brought to the altar should have been only the 'tip of the iceberg' of a life lived in God's service. As Samuel said, 'Has the Lord as great delight in burnt offerings and sacrifices as in obeying the voice of the Lord? Surely, to obey is better than sacrifice' (1 Samuel 15:22). Worship is not just something to be done in the sanctuary; it is a way of life.

The apostle Paul expresses this graphically when he urges the Christians in Rome to 'present your bodies as a living sacrifice, holy and acceptable to God, which is your spiritual worship' (Romans 12:1). He uses 'bodies' here to signify our existence as embodied beings in this world. The way we live out this existence day to day, not just what we do in church, is to be sacrificial worship offered to God. That means living holy lives at home, at work, at leisure, and so on. Paul goes on to explain the basis for achieving this: 'Don't let the world around you squeeze you into its own mould, but let God remould your minds from within' (Romans 12:2, J.B. Phillips). This remoulding takes place as we prayerfully read, study and meditate upon the Bible and seek to live it out in practice.

PRAYER

Lord, I want to be a living sacrifice. Please give me the strength to resist the temptation to crawl off the altar when the demands of holy living get tough.

ADMISSION *to the* SANCTUARY

Ezekiel's guide brings him back to the east gate in the outer wall. He is told that the gate is to remain shut (v. 2). This would stand as a reassuring sign for two reasons. First, it would be a reminder that God had returned to the sanctuary. Second, it implies his intention never to leave it.

The prince can use the space within the gatehouse to eat his sacrificial meals, but he has to enter the gatehouse through the vestibule that opens on to the outer court (v. 3). This privilege marks the prince's unique position among the laity. However, it is clear from these chapters that the prince was to have much less freedom of access to the temple precincts than did the pre-exilic kings. This introduces the issue of who may have access to which parts of the complex.

Ezekiel and Moses

The prophet returns to the front of the temple where once again he falls down before the glory of the Lord. God then gives him a series of 'ordinances of the temple of the Lord and all its laws' (v. 5). Ezekiel plays a role somewhat similar to that of Moses. Moses went up on to a mountain that was wreathed in smoke and fire because the glory of the Lord had settled on it (Exodus 24:15–18). There he received laws and ordinances to give to the Israelites. He was also shown the pattern of the tabernacle, the temple's forerunner. Ezekiel was taken to a very high mountain and shown the pattern of the new temple, and now, in the presence of the glory of the Lord, he is given laws and ordinances to pass on to the people. This is part of the symbolism of God giving his people a new start.

Privileged access

The Israelites had always accepted that access to God's presence in the temple was a privilege. Worshippers coming to the temple asked, 'Who shall ascend the hill of the Lord? And who shall stand in his holy place?' (Psalm 24:3). Ezekiel is told that 'foreigners, uncircumcised in heart and flesh' (v. 7) are completely excluded. This refers to people who are not members of the covenant, both in their outlook and because they have not accepted the rite of entrance into the covenant community. The reference to their having been allowed admittance in the past refers to the use of foreign mercenaries as temple guards (2 Kings 11:4). Also, other foreigners seem to have been used to do menial tasks in the temple, to judge by the number of non-Israelite names in the lists of temple servants in Ezra and Nehemiah. The Levites, other than those descended from Zadok, are to take over the guarding and menial duties that these foreigners did in Solomon's temple, as well as slaughtering the sacrifices. They are not to be allowed into the inner court or to officiate at the altar. The reason given in verse 12 refers to the period before Josiah's reform in Judah when many Levites served at shrines out in the countryside where there was either a mixture of worship of the God of Israel and the local Canaanite gods, or outright idolatry.

Keeping the balance

The exclusiveness of the regulations here sounds intolerant to modern ears, but the historical context needs to be borne in mind. Assimilation to non-Israelite cultures, and the consequent idolatry, had brought disaster on Judah. Hence there was a need to ensure that the same did not happen again. As one commentator (Iain Duguid) says, the attitude expressed is rather like the perceived need to tighten up on safety procedures in nuclear power plants after the Chenobyl disaster. Moreover, the remnants of Judah, whether in exile or in Judah, were a demoralized minority in a hostile environment and felt the need to take measures to preserve the uniqueness of their faith. If they had not taken such steps, Judaism and its offshoot, Christianity, might not be with us today. However, there is a fine balance between having clear boundaries that mark and preserve what is precious, so that it can be shared with other people, and becoming narrowly and selfishly exclusive. The early Church struggled hard over this issue before concluding that the good news of Jesus Christ was for all people, Jew and Gentile alike. The struggle has continued down the ages in various forms.

MEDITATION AND PRAYER

Think of some issues on which you see the Church struggling with the balance between staying distinct and becoming wrongly exclusive. Pray about them.

The ZADOKITE PRIESTHOOD

The section on access to different parts of the temple complex concludes with regulations that limit the performance of duties within the inner court to Levites descended from Zadok. This restriction did not apply before the exile. In Deuteronomy all Levites were allowed to perform priestly duties (Deuteronomy 18:1–8). Zadok was a leading priest during David's reign, together with Abiathar. Following Abiathar's expulsion by Solomon (1 Kings 2:26–27), Zadok was the chief priest. After the return from exile, Joshua, son of Jehozadak, a Zadokite, became high priest. The Zadokites remained in control of the temple and the high priesthood until 171BC, when Jason the high priest was deposed by Antiochus IV. Disputes over the legitimacy of subsequent high priests was one factor in the rise of different sects within Judaism, such as the Qumran Community, some of whom were Zadokites. In the light of the criticism of the Jerusalem priesthood in Ezekiel 22:26 and chapters 8—11, the reason given for the restriction of priestly duties to the Zadokites in verse 15 may seem a bit strange. Clearly the Zadokites were innocent of the charges laid against the rest of the Levites only in a relative sense, not an absolute one.

Dress and behaviour

The privilege of serving in the inner court and officiating at the altar brought with it the responsibility to protect the holiness of the area. This meant observing certain restrictions. When in the inner court, the priests were to wear only linen clothes in order to avoid sweating (vv. 17–18). Presumably sweat was put in the category of bodily emissions that made people unclean. These linen clothes were not to be taken out of the inner court (v. 19), but were to be left in the special rooms mentioned in 42:13–14. The restriction against drinking wine in the inner court (v. 21) was no doubt intended to avoid any unseemly drunken behaviour. The regulations about hair (v. 20) may have been related to mourning customs, and so be linked with the regulations concerning contact with the dead (one of the greatest sources of uncleanness) in verses 25–27. The restriction of marriage to an Israelite virgin or the widow of a priest (v. 22) would ensure that no child conceived by a former husband of a non-Zadokite family could ever mistakenly be made a priest. These restrictions on the Zadokites would serve to remind the worshippers of the need for care in approaching God, and the need for purity, both ethical and ritual.

Teachers and judges

Besides their duties in the inner court, the priests had the responsibility of teaching the people (v. 23). In particular they were to help the people to understand the differences between the holy and the common, the clean and the unclean. (As we have noted earlier, the clean and the common are in fact two different ways of describing the normal state of God's people.) The priests were also responsible for teaching the people about the religious festivals and how to keep them. Their expertise was not limited to the ritual law. It encompassed the whole of God's law, and so they acted as the community's judges (v. 24).

A special inheritance

The priests were not allotted inheritable ancestral land from which to make their living. Instead God was their 'inheritance' (v. 28). They made their living by serving God in the temple and their needs were met through the sacrificial system. This special position of having God as one's 'inheritance' is taken up in a significant way in Psalm 16:5–6: 'The Lord is my chosen portion and my cup; you hold my lot. The boundary lines have fallen for me in pleasant places; I have a goodly heritage.'

These verses evoke the apportioning of the land of Canaan to the different tribes by drawing lots. The psalmist is a priest, one who received the Lord, not land, as his portion. (The psalm heading 'Of David' may mean 'for David', or indicate that the psalm comes from a collection belonging to David.) The psalmist is satisfied with this as 'a goodly heritage'. As the psalm goes on, it becomes clear that this is because of the personal relationship he has with God: 'I keep the Lord always before me; because he is at my right hand, I shall not be moved' (Psalm 16:8). This relationship is so real that he is sure that even death will not be able to end it. Instead he looks forward to 'fullness of joy' and 'pleasures' at God's right hand for evermore (Psalm 16:11). This psalm gives us a glimpse of the vibrant spiritual life that could arise from keeping the ritual and regulations of the temple.

MEDITATION

Meditate on Psalm 16, turning it into your own prayer.

The ALLOCATION of the LAND

(Refer to figure 3, page 231, while reading this section.) The prophet's vision moves from the temple complex itself to the allocation of one portion of the restored land as its setting. The division of the land among the various tribes is the subject of chapters 47—48, where some of the material given here is repeated. The reason for anticipating that later section is to emphasize the holiness of the sanctuary.

The Hebrew word used for the 'portion' of land to be set aside for the Lord *(terumah)* is also used of the choice portion of a sacrifice that was reserved for the priests. This piece of land forms a square with sides of 25,000 cubits (about 13 kilometres). It is made up of three strips, aligned in a east–west direction like the temple. To the north is a strip 25,000 cubits long and 10,000 wide, where the Levites were to live (v. 5). The middle strip, of the same size, contains the 500-cubit-square temple complex, which is surrounded by a 'buffer zone' 50 cubits wide. The rest of this strip is where the priests live (vv. 1–4). In the light of 44:28 this is not intended as inheritable ancestral land, nor as land to be farmed by the priests. The third, southern, strip is only 5,000 cubits wide. At its centre is the city, 4,500 cubits square, with a 250-cubit 'green belt' around it (48:15–18). The land to the east and the west of this sacred square, stretching to the boundaries of the holy land, is allocated to the prince (vv. 7–8).

Protecting the temple

This distribution of the land follows a pattern similar to that of the temple. The temple complex itself becomes a kind of 'most holy place' (v. 3). The surrounding territory of the priests is the 'holy place' (v. 4) and the land allocated to the Levites is like the vestibule of the temple. Thus the holiness of the temple is expressed in the geography of the land. It is also significant that both the city and the prince's land are clearly separated from the temple complex. As we have noted, Solomon's temple was really part of a larger palace complex. Originally this lay on the northern side of the city of David, but as the city grew, the complex was incorporated into it. In the thought of the Judeans prior to the exile, there was a tendency to think of the temple and Jerusalem as one entity, with the sanctity of the temple guaranteeing the protection of the city by God. In this vision of the future, royal prerogatives over the temple are removed and it is made clear that God is the true King who rules from his throne-room, the most holy place in the temple.

Tenants, not owners

Enshrined in Israel's law was the recognition that the land did not belong to them but to their God: 'The land shall not be sold in perpetuity, for the land is mine; with me you are but aliens and tenants' (Leviticus 25:23). In the allocation of tribal territories, each tribe was supposed to be given land according to its size, so that each family had enough land to support itself. The land was seen as God's gift to them. This was remembered annually in the ceremony of offering the 'first-fruits' of the harvest to God (Deuteronomy 26:3–10). The theological truth that the land belonged to God, and that the people of Israel were his tenants, would now be expressed by its geographical layout. A portion of the land itself, not just of its produce, was to be set aside for God as a constant reminder of who the true owner was.

Israel's apprehension of the nature of the relationship between God, the land and his people is a microcosm of the wider truth of the relationship between God, planet earth and humankind. In the Genesis creation story, God gives the earth and its creatures as a gift to humans made in his image, to manage it as his tenants. Being made in God's image, we should do this in ways that express God's character—showing love, wisdom and justice. Sadly, we have too often done it in selfish, greedy and exploitative ways, and are reaping the results in the ecological problems that we face.

PRAYER

Lord, teach us to accept gratefully the gifts of your creation. Through selfishness and greed we woefully misuse them. Change our attitudes so that we use your gifts wisely and with due care, sharing these resources so that the needs of all are met fairly.

The DUTIES *of the* PRINCE

The description of the land allotted to the prince leads naturally to a consideration of the duties of the prince in the restored community. This begins with a prophetic oracle calling for the end of the corrupt use of power (v. 9). When the Israelites first asked for a king, Samuel warned them that rulers were prone to exploit their position and power (1 Samuel 8:10–18). Solomon changed the twelve tribes into twelve tax districts to provide for the needs of his court (1 Kings 4:7), and he conscripted forced labour gangs to carry out his building programme (1 Kings 5:13). Jezebel had Naboth judicially murdered when he refused to sell his ancestral land to Ahab, who coveted it (1 Kings 21). Amos denounced the leaders of Israel and Judah for living in self-indulgent luxury while their nations slid into ruin (Amos 6:1–7). Isaiah denounced those who built up large estates (Isaiah 5:8), which could be done only by dispossessing the peasants of their lands. This kind of abuse of power was not to be repeated. Instead the prince is called upon to rule with justice and righteousness.

Promoting justice

The prince is also urged to promote justice in commercial dealings, by ensuring honest weights and measures (v. 10). Amos condemned those who 'make the ephah small and the shekel great, and practise deceit with false balances' (Amos 8:5)—in other words, who sold short measures and overcharged for goods (goods were paid for by weighing out the required amount of silver or gold). The ephah and bath were volume measures for dry goods and liquids respectively. The standard measure, which the prince was to regulate, was the homer (literally an ass-load, about 220 litres). The standard weight was the shekel (about 11.5 grammes). In verse 12b the minah is set at 60 shekels, which was the Babylonian standard, though a 50-shekel minah is attested elsewhere.

Providing sacrifices

The prince was to be responsible for making sacrificial offerings on behalf of the people at the various religious festivals (vv. 13–17). He was to provide these offerings out of a levy that the people made to him. To avoid the kind of exploitation that had occurred in the past, the levy is clearly specified—a sixtieth of the cereal crop, a hundredth of the oil, and one sheep out of two hundred. These sacrifices are to be offered 'to make atonement for the house of Israel' (v. 17).

Justice, righteousness and honesty

In a book in which the ritual purity aspect of holiness is often to the fore, this passage is a reminder that social justice is also an important aspect of what it means to be 'a holy nation'. As the civil leader of the community, the prince has the responsibility to promote justice. It is notable that Ezekiel prefers the word 'prince' to 'king', probably because it does not carry the same connotations of political domination and exploitation. Justice, righteousness and honesty are the three qualities emphasized in this passage. They are certainly necessary foundations for a stable and healthy society, and the pre-exilic prophets had declared that the lack of them was leading the nation towards judgment. '[God] expected justice, but saw bloodshed; righteousness but heard a cry [of the oppressed]!' declared Isaiah (Isaiah 5:7), and Jeremiah said of the Judeans, 'They all deceive their neighbours, and no one speaks the truth; they have taught their tongues to speak lies' (Jeremiah 9:5).

God's gracious gifts

Because no society is perfect, there is need for a means of atonement, the restoring of its relationship with God. This passage gives evidence of God's grace. The ability to make such offerings is the direct result of God's gift to his people of the land and the crops and animals it produced. The people's relationship with God is restored by returning to God a portion of what he provides. The principle of God providing the means of atonement found its fullest and final expression in Jesus, 'whom God put forward as a sacrifice of atonement by his blood, effective through faith' (Romans 3:25). If we accept this means that God has provided, our relationship with God will be restored. As the apostle puts it, God 'justifies the one who has faith in Jesus' (Romans 3:26b).

PRAYER

Make a list of the leading politicians whose names you know.
Pray for each one personally, that he or she will promote justice,
righteousness and honesty within the nation.

PURIFICATION, PASSOVER &
TABERNACLES

Mention of the prince's responsibility to provide animals for the sacrifices associated with various festivals leads to consideration of the ritual calendar. Ezekiel's calendar is somewhat different from the one that had been observed before the exile.

Purifying the temple

To begin with, there is a new ceremony for purifying the temple (vv. 18–20). The 'first month' is the month Nisan. The ceremony is similar to that already described for purifying the altar (43:18–27). The blood of a sacrificed bull is smeared on the doorposts of the temple, the corners of the upper ledge of the altar and the doorposts of a gate of the inner court—probably the east gate since it was in line with the temple and the altar. It is implied that, unlike the purifying of the altar, this is not a once-for-all ceremony, but one to be repeated annually. According to the Hebrew text it is to be done on the first day of the month and repeated on the seventh day. The early Greek translation of the Old Testament has the repetition take place on the first day of the seventh month. However, this looks like a 'tidying up' of the calendar so that the ceremony is held before each of the two major festivals mentioned in verses 19–25.

Two festivals

What is said of the two festivals in verses 19–25 is brief. It probably presupposes a wider background knowledge of these festivals, and only specifies what is to be done differently from the past. The regulations for the sacrifices at the Passover feast make a considerable increase in the sacrifices to be offered, compared with the legislation in Numbers 28:16–25. Passover is the festival commemorating the exodus from slavery in Egypt into freedom. The unnamed festival of the seventh month, the month Tishri (v. 25), is the festival of Tabernacles or Ingathering. It celebrated the end of the olive and grape harvest, and therefore God's provision of the land and its produce. This time the quantity of sacrifices required is less than stipulated in Numbers

29:12–38. Although there is no reason to think that Ezekiel has forgotten the original significance of these two festivals, the fact that he mentions the sin offering at the head of the lists of offerings for each of them suggests that this is his primary interest in them. They are major opportunities 'to make atonement for the house of Israel' (45:17). It is surprising that there is no mention of the festival of Weeks (Numbers 28:26–31), which celebrated the grain harvest. The calendar seems to have been reduced to two major festivals marking each half of the year, with the purification of the temple at the start of the New Year.

Salvation and creation

Whatever may have been Ezekiel's reason for mentioning only the festivals of Passover and Tabernacles, it does in fact produce a ritual year in which there is a balance between celebration of God as Saviour and of God as Creator, between salvation and creation. In the Christian tradition there has been a tendency to concentrate on salvation and to give relatively little attention to creation. No doubt this is partly because the high point of the Christian year is Easter, with its celebration of God's great act of salvation in Christ. Celebration of God as creator can be associated with our harvest festival. However, with the growth of urbanization, this has become a less and less meaningful festival for most people.

One harmful effect of this tendency to stress salvation and ignore creation has been a relative neglect of our responsibility to care properly for God's world. Many Christians think of salvation in purely personal terms, and of this world as a 'disposable item' in God's plans. In the Bible, however, God's plan of salvation embraces all his creation, and indeed is seen as the consummation of his creative purposes. 'For the creation waits with eager longing for the revealing of the children of God... the creation itself will be set free from its bondage to decay and will obtain the freedom of the glory of the children of God' (Romans 8:19, 21). Related to this is the fact that the Christian future hope is not existence as a disembodied spirit in heaven, but life in a resurrected body in a renewed heaven and earth.

MEDITATION

Meditate on Colossians 1:15–19. Here Christ is presented as God's agent in both creation and salvation and his death as the means of reconciling all creation to God.

FURTHER REGULATIONS *for* WORSHIP

As well as his responsibility to provide the animals for sacrifices at the great festivals, the prince was required to provide them for the sacrifices that took place at the new moon (the beginning of each month, since the calendar was a lunar one), on the weekly Sabbath and on a daily basis (vv. 4–7, 13–15). Once again there are differences between the sacrifices specified here and those laid down in the book of Numbers for the Sabbath (Numbers 28:9–10) and the new moon (Numbers 28:11–15). Also, legislation in Numbers 28:3–8 specifies that a lamb should be sacrificed morning and evening. This seems to have been the normal practice both before and after the exile in Babylon. According to Ezra 3:2–3, the daily morning and evening sacrifices were the first to be resumed after the return from exile. Ezekiel's silence about the evening sacrifice is surprising, but maybe he means that the prince was responsible for the lamb for the morning sacrifice alone. The provision of even one lamb a day would have been quite a drain on his resources.

Ezekiel and the Mosaic Law

The differences between the regulations for festivals and sacrifices in Ezekiel and in the Mosaic Law greatly worried the early rabbis. A well-known rabbinical tradition tells how, when the book of Ezekiel was in danger of being excluded from the Hebrew canon of Scripture, Hananiah ben Hezekiah shut himself in his upper room and burned 300 jars of oil while labouring to reconcile Ezekiel's regulations with those in the *Torah* (the first five books of the Hebrew Bible). The results of the learned rabbi's labours are now lost, but they must have carried conviction with his contemporaries since the book remained in public use. This debate is an example of a tension that often exists with regard to religious worship, namely how to preserve what is good and important in a tradition, while at the same time being willing to adapt to the needs of a new situation. The reasons for the differences between Ezekiel's legislation and that in the Torah is often not obvious, but one factor that is clear is the need, following the experience of the exile, to reassert the holiness of God in the widest sense, and the consequent importance of the provision for atonement for sin.

The need to safeguard God's holiness is evident in the regulations about the east gate of the inner court. This was the gate that looked directly on to the entrance to the temple on the other side of the altar. It was to be opened only on the Sabbath and the day of the new moon (vv. 1–2). Apart from the priests, only the prince could enter the gate-house, but he was not allowed to cross its threshold into the inner court. He could stand by the doorpost at the threshold to watch the priests offering on the altar the sacrifices he had brought. The ordinary worshippers could make their obeisance to the Lord at the entrance to the gate, which would give them a glimpse of the altar and the temple. Although these were the only days when the east gate was kept open all day, it was also opened when the prince wanted to make freewill offerings (v. 12).

The regulations in verses 9–10 seem intended to ensure orderly conduct at the major festivals when large crowds would come to the temple. One procession of worshippers would enter by the north gate and pass through the outer court to leave by the south gate. At the same time another procession of worshippers would enter by the south gate and leave by the north gate. The exact sense of verse 10 is unclear. It might mean that the prince would lead one of the processions.

Worship and life

These regulations express a number of important things about worship. There is its centrality to life, in the practice of daily worship. The helpful practice of morning and evening prayer seems to have developed from that of the morning and evening sacrifice in the temple. Then worship is also woven into the rhythm of life with the weekly and monthly offerings. The development of physical and spiritual life are to flow together. The annual festivals provide special high points and are reminders of fundamental truths of the faith. The Christian version of this is the daily offices of the Church and its liturgical year, with its cycle of seasons and festivals.

PRAYER

Try writing some special prayers for the first day of each month of the year, relating them to the rhythm of the seasons and the pattern of your own family and work life as it unfolds through the year.

The PRINCE'S LAND

This short piece of legislation returns to, and expands upon, the brief charge made to the prince in Ezekiel 45:9: 'Cease your evictions of my people, says the Lord God.' The common thread in 45:9—46:18 is the privileges and responsibilities of the prince. The fact that the section is bracketed by verses concerning the issue of land-holding by the prince and the people shows how important this was in Israel.

The land and economics

It was important for socio-economic reasons. Israel's economy was based largely on subsistence agriculture. The land provided people with the means to live, and there could be some produce left over to barter for other goods. That is why it was important for each family to have enough land to subsist on. In the apportioning of the land in Joshua 14—21 the tribes were allotted portions 'according to their families', so that each had sufficient land for its support. Any land that was sold or leased reverted to its original owner in the year of Jubilee, so that a family's ancestral land-holding was periodically restored to it. If for any reason a family lost its land—and the most common reason would be debt—it would become destitute. In this situation a person could enter a form of 'slavery', as a form of social welfare provision: 'If any who are dependent on you become so impoverished that they sell themselves to you, you shall not make them serve as slaves. They shall remain with you as hired or bound labourers' (Leviticus 25:39–40a). In Leviticus, all such 'slaves' were to be set free in the year of Jubilee. In Exodus 21:2 and Deuteronomy 15:12, the period of servitude is limited to six years. According to Deuteronomy 15:14, when set free they should be provided for generously so that they could make a fresh start and not immediately fall back into servitude. There are principles at work here that might have relevance for social welfare provision today.

The land and politics

The land was important for socio-political reasons. Rulers have always used gifts of land as rewards and bribes to bolster their own power. To do this, they have often had to expropriate the land of other people— their political enemies or powerless peasants. The Hebrew prophets roundly denounced such expropriation of land, whether for political or purely selfish purposes (Isaiah 5:8; Micah 2:2). The legislation in Ezekiel is clearly intended to prevent this from happening in the future. The prince cannot alienate the royal lands. He can give royal land to his sons as an inheritance, but can only lease it to other people. The leases would terminate in 'the year of liberty' (v. 17), probably the year of Jubilee, so that all the royal land would then revert to the crown. The prince is prohibited from seizing land belonging to anyone else (v. 18).

The land and theology

The land was also important for theological reasons. As we have already noted, it was God's property (Leviticus 25:23). He had commanded that it be allotted fairly, to meet the needs of all, and things were meant to stay that way. Each family held their land as a gift from God, evidence of his grace and love toward them. Its produce provided them with the means to express their worship of God and to make atonement when they had sinned. Therefore the issue of land, and land use, had an important spiritual dimension.

Land today

The possession of land is a major political issue today between the Israeli Jews and Palestinian Arabs. There is no simple solution to this problem. Maybe consideration of the principles outlined here, taking into account what is said in Ezekiel 47:22–23 about the rights of the resident alien, would provide a way forward.

To see the wider relevance of the issues and principles raised by this piece of legislation for us today, we need to think not just in terms of land, but of natural resources. For many, perhaps most, people in the world today, land is still the major natural resource that concerns them, but in urbanized societies we depend on other natural resources, which are no less the gifts of God to be shared fairly and justly.

PRAYER

Lord, we are faced with global ecological crises because of the way we have misused the natural resources you have given us. Please give the leaders of the world the political courage to seek solutions before it is too late, and the moral courage to adopt those that are fair and just to all nations.

The TEMPLE KITCHENS

The heavenly guide, who has been absent since 44:4, reappears and Ezekiel's tour of the temple complex continues. The lengthy intervening section (44:5—46:18) forms a distinct collection of laws in which God, not the guide, speaks. This is emphasized by the occasional use of the prophetic oracle formula (44:6, 9; 45:9, 18; 46:1, 16). As we have noted (commenting on 44:1–14, pp. 206–207), this section gives Ezekiel a role similar to that of Moses. The laws cover various issues: who may go where in the temple, the roles of the priests and Levites, the privileges and responsibilities of the prince, the allocation of the land around the temple, and regulations for the festivals. At the heart of it all is the concern to protect the holiness of the divine presence that has returned to the temple.

The priests' kitchens

During the giving of the laws, Ezekiel has been standing in front of the temple (44:4). In the resumed tour, the prophet is first taken through the priests' rooms on the north side of the temple, presumably along the passage between the two blocks of rooms (42:4), to see a building on the north side of the large building to the west of the temple (41:12). In view of the symmetry in the layout of the temple complex, there was presumably a similar building on its south side. This building was the kitchen where the priests' portions of the sin and guilt offerings and of the grain offering were to be cooked (see figure 1). We have already been told that these portions were to be stored and eaten in the priests' rooms in the blocks on either side of the temple (42:13). As with the requirement for the priests to change their clothes before leaving the inner court (42:14), the purpose of these arrangements for cooking and eating the sacrificial offerings was so that the priests should not 'communicate holiness to the people' (v. 20). The prophet is then taken to the outer court where, in each corner, he sees more cooking areas, each forty cubits by thirty cubits. These areas are where the Levites cook the portions of the sacrifices that the worshippers eat. They would be portions of the 'offering of well-being' (46:12).

Some scholars argue that this short section is out of place here and would, for example, fit better somewhere in chapter 42. However, this may be applying the wrong kind of logic to the arrangement of the material. From a priestly point of view it makes sense to delay the description of how to deal with the portions of the sacrifices that are to be eaten until after the detailed regulations governing the sacrifices themselves. It has also been pointed out that, placed here, the section rounds off a second cycle in Ezekiel's tour of the temple. In each cycle there is a movement from the outside to the centre (40:5—41:4; 43:1–5) and then back from the centre to the outside again (41:5—42:20; 43:13—46:24). Like everything else in this vision of the future, the tour follows a well-ordered plan.

The idea that the portions of the sin and guilt offerings not burnt on the altar are 'holy' may seem odd (v. 20). Surely they ought to be 'unclean', since the animal concerned was vicariously bearing the sin of the offerer. However, the sin was dealt with by the shedding of the animal's blood: 'The life of the flesh is in the blood; and I have given it to you for making atonement for your lives on the altar' (Leviticus 17:11). Presumably it was because the animal was given to God as an act of 'compensation' that it was eaten by the priests alone.

God's guests

As mentioned above, the sacrifices referred to in verse 24 would be for the offering of well-being, which was eaten as a meal shared with God. After the animal's blood had been shed and applied to the altar, the fatty parts were burnt and the rest was cooked and eaten by the worshipper, no doubt along with family and friends. In all cultures, sharing a meal seems to be an important way of building up relationships. By making the meal into a sacrificial one eaten in the temple complex, the worshippers' relationship with God is included in this fundamental social activity. Since it was eaten in 'God's house' with food provided by his land, the worshippers ate it as his guests.

PRAYER

'Saying grace' at meals can become a mere formality.
Try to make it a genuine recognition that we eat our meals
in God's presence as his guests.

The RIVER *of* LIFE

As the prophet's tour continues, he is taken to see water springing up from under the southern side of the temple platform. It flows east, to the south of the altar, and passes under the wall of the temple court (v. 1). He is led out of the north gate of the temple and, going round to the closed east gate, he sees the water flowing out from under its south side (v. 2). Ezekiel and his guide then walk east along the river, stopping every 500 metres or so to measure its depth. At the first stop it is ankle-deep, at the next it is knee-deep, at the third it is waist-deep, and at the fourth it is too deep to cross without swimming. The guide's question, 'Mortal, have you seen this?' (v. 6) focuses our attention on the amazing fact that here is a river without tributaries which nevertheless gets deeper the further it flows from its source! This is a physical impossibility, reminding us that what we have in this vision is a series of symbolic pictures. The river is a picture of the abundant blessings that flow from God's presence. In the temple God's presence is focused on earth in a special way (43:7), and so from it his blessing flows out to his people and his land. That blessing is not weakened by distance, but expands to meet the needs encountered.

A life-giving river

Ezekiel and his guide turn back, and as they walk alongside the river the prophet notices that there are many trees growing along both banks. He is told that their fruit is a continuous source of food and that their leaves have medicinal properties (v. 12). There are echoes here of the garden of Eden, with its river and fruit trees (Genesis 2:9–10). That too was a place where God could be met regularly.

The guide tells Ezekiel the course that the river takes as it flows away from Jerusalem. It goes through the wilderness east of the city and drops down into the deep rift valley containing the River Jordan. Here it flows into the Dead Sea, whose very salty waters cannot support any kind of life (vv. 7–8), but wherever the fresh waters of this symbolic river flow they bring life. Even the waters of the Dead Sea will be transformed so that fish and all kinds of aquatic creatures flourish in it, and there is a thriving fishing industry on its shores

(vv. 9–10). However, the salt marshes around the sea remain, because the salt they provide is a vital commodity (v. 11).

A promise symbolized

What the prophet is seeing is not a prediction of a physical and geographical transformation but a promise, given in symbolic form, of the amazing transformation that will come about in God's people and their fortunes when God is once again able to dwell in their midst because their sin has been dealt with and they have been restored to a right relationship with him.

This same symbolism is taken up and used in the New Testament, in John's vision of the new Jerusalem (Revelation 21—22). In this vision there is no temple in the city, 'for its temple is the Lord God the Almighty and the Lamb' (Revelation 21:22). But there is the river of life, with its tree-lined banks, flowing from the throne of God, a symbol of God's blessings made abundantly available to those whose names are in the book of life (Revelation 20:12).

Living waters

Ezekiel's vision can help us to understand what Jesus meant when he said, 'Let anyone who is thirsty come to me, and let the one who believes in me drink. As the scripture has said, "Out of the believer's heart shall flow rivers of living water"' (John 7:37–38). It is not clear what scripture John intends here. It may not be any one single passage, but probably includes Ezekiel 47:1–12. Jesus spoke of his body as 'this temple' (John 2:19–21) because God was present on earth in him. Paul speaks of both the fellowship of the Church (1 Corinthians 3:16–17) and the individual believer (1 Corinthians 6:19) as God's temple, where the Holy Spirit dwells. If God is really present in the fellowship of the Church, and in the lives of its members, then God's transforming blessing can flow out from these sources to bring new life to those whom it touches.

PRAYER

Lord Jesus, I am thirsty. Give me your living water in abundance so that it may flow out of me to those whom I meet day by day.

The BOUNDARIES of the LAND

After the detailed description of the temple complex, Ezekiel's vision ends with a description of the restored land of which the temple is the focal point. The description begins by delineating the boundaries of the land. It moves in a clockwise direction, beginning at the north-west extremity, which is somewhere on the Mediterranean coast to the north of Tyre. The northern boundary (vv. 15–17) is very unclear because none of the places named can be identified with any certainty. There are two main interpretations. It may be that the boundary runs north-north-east to near Hamath (modern Hama), some 180 kilometres north of Damascus. However, Lebo-Hamath ('entrance of Hamath') may be the Beqa' Valley, a long depression running north-east between the Lebanon and Hermon-Antilebanon ranges for more than 150 kilometres and leading to Hama. In that case the northern boundary could run from the Mediterranean coast north of Tyre to some point near the headwaters of the Jordan to the south-west of Damascus. The eastern boundary seems to start somewhere south of Damascus and then run down the Jordan valley to the south end of the Dead Sea (v. 18). The southern boundary runs from just south of the Dead Sea to the oasis of Meribah-kadesh (v. 19). This is better known in the Old Testament as Kadesh-barnea. Ezekiel gives it the name that commemorates the rebellion that happened there (Numbers 20:13). The boundary then runs along the 'river of Egypt' (the Wadi el-Arish, not the Nile) to the Mediterranean coast. That coast forms the western boundary (v. 20).

The covenant restored

This delineation of the land corresponds to the greatest extent of Solomon's kingdom ('from Lebo-Hamath to the Wadi of Egypt', 1 Kings 8:65) and the more detailed description given by God to Moses in Numbers 34:1–12. The territory to the east of the Jordan where the tribes of Reuben, Gad and the half-tribe of Manasseh settled is not included in the delineation of the promised land in Numbers. The fact that, despite having been occupied by Israel for centuries, it is not included by Ezekiel shows that the purpose of Ezekiel 47:13–21 is to reaffirm the promise given to Moses. This is part of the re-establishment of the covenant. Banishment from the promised land was the ultimate in the covenant curses (Leviticus 26:27–33). Restoration to it indicates that the curse is no longer operative and the covenant has been re-established.

The statement that the land is to be divided 'according to the tribes of Israel' (v. 21) indicates a return to the pre-monarchic state. There is to be no return to the pre-exilic situation of two divided kingdoms, in each of which the tribal structures were eroded. It is notable how, throughout the Old Testament traditions, the figure twelve is retained for the number of the tribes, even though the exact configuration that makes up this number changes. Here the configuration is the most common one in which Joseph's two sons, Ephraim and Manasseh, are represented by separate tribes and Levi is left out of the list since it is not given any tribal land. In the future, the twelve tribes are to be united under a single leader, the prince.

Care for the alien

Before the division of the land between the tribes is described, there is a surprising piece of legislation. Families of resident aliens are to be allotted land within the tribal territory in which they have settled (vv. 22–23). The Mosaic Law is remarkable in its generosity towards resident aliens. The fundamental reason for this is given in Deuteronomy 10:19: 'You shall also love the stranger, for you were strangers in the land of Egypt.' They were allowed to take part in worship alongside Israelites (Exodus 12:48; Leviticus 22:18). In the laws, they are linked with widows and orphans as those in special need of care and protection.

In Jesus' day there was disagreement over how the command 'You shall love your neighbour as yourself' (Leviticus 19:18) should be understood. How wide was one's community of 'neighbours'? This is why Jesus was asked the question, 'Who is my neighbour?' (Luke 10:29). Jesus' answer was the parable of the good Samaritan. Radical though it is, it can be seen as developing the attitude encouraged by the Old Testament command, 'You shall love the alien as yourself' (Leviticus 19:34).

PRAYER

War, persecution and poverty have spread resident aliens around the world today. Do you know of any for whom you and your church can pray? This may lead to other ways of expressing love for them.

The DIVISION *of the* LAND

Ezekiel now moves on to the division of the land itself among the twelve tribes. Each tribe is assigned an equal portion (47:14a), running in a strip from east to west. This parallels the temple's orientation. No dimensions are given for the tribal strips, and no geographical markers are given for the boundaries between them. There are marked differences compared with the division of the land described in Joshua 14 to 21. Then the land was shared out according to the size of each tribe. This principle is spelt out in Numbers 26:52–56, which also says that the apportioning is to be done by drawing lots. In Joshua the boundaries of the tribal territories are described in detail by reference to towns and significant topographical features. Ezekiel's vision totally ignores socio-economic and geographical considerations. It is a theological construct which was never meant to be applied literally.

The tribal lands

The tribal lands are separated into two blocks by the sacred portion. Seven tribes have land to the north of it (vv. 1–7) and five to the south (vv. 23–29). The arrangement of the tribes is not random. Those furthest from the sanctuary, Dan, Asher and Naphtali to the north and Gad to the south, are the sons of Jacob's concubines, Zilpah and Bilhah (Genesis 30:1–13). Judah and Benjamin flank the sacred portion. No doubt Judah has this privilege because Jacob's blessing gave him the place of the ruler among his brothers, a promise that came to be seen as messianic (Genesis 49:8–12). Benjamin was Jacob's youngest and favourite son. He and Joseph were Rachel's sons. Historically, the territory of Judah and Benjamin lay to the south and north of Jerusalem and the temple. The order is now reversed. This may be intended to stress the unity of the tribes in the new nation. No longer will 'north' and 'south' correspond to 'Israel' and 'Judah'. Judah, the royal tribe, is now in the northern part of the land. Reuben, Jacob's firstborn, lies next to Judah, on the north. The two remaining portions in the north go to the sons of Joseph, Ephraim and Manasseh. South of Benjamin, between its territory and that of Gad, are the lands of three of Leah's sons, Simeon, Issachar and Zebulun. Although the arrangement bears little resemblance to the allotment of territory made by Joshua, the inclusion of these details of the division of the land makes the point that the return from exile will be a new beginning and all Israel will have a part in it.

The sacred portion

The details given of the sacred portion expand on what has been said in Ezekiel 45:1–8. Now it is said that the temple is in the middle of the priests' lands (v. 10). It is also explicitly stated that none of 'this choice portion of the land' belonging to the priests and Levites can be alienated by sale or exchange (v. 14). More details are given than earlier about the city and its land. The city does not belong to any tribe and its citizens are to be drawn from all the tribes (v. 19). The arable land beyond its 'green belt' is there to be cultivated by its citizens to provide for their needs. They are not to be dependent on 'charity' from the tribes. Nor, on the other hand, are they to 'tax' the tribes for their upkeep. The city is not referred to as Jerusalem. If we take seriously the equal size of each tribal portion, the city of Ezekiel's vision would lie some way north of Jerusalem. The temple would then be near Shiloh, where the ark of the covenant was kept in pre-monarchical times before it was captured by the Philistines (1 Samuel 4). This, too, may be an indication of making a new start, free from the defilements of the temple's former home depicted in the vision in Ezekiel 8—11.

A new start

Ezekiel's vision might be dismissed as unrealistically utopian—but only if it is taken with a literalism that was never intended. Rather, the vision enshrines in concrete images and detailed legislation principles and ideals intended to inspire the exiles to work for something different and better than simply a return to the past. Moreover, it puts before them the promise that God will give them a new start.

PRAYER

Lord, we thank you that we need not be trapped in the past, with its failures, because you give us new opportunities to put right what is wrong and to begin again. Help me to see and grasp those opportunities.

The CITY *of* GOD

Ezekiel's vision ends with a brief description of the new city. Like many of the structures in his vision, it is perfectly square, with sides 4,500 cubits long (about two-and-a-quarter kilometres). There are three gates in each side, named after the twelve tribes. This list is the 'classic' one of the twelve sons of Jacob, with Joseph instead of Ephraim and Manasseh, so making room for Levi. This, no doubt, is to symbolize the unity of the whole nation, of which the city is the capital.

There is a discernible logic to the grouping of the tribes with regard to the gates. On the north side, facing the temple, are the three most significant sons of Leah—Reuben, the firstborn; Judah, the royal tribe; and Levi, the priestly tribe. All have territory to the north of the city. On the south side are Leah's other three sons, Simeon, Issachar and Zebulun. Their territories lie to the south of the city. On the east are Rachel's two sons, Joseph and Benjamin, and Dan, a son of her maid Bilhah. The other three sons of the concubines are on the west—Gad, Asher and Naphtali. The fact that, in both the placing of the tribes in the land and the positions of the gates bearing their names, there seems to be a remembrance of the differences in origin and history of the tribes makes the point that, although in the new land there is a new beginning and things are transformed, there is also a continuity with the past.

'The Lord is there'

The most important thing about the city is its name, 'The Lord is there' (v. 35). This stands in tension with the earlier assertion that God's presence is in the temple, some way to the north of the city and separated from it by various buffer zones and barriers. Once again we have the tension of God's transcendence, particularly emphasized in the structure and situation of the temple complex, and God's immanence, asserted in the name of the city. God is with his people not just in worship but in the day-to-day living of their lives. This name is the climax towards which the book of Ezekiel has been building. In chapters 1—24 the prophet was constantly seeking to undermine false hopes based on the belief that as 'the city of God', the place of the temple, Jerusalem was inviolable. He insisted that the abominations going on in the city and the temple had driven God out of the city and, as a result, it would be given up to its enemies to be destroyed. When these things had happened, he was able to bring oracles of hope (chs. 33—37), promising that God would purify his people, bring them back to the land, and re-establish the covenant with them. The visions in chapters 40—48 fill out the promise in 37:27–28 that God will once again dwell with his people.

The new Jerusalem

The vision of the new Jerusalem in Revelation 21—22 clearly draws on Ezekiel's vision, but transforms it in important ways in the light of the coming of Jesus Christ. The city is 'the bride, the wife of the Lamb' (21:9). It represents the consummation of Christ's work—all those he has ransomed from 'every tribe and language and people and nation' (Revelation 5:9). It has twelve gates on which are the names of the tribes of Israel (Revelation 21:12). However, it also has twelve foundations bearing the names of the 'apostles of the Lamb' (21:14). The old covenant is fulfilled in the new covenant sealed by the death of Jesus, resulting in a new people of God embracing both Jew and Gentile. Most strikingly, the city has no temple because the Lord God and the Lamb are its temple (21:22). Therefore the river of the water of life flows out through the city from 'the throne of God and of the Lamb' (22:1–2). This reminds us of those places in John's Gospel where Jesus speaks of his body as the temple (John 2:19–21) and of himself as the source of living water (John 7:37–39). In his vision, John sees what Ezekiel saw, fulfilled in the person and work of Jesus Christ.

PRAYER

Lord God, salvation belongs to you and the Lamb. Blessing and glory and wisdom and thanksgiving and honour and power and might be yours for ever and ever! May your kingdom come on earth. Come soon, Lord Jesus!

Based on Revelation 7:10, 12; 22:20

Figure 1: Ezekiel's temple area

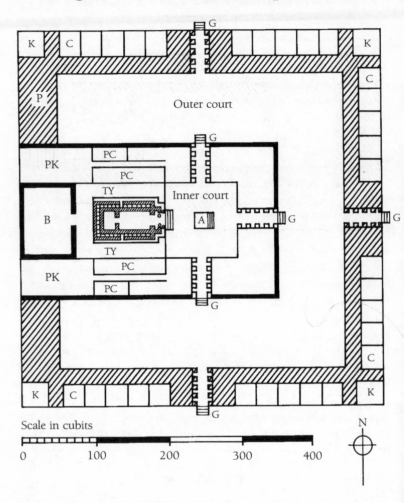

A:	Altar	
B:	Building	
C:	Chamber	
G:	Gateway	
K:	Kitchen	

P:	Pavement
PC:	Priests' chambers
PK:	Priests' kitchens
TY:	Temple yard

Figure 2: Ezekiel's temple

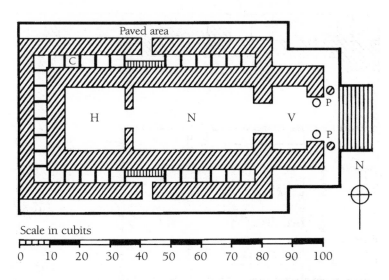

Scale in cubits

| 0 | 10 | 20 | 30 | 40 | 50 | 60 | 70 | 80 | 90 | 100 |

C: Side-chambers
P: Pillars
V: Vestibule

N: Nave, or holy place
H: Inner room, or most holy place

Figure 3: Apportionment of the land

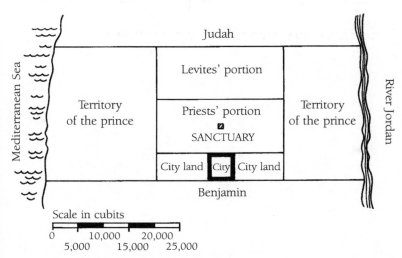

Scale in cubits

| 0 | 5,000 | 10,000 | 15,000 | 20,000 | 25,000 |

(86) A HOLY GOD
(not personal)
Not like other gods
Morality now not holiness

(100) A FLOWING RIVER
Of life
Thirsting & drinking
John 4 Samaritan woman at well
Freshness of water.
Rain.

(103) "The Lord is there"
The name of the city
God is with his people not just in the
worship but into the day to day living of the
lives. The old covenant is fulfilled in the new
covenant sealed by the death of Jesus
resulting in a new people for God embracing
both Jew & Gentile.

NOTES

NOTES

NOTES

NOTES

THE PEOPLE'S
BIBLE COMMENTARY

VOUCHER SCHEME

The People's Bible Commentary (PBC) provides a range of readable, accessible commentaries that will grow into a library covering the whole Bible.

To help you build your PBC library, we have a voucher scheme that works as follows: a voucher is printed on this page of each People's Bible Commentary volume (as above). These vouchers count towards free copies of other books in the series.

For every four purchases of PBC volumes you are entitled to a further volume FREE.

Please find the coupon for the PBC voucher scheme opposite.

All you need do:

- Cut out the vouchers from the PBCs you have purchased and attach them to the coupon.

- Complete your name and address details, and indicate your choice of free book from the list on page 256.

- Take the coupon to your local Christian bookshop who will exchange it for your free PBC book; or send the coupon straight to BRF who will send you your free book direct. Please allow 28 days for delivery.

Please note that PBC volumes provided under the voucher scheme are subject to availability. If your first choice is not available, you may be sent your second choice of book.

THE PEOPLE'S
BIBLE COMMENTARY

VOUCHER SCHEME COUPON

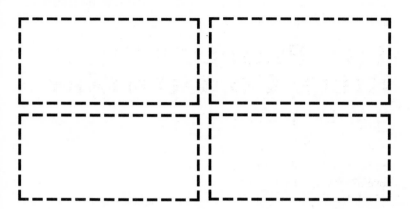

Customer and bookseller should both complete the form overleaf.

TO BE COMPLETED BY THE CUSTOMER

My choice of free PBC volume is:
(Please indicate a first and second choice;
all volumes are supplied subject to
availability.)

❏ 1 & 2 Samuel
❏ 1 & 2 Kings
❏ Chronicles to Nehemiah
❏ Job
❏ Psalms 1—72
❏ Psalms 73—150
❏ Proverbs
❏ Jeremiah
❏ Ezekiel
❏ Nahum to Malachi
❏ Matthew
❏ Mark
❏ Luke
❏ John
❏ Romans
❏ 1 Corinthians
❏ 2 Corinthians
❏ Galatians and Thessalonians
❏ Ephesians to Colossians
   and Philemon
❏ Timothy, Titus and Hebrews
❏ James to Jude
❏ Revelation

Name: . . . .
Address: . . . .
. . . .
Postcode: . . . .

TO BE COMPLETED BY THE BOOKSELLER

(Please complete the following.
Coupons redeemed will be credited to
your account for the value of the
book(s) supplied as indicated above.
Please note that only coupons correctly
completed with original vouchers will
be accepted for credit.)

Name: . . . .
Address: . . . .
. . . .
Postcode: . . . .
Account Number: . . . .

Completed coupons should be
sent to: BRF, PBC Voucher
Scheme, First Floor, Elsfield Hall,
15–17 Elsfield Way, Oxford
OX2 8FG.

Tel 01865 319700; Fax 01865
319701; e-mail enquiries@brf.org.uk
Registered Charity No. 233280

**THIS OFFER IS AVAILABLE IN THE UK
ONLY**
**PLEASE NOTE: ALL VOUCHERS ATTACHED
TO THE COUPON MUST BE ORIGINAL
COPIES.**